Bon appetit

Norma Lee Browning

BE A GUEST
AT YOUR OWN PARTY

....

BE A GUEST
AT YOUR OWN PARTY

....

FLORENCE LOWELL
AND
NORMA LEE BROWNING

M. EVANS and Company, Inc.
New York

Library of Congress Cataloging in Publication Data

Lowell, Florence, 1914–
  Be a guest at your own party.

  Includes index.
  1. Entertaining. 2. Cookery. I. Browning, Norma
Lee, joint author. II. Title
TX731.L64   642'.4   80-11181
ISBN 0-87131-318-9

M. Evans and Company, Inc.
216 East 49 Street
New York, New York 10017

Designed by RFS Graphic Design, Inc.

Manufactured in the United States of America

9 8 7 6 5 4 3 2 1

Contents

Introduction

· ·

by
Norma Lee Browning

· ·

My idea of how to Be a Guest at Your Own Party is to hire Florence Lowell to cater it.

When Florence asked me to help her put this book together, my initial reaction was, "You've *got* to be kidding!" Sure, I love parties—when someone else does the work. For me, cooking has always been a crashing bore. I'm a total disaster in the kitchen.

But Florence has a special knack of making everything seem so easy and such fun that she'll have you running to the kitchen in no time; she did it for me.

For years, Florence was entrusted with the care and feeding of the world's celebrity superstars—shahs and sheikhs, presidents and princes, captains of industry and kingpins of the entertainment world. These aren't the kind of people most of us will ever find on our guest list, but we all may want to treat our guests as if they were royalty.

For the price of this book, Florence will tell you her favorite menus, recipes, and party plans, adapted to *your* needs. A few of

7

the recipes might seem a little outrageous, but that's what you call a caterer for anyway.

Florence will tell you how to cater your own party and remain cool, calm and collected in the process. No one has more expertise at this. I can personally vouch for that, having watched her in action for many years.

She was a great favorite of both President Eisenhower and Mamie, former Governor Ronald Reagan and Nancy, the Walter Annenbergs, composer Frederick Loewe (and he's a bear to please!), Lily Pons, Gerald Ford, and of course such film and TV stars as Dinah Shore, Lucille Ball, Kirk Douglas, Bob Hope and Frank Sinatra.

From years of experience Florence has mastered all the secrets of entertaining. There's nothing to throwing a beautiful party that Florence Lowell can't teach you. So read on, and Happy Partying!

How I've Been a "Guest" at Some of the World's Most Fabulous Parties

· · · · · · · · · · · · · · · · · · · ·

by
Florence Lowell

· · · · · · · · · · · · · · · · · · · ·

Probably my most expensive party, for its size, was one I catered for a jet-setting Frenchwoman. She had only forty guests, but her party (back in 1972) cost $134 per plate. She ordered five pounds of fresh Russian caviar, and that blew $500 right there. She ordered fresh Georgia strawberries the size of golf balls and floated them in Dom Pérignon Champagne which at that preinflation time was only $34 a bottle.

Each table for four guests had its own chef to carve the meat, its own wine steward (with white gloves, of course), and its own waitress.

She had borrowed a friend's home for the party, then discovered it was surrounded by a redwood fence which she didn't like at all. So she ordered the fence covered with orchids flown in from Hawaii just for the party. The florist's bill was $10,000.

When she first asked me to cater the party, I refused. I told her I had a wedding reception to do at my place, Lowell Manor, and I couldn't possibly be at her house in time to serve dinner before 10 P.M. She said 10 P.M. would be just fine! So I was stuck.

The reception at Lowell Manor, which I generally referred to as my "shop" though it was quite a nice establishment, was a modest affair, with a budget of $1.35 per guest. When it was over, I packed a little hamper with sandwiches, cakes, and a bottle of Champagne for the young couple to take on their honeymoon. I went directly from the reception to the lavish party I had prepared for the $134-a-plate jet-setters. What a contrast! I couldn't help comparing their party faces with those at my $1.35-a-plate reception.

Fame, fortune and social status have nothing to do with your ability to imbue others, as well as *yourself* with an exhilarating sense of *joie de vivre* when you're entertaining either friends or strangers. Some of us, perhaps by birth, breeding, natural instinct, inclination or conditioning, may enjoy it more than others, but with expertise comes the enjoyment and nobody is born with expertise in anything. Expertise is something you acquire, cultivate and enhance with practice.

Fortunately I had a head start with my heritage. My mother was the most fastidious lady I've ever known. She insisted on nice linen napkins even with her lunchtime pumpernickel and caviar and glass of beer. I never knew what a paper napkin was as a child. I grew up in Milwaukee, a beer-drinking town, but my parents were European born and bred, so we had the best of all worlds at our house, especially in the kitchen and around our dining room table.

My Russian mother adapted easily to the Milwaukee-German style of hospitality. The minute anyone walked into our home, she would put on the coffeepot or teapot and bring out her home-baked breads and coffee cakes, or tea cakes, or *Schnecken* (German sweet rolls). Her *Schnecken* and strudels were always my favorites. She taught me how to make them. They were to become favorites of my clients in the catering business and are still among my specialties today.

In such an environment it was only natural that I would grow up loving the aroma of a kitchen and the ambience of a party. I've always felt sorry for people who say they hate to cook and dread entertaining and won't go near the kitchen. All of these things were associated only with pleasure throughout my childhood and growing-up years, thanks to my mother. By her example I was exposed early to the gentle and genteel art of being a guest at one's own party and being at home with equal ease in the kitchen or at the dining table.

Luckily my education in cookery continued at the University of Wisconsin in Madison, where I officially majored in psychology. But I spent more time in the kitchen of the girls' dorm than I did with my books.

Sena, the cook in our dorm, was not only fabulous at her job but a fascinating woman as well, with a beautiful philosophy of life. As soon as my classes were over, instead of going up to my room, I would make a beeline for the kitchen to philosophize with Sena and to "audit"—for no credit—her ovenside seminars. Before long I became Sena's unofficial, unpaid student assistant on a part-time but regular basis, helping with the cooking and menus for our dorm. Most girls would have considered it drudgery. I loved it!

After college, I married, had two babies, and then became active in P. T.A., Women's Clubs, charity organizations. I always wound up doing the cooking for their fund-raising events. When we moved to California, I simply continued the same routine of getting myself involved.

Some of my friends began bugging me. "Hey, why don't you do this for yourself? Go into business on your own?"

Finally I did. I opened a small pastry shop and started baking *Schnecken.*

My place was next door to the world's largest barber shop; at least that's what it was called. No sooner had my caramel and cinnamon aromas wafted over there than I had 35 barbers as steady customers, along with *their* clients.

Naturally they wanted coffee with their hot rolls so I put in a coffee maker. Next they coaxed me for sandwiches and ice cream. Before I quite realized what was happening, I had a booming little tearoom business going, with small tables and chairs in an attractive, homey setting.

One of my first regular customers was Cass Daley. She thought I made the world's greatest tuna salad, and so every Thursday she would bring her mother and a couple of friends in for lunch. They always ordered the same: tuna salad, *Schnecken* and tea.

One day Miss Daley called me over to her table and told me that tomorrow would be her son's seventh birthday and she had to be on the studio lot all day. Please, would I *cater* her son's birthday party?

And *how,* pray tell, does one cater a party for a bunch of seven-year-olds? I hadn't the remotest idea. Nor do I remember what I served or did for the birthday party kids, but it must have been all right because the mother of one of the child guests said to me when the party was over, "I like the way you handle things. We're having a christening a week from Sunday. Would you cater it for us?"

How does one cater a christening? I called a friend who was a priest and asked. Nothing to it—finger sandwiches and Champagne. As a result of that party I was asked to do five more within a week. Before I knew it, I was embarked on a whole new career in catering. It just took off. I had to hire a woman to help me at my shop, called the Camellia House. Then the Bel Air Hotel engaged me to make the hors-d'oeuvre and finger sandwiches for all their weddings.

As my business grew, it also changed radically—from coffee and *Schnecken* to cocktails and hors-d'oeuvres. This led to another business—Florence Lowell's Frozen Hors-d'Oeuvres. I had some big accounts; Jurgensen's on the West Coast, the Palmer House, Marshall Field's, and Stop 'N Shop in Chicago. But I sold the business when I realized it was growing into more than I could handle. I preferred the personal contact of catering.

I often think how lucky I am that I really love cooking and baking; how lucky I am to be able to turn a hobby into a vocation; and how *very* lucky I was when I made the big decision to move to Palm Springs, which is undoubtedly the most partying town anywhere on earth.

I'll never forget the first party I catered for Jolie Gabor in her mountainside home. It's truly a dollhouse in a magnificent movie-like setting. She had told me to plan for 85 to 90 guests; about twice that number showed up. She told me that she had a double oven for her goulash, and sure enough, she did. The only problem was that after the tables were all set, ready for the goulash to be served hot from the double oven, I discovered the oven wasn't working. There was nothing wrong with it. Merely, *the gas had never been connected* in Jolie Gabor's kitchen! Though she had lived in that house for two years, this grand lady had never stepped into her kitchen. She apparently used her electric coffeepot for breakfast, dined out the rest of the time, never cooked at all, and she wasn't even aware that her gas stove had never been connected.

After recovering from the initial shock, I hastily dispatched my helpers to round up every electrical appliance that I owned. We started plugging them in and wham! All the fuses blew.

That was the night I really learned to jitterbug.

I doubt that any of you who are reading this book will find yourselves in a similar predicament, but party disasters can happen to all of us, if on a smaller scale. One of the purposes of this book is to help you prevent them, or to cope with them when they do happen.

In this book I have tried to distill from my twenty years of experience in the catering business the guidelines I believe to be most practical and helpful to the average woman in planning a party, whether it's for six or sixty guests—or more. Even the smallest party can be a headache to the hostess who isn't prepared.

Some people panic at the thought of dinner for six. Some women don't consider it a "party" unless there are at least twenty or thirty guests; others call it a party if they're only having eight or ten. Some prefer to bring in a professional caterer for large parties; others enjoy doing their own thing.

A few years ago my son decided I had worked long enough and I let him talk me into an early "retirement." It lasted nearly a whole month. I saw a "For Sale" sign in a small bakery shop in LaJolla and soon there I was again back in the kitchen rolling dough for *Schnecken* and strudels. Within a year I had another flourishing business with three shops called The Queen of Tarts, specializing only in Quiches, Tarts, Tortes and Trifles.

I find that more and more young people are coming into my shops not only to *buy* the makings for their parties but for over-the-counter advice on how to bake these things themselves, what to serve with them, how to plan their own parties.

I've also observed that more of these young people are planning *bigger* parties and they're *not* hiring caterers; they're putting the whole number together themselves. I think there's been a fantastic revolution in entertaining. More people are doing it, more *young* people are doing it, and they're going at it as if they really *care* about it, almost as if they're competing with each other for ideas. I think this is good—good for them and for me too because it still keeps me on my toes.

I have tried in this book to cover all the bases of entertaining in a way that will, I hope, encourage *you*, the hostess, to stay flexible, to be creative, and to tailor your party to your needs.

Most of the menus and recipes are planned for eight but can be easily doubled, tripled or quadrupled. For larger parties I've tailored the menus for thirty people; these also can be doubled or tripled if you're going all out, or cut into halves or thirds if you can do simple arithmetic. By including a wide range of recipe specifications, I'm sure that even a novice at entertaining can handle most of them with ease and confidence. Don't let it throw you if my marketing sheet calls for fifteen stalks of celery. Just cut down the recipe, or turn to another one for smaller portions.

All the recipes are from my own files and include only those which I have tried and used. The menus are those that have been the most successful from the standpoint of execution, taste and visual appeal.

There are no guarded secrets in my business, at least not for me. Whenever anyone asks me for a recipe, and many have, I consider it a compliment. If I thought my business would collapse by giving away my recipes, I shouldn't be in the business.

New trends in anything may come and go but one basic element of entertaining remains unchanged: The secret of a successful party is a relaxed hostess; and the secret of a successful hostess is proper planning and pre-preparing.

The book is organized to help *you* get yourself organized for your parties and make your role easier. Part I, for example, will summarize the tricks of the trade, the short cuts and time savers, so you'll know how to get it all out to the table at the proper time. You will need to pay special attention to the *Equipment Work Sheet* and the *Marketing Work Sheet* for each party menu you plan; and to my "Flo charts" which operate on the principles of a businessman's "flow" chart. Following the Flo charts, you'll find some helpful hints on some of the trickier aspects of cooking and catering—answers to questions you've always wanted answered and didn't know whom to ask: how to judge the freshness of an egg, where to buy the best seafood, tips on setting up a bar, etc. These topics are also listed in the index for handy reference.

It's really no big deal to be sufficiently well organized to cater your own party. Don't be afraid! I promise you, all it takes to turn your party from a pain in the neck, for you, the hard-working hostess, to the time of your life is the confidence that comes from knowing how. This is what I hope my book gives you. Be a guest at your own party! Good luck and enjoy!

PART I

. . . .

TRICKS OF THE TRADE

. . . .

CHAPTER I

. . . .

So You're Going To Throw A Party

. . . .

The first thing I do when someone asks me to cater a party is ask, "How many people do you want to have?"

And this is the first question you must ask yourself. The number of guests determines to a great degree the type of party you should plan, and vice versa. Do you want a sit-down dinner, a brunch, a buffet supper, a cocktail party?

The second thing I do when I'm hired to cater a party is make an appointment to look over the physical facilities and accommodations at the place where the party is to be held. And this, of course, is what you *must* do. If it's in your own home, only you know how much traffic your kitchen will bear, how much your ovens and refrigerators can handle, what kind of bar space, serving and seating arrangements you already have or can improvise; in short, how you can accommodate guests comfortably in your house.

And I do mean *inside* your house. Forget the porch and patio unless they're enclosed and weatherproof, in which case you can consider them part of the house. Patio parties, lawn and garden parties can be sensational when the weather cooperates, and disastrous when it doesn't. It's simply wishful thinking to count on the weather for an outdoor party.

So, my very first piece of advice in planning your party is this: *Don't invite more people than your house will hold.*

My second is this:

Always cook for more guests than you've counted on.

I know there are people whose idea of a good party is a mob scene: the bigger the crowd the better. I have a friend in Palm Springs, Allan Keller, a marvelous host who throws great fun parties, usually for at least 150. His theory is that you should always invite more guests than you have places to seat them; this keeps the party moving. They can eat lap-style on the piano bench, hassocks, brick patio ledge, wherever they land; they can eat standing or they can sit on the floor and many do.

But Allan has an advantage most of us don't have; he's a former opera singer with a large nucleus of professional showbiz friends he always invites to his parties, as well as a lot of aspiring would-bes or might-have-beens who don't need to be coaxed into doing their song and dance routines. Thus each party is a continuous impromptu floor show, some of them better than you'll see in Las Vegas. Moreover, his menus are confined to only a few dishes which he specializes in (he's a superb cook) for easy self-service at the buffet table. His parties are coordinated with certain festive holiday themes—Valentine's Day, St. Patrick's Day, May Day (he always has a Maypole dance), Fourth of July, Halloween—all of which offer infinite possibilities to a creative host or hostess.

In between these large bashes, Allan frequently hosts quite elegant sit-down dinners for 8 or 12, either formal or informal. He does both with great style.

The important point is that he knows the difference between the kinds of parties that should or can be planned according to your guest list or guests of honor. Most of his large parties fall in the category of *casual* entertaining.

If you're planning a large party and want to keep it as casual as possible with a minimum of hired help, self-service at the buffet table, and catch-as-catch-can seating space, then I strongly recommend that you have a focal point of interest and a simple, easy-to-serve menu with a motif that your guests can handle and which may also amuse or entertain them. One woman I know, for example, always has a casually elegant or elegantly casual Black-Eyed Pea Party on New Year's Day. Eating black-eyed peas on New Year's Day is an old Southern custom; it's supposed to bring you good luck all year. So there's nothing new about black-eyed pea parties in the South. But in this case the setting is a swank Thunderbird Country Club villa near Palm Springs and the hostess is Countess Marajen Chinigo, a lady publishing tycoon who throws fabulous formal parties; her Black-Eyed Pea Party is the biggest hit of them all because it's a novelty, and fun.

There are all sorts of occasions that lend themselves to casual entertaining on a large scale. Besides holidays, there are birthdays, anniversaries, Bon Voyage and Welcome Home parties. You really don't need a *reason* for a party but if you think you need one, you can always invent one.

In any case, it is most important that you *give special consideration to the type of party you want to give.*

Ask yourself these questions:

Is it a special occasion that calls for a certain type of party?

If you're having a guest or guests of honor, what type of party would they prefer?

If the occasion calls for a large guest list, how will you handle it?

In general, if a large party is an absolute must for a special occasion, then *I recommend that you divide it into two parties.* Unless, of course, you're *absolutely sure* you can handle it in one.

So okay, you're groaning—that means double the work, headaches and expense. Not necessarily so. In fact there are certain advantages to having two parties, either on the same day or suceeding days.

Your cost for food and beverage will be the same for 100 guests, whether they come all at the same time or in two parties. Your flower and fruit arrangements, nut bowls, decorations et ceteras all will stay fresh or at least look fresh with a little touch-up for your second party. Your expenses for rental equipment, hired help, even musicians if you make a deal with them, shouldn't amount to much if any more for two parties than for one. Economically it makes sense to have two parties, one after the other, instead of one big party with so many guests that nobody enjoys it.

But back to Jolie Gabor's goulash: When Jolie asked me to do her party, I had never made goulash in quantity before. However, knowing her predilection for collecting stray Hungarian houseguests (especially if they play the violin) and being fully aware of her fame and popularity as a hostess, I had figured (quite wittily, I thought) on quite a few more guests than the number she gave me. I knew everyone who was invited would come and probably a lot more who weren't invited. So I made almost double the amount of goulash she had asked for, thinking I could always freeze any that was left over.

It proved to be more than a slight miscalculation on my part. Fortunately, I had prepared my Hawaiian chicken dish for a party I was catering the next day. I could see the goulash going, going, almost gone. There was nothing to do but bring in the Hawaiian chicken dish to have enough food for Jolie's party. So I sent my helpers to fetch it. Then I spent practically the whole night starting over again for my next night's party.

Inevitably, there will be those last-hour or last-minute extras who show up. This happens at smaller parties as well as larger ones. I once threw a small, sit-down dinner for which only 18 were invited and about twice that number showed up.

This sort of thing doesn't happen very often. But it taught me a lesson I've never forgotten and one anyone can learn from: *Be prepared; always cook for more guests than you've counted on.* You can safely predict how a soufflé will turn out with the oven at the right temperature, but the only thing you can predict about guests is that they will be unpredictable.

I have another rule that will get you through any crisis: *stay cool, calm and collected; ACT as though you're having fun and you will; adapt to the role of being a guest at your own party.*

When I say *adapt to the role* of being a guest, I mean just that. As I've mentioned before, a good hostess at times also has to be a good actress. We've all heard professional actors say that the longer they act a role the more they feel like the character they're portraying. It's the same with a hostess.

But the secret to being a guest at your own party is *control*, and you only get control when you know specifically what you're doing.

This brings us back to the nitty-gritty: the real secret is to start being cool, calm and collected right from the beginning, not five minutes before the guests walk in the door. You begin the moment you even start *thinking* about your party, which generally should be at least a month before the event.

Everything about a party requires planning, from the invitations and the guest list to where the guests can get their coats when they leave. Handled carefully, everything will come off smoothly and stay in your control.

In spite of any eruptions at a dinner party with six extra guests, I'm able to stay in control because *I am prepared.* I have ample space, an extra table and chairs, enough dinner plates, goblets and silverware, as well as a linen closet filled with napkins and tablecloths. My liquor and wine cabinet is always well stocked; so is my freezer. I *always* make extra portions for second helpings.

Naturally it is easier for me to stay in control of a party than it may be for you because I've had more experience. But I can make it easier for you, too, if you'll follow my suggestions step by step.

Let me summarize a few points to help you get the overall *big picture* about your party. Before you start actually planning it, set yourself down and do a lot of thinking about it. Or better yet, do your thinking while you're walking around your house and looking at it with your "party" eyes. Are there any overlooked nooks and crannies you could fit your guests into? I have a writer friend who absolutely never allows visitors in her study, not even her husband. It's filled with rare books, treasured antique music boxes, shelves of research materials. She gave a big party recently for a VIP houseguest (who incidentally wasn't permitted to set foot in the study) and went to great expense covering her outdoor patio with red-striped circus awning, balloons and clown motif. Came the winds and a sudden battering rainstorm and whoosh went the awning. The hostess kept a jittery eye on her guests as they jammed into her study, dripping wet and with plates of food. And of course with no place to put them down except on the music boxes! Fortunately none was damaged though the hostess must have had a fine case of jangled nerves by the end of her party.

While you're still in your thinking stage, make a *mental* checklist (you'll have plenty of *written* checklists later on) of the rooms and areas that can be expanded, converted, and used for sitting and eating. Can some of your furniture be moved to the garage? Or can your garage be attractively camouflaged for your party? (It's often done.)

Mentally check out everything from bar to bathroom with your "party eyes" while you're still thinking about it; and don't forget that closet or bedroom for coats and wraps. Even in nice weather the ladies love to show off their mink stoles; you'll need a place for them.

After thinking it all over, getting the big picture, and deciding on the kind of party you're going to have, you'll be ready for the actual planning of the party. This is where the real work begins, but you can turn the work into fun by following my "Flo Chart" which is explained in the next chapter and my "Work Sheets" that accompany each of the party suggestions in this book. One is an *Equipment* Work Sheet that lists everything you'll need for a particular party; the other is a *Marketing* Work Sheet that itemizes what you'll need to buy, how much and when, for that particular party menu. Also there is a *Staples Checklist*.

So relax, enjoy, get in the mood! There are a lot of very important ABCs to giving a successful party but I like to think of the first ABC as:

A for *ATTITUDE*. Get in the mood to have a party and feel enthusiastic about the type of party you've chosen. Look forward to having as good a time as your guests will have, backed by your own confidence that you *will* be a guest at your own party because of

B for *BEING PREPARED* and

C for *CONTROL*.

Thus, if you start with the right *attitude,* you'll have no problem *being prepared* in advance and this insures your remaining relaxed and in *control* of your party. You will know that when the last guest leaves, you can congratulate yourself on a job well done!

CHAPTER II

. . . .

The "Flo" Chart

. . . .

A successful party depends on a combination of planning, organizing, advance preparation, and executing your ideas and plans in an orderly fashion.

All of this makes the difference between a happy hostess and the one who winds up a nervous wreck. It makes the difference between a joyful party or just another ho-hummer, at best a bore, at worst a clunker.

No hostess can handle all the details of a party without careful organization; this requires day-by-day, hour-by-hour planning and there are certain details that should be taken care of even weeks before the party.

The crux of it all is *TIMING*. So be prepared for *TIMETA-BLES*, lots of them. They'll give you the important "whens" for your party—when to check your supplies, when to order food and flowers, when to have your "dress rehearsal."

I call my timetables my "Flo" charts. They work on the principles of a businessman's "flow" chart designed to organize his

26

schedule with blocks of time set aside for specific purposes and with one event leading into another smoothly, in orderly fashion. What follows is a prototype of a "Flo" chart. Of course, each hostess and each party has its own special timing. What's important is that you think everything out, and plan ahead.

THE "FLO" CHART

FOUR WEEKS BEFORE Decide on date, invitations, type of party, guest list, space requirements, equipment, other needs. Check on hired help.

THREE WEEKS BEFORE Prepare equipment and marketing sheets. Check liquor supplies and kitchen staples. Send invitations this week. Make complete arrangements for help, and for musicians if necessary.

TWO WEEKS BEFORE Make final decision and arrangements for flowers, decorations, wardrobe, etc. Make appointments for hair, manicure, etc. Order specialties from butcher and liquor store.

ONE WEEK BEFORE Double-check everything done so far (especially the help and the musicians). Early in the week prepare any frozen foods or decorations that can be set aside.

THREE DAYS BEFORE Baking and freezing. Dress rehearsal.

TWO DAYS BEFORE Prepare any foods that can be refrigerated.

ONE DAY BEFORE Check marketing and equipment lists. Pick up any items not already used; especially fresh fruits, greens, cheeses, etc. Assemble equipment items: chairs, trays, platters, glassware, etc. Set up tables, centerpieces, bar. Write out timetable for tomorrow.

DAY OF THE PARTY Relax. Get your hair done. Take a nap. Spend some time fixing the "perishables" in the menu. Buy fresh flowers. Double-check today's timetable. Make a final check of the bar.

You shouldn't have to wear yourself out on last-minute errors if you've followed your plans all along.

You will need to work out your own timetables according to your individual requirements and preferences. Only *you* can decide, for example, whether you're going to send written invitations, hire musicians, buy a new party dress or have an old one altered. In this chapter you'll find general guidelines on when to do what in your pre-party preparations. You'll find tips on how to save time and work in *planning* your party, and more importantly, how to organize yourself so you can spend a maximum amount of time with your guests on the actual Day of the Party.

Following are some important guidelines that can be incorporated in your own "Flo" charts:

Invitations: If you're sending written invitations, it will take time to have them printed and addressed. You may need to allow a week or two for this. Invitations should be mailed so guests will receive them no less than two weeks before the party. Don't forget the RSVP. You may specify "Regrets Only." But save time to doublecheck RSVPs during the week before the party so you'll know how many guests to count on, at least more or less. You can never be sure.

If you should decide on the spur of the moment to throw a party without too much advance notice, as many people do, it's best to telephone your invitations and get an immediate RSVP.

Be sure to state the type of attire for guests—whether casual or dressy, informal or black tie. You can do it tactfully but don't leave your guests guessing about what to wear. Also be sure to indicate whether there will be *food* at your party. I've seen many *cocktail* party invitations that leave guests wondering: Is it for cocktails only? Cocktails and buffet? Cocktails and canapés? If it's for cocktails only or with light refreshments to nibble on, a tactful way to indicate this is to specify a given time, such as: Cocktails, 5 to 7, or 6 to 8. This will let the guests know they should plan on going somewhere else for dinner.

Music: If you're having music at your party, be sure to confirm plans well in advance. Some musicians with busy schedules are booked up weeks ahead. Make sure you have a firm understanding with your musicians as to the number of hours they will play for a certain fee and the *timing* of the music at the party.

I have always encouraged my clients to have music at their parties. I feel that the right music *at the right time* can turn an otherwise good party into a great one. But I've had plenty of problems with the musicians.

Most musicians are hired for three to four hours and it is understandable that they need to take a break every so often. A good time is while the guests are dining, especially if the musicians also are to be fed. This often depends on the hours of the party, whether the musicians will have already had dinner or may be going on to another engagement. In any case, if they take a break while your guests are dining, they must resume their playing by the time dessert is served. This is a *very* important tactic to keep a party from breaking up immediately after guests finish their food.

Flowers and Decorations: Flowers are very important to any party. Check your local florists and nurseries about *two weeks before* your party to see what kind of cut flowers or plants are in season so you can plan your decorations, coordinate color schemes, decide exactly what you want. Do your ordering early. It is *not* necessary to float your party in orchids or buy the most expensive plants available. With a little ingenuity, you can make your own charming centerpieces and floral arrangements with branches, leaves or blossoms from your own garden and trees, if you have any.

Fresh-cut flowers, however, should be fresh the day of the party. Leave yourself time to arrange these a few hours before the event, though you should have all your flower pots and vases ready for them the day before and know exactly where they're to be placed. You can also make attractive arrangements of inexpensive potted flowers.

Many people these days are talented and creative in doing all sorts of homemade decorations with almost anything from spools of yarn to papier-maché to tinsel and tin-can tops. If you're one of the lucky ones with any talent at all in this direction, put your creative juices to work for your party. But start this very early in your Flo chart too. If you're planning a party with a theme, for example, there's no reason you can't get many of your major decisions made and your production schedule well on its way during the first week of your Flo chart or timetable.

You should allow enough flexibility in your timetables to change your mind or switch plans if you need to or want to, but don't wait until the last week to do this. A party with a theme is very good for flexibility; it lends itself well to adjustments in color coordination of decorations and menu; it has the advantage of allowing you to get a lot done at the beginning of your timetable, especially with your homemade decorations, centerpieces, arrangements of "theme" ideas. You can decide early on, for instance, whether to use your big Chinese vase to hold a bunch of balloons (they should be blown up only hours before the party) or Bird of Paradise flowers (they should be fresh-cut the day of the party) or imitation pussy willows that can be made to order weeks in advance.

Hiring Help: Whether you will need to hire someone to help you with your party depends entirely on two very important factors: (a) the number of guests you're inviting, and (b) your own competence and confidence. As I've mentioned, some people panic at the thought of a party for 8; some can handle up to 20 or 30 single-handedly with ease. Whether you're *hiring* an extra hand or two or three, or recruiting nonprofessionals to help you, it's best to have all this settled ahead of time.

There are generally three kinds of extra help considered essential to ease the load on the hostess: kitchen help, bartender, and clean-up crew. Of these the last is the most important. Even for a small party that you think you can handle by yourself, I would personally recommend that you hire one or two helpers, preferably two, if for no other reason than to keep the place tidy during the party. They needn't be professionals. Any schoolgirl or neighbor's daughter should be able and willing for a few dollars to pick up and clean up glasses, ashtrays, plates and trays. They could also help clean up your post-party debris. The happy host and hostess should not be left with stacks of dirty dishes when the guests have gone, so make sure you take this into consideration when you're thinking of helpers.

If you're planning a large party you will, of course, need trained helpers to assist you in the kitchen and with serving; they could also take care of the pick-up and clean-up chores. There is an advantage to hiring trained helpers who will know how to do double duty in the kitchen and bar areas as well as serving drinks and food, and picking up,

Whether they're "hired help" or "friendly recruitments," they should be engaged no later than *two weeks* before your party. Your Flo chart should indicate by then who will be tending bar or helping you in the kitchen. But, *important,* make a note in your timetables a week before the party to *double-check* with your helpers and reconfirm that they're coming. Hired or volunteer helpers are often as unpredictable as the guests; you don't know how many will show up. It's a good idea to have some standby help ready to come if needed.

Your helpers should come at least an hour before the guests arrive. They should be given two written lists: one is your complete menu, the other a Flo chart timing schedule that now gets down to hours and minutes. It specifies all the "whens" of getting this-and-that out of the refrigerator, into the oven, onto trays, platters, tables, etc.

IMPORTANT: *Post your menu and timetable on the refrigerator* door so you don't forget anything. It will help you get everything together on time. These written lists are very important for your helpers but they are even more important, an absolute *must,* when you're doing a party by yourself.

When your guests are gone you don't want to open that refrigerator door and see the gorgeous gelatin mold you forgot to serve; and the rolls that should have gone in the oven to coincide with the serving of the casserole.

Dress Rehearsal: Somewhere in your last week of Flo charts, possibly two or three days before the party, save some time for a dress rehearsal with your trays and casseroles, your dinner table or buffet table. I cannot stress too emphatically the importance of this kind of "party dress rehearsal" so that you will know exactly which of your bowls, trays and dishes you're going to use, what they are to be used for, and where you're going to put them and when. Could anything be more devastating than to find, while you're holding a hot and heavy tray in your hands, that you have no place to set it down? Place everything (trays, casseroles, dishes, silver, etc.) you plan to use on your buffet table in the order and the position they will be used. Practice and play-act and try to visualize the most efficient and most attractive placements for serving. At this calm, cool time, as you arrange and rearrange your table, I recommend that you mark each platter, bowl, and tray according to what they will be used for. You can do this by Scotch-taping a small piece of paper on each bowl and tray, indicating what is to be put in it. This will prove a tremendous help when that crucial time of serving arrives, and most particularly for your helpers. *But don't forget to remove the taped memos!*

Dress Rehearsal for Yourself: Check your wardrobe. Does anything need cleaning or pressing? Alterations? Don't wait until the last minute to discover you can't get into the outfit you had planned to wear. Try it on. Does it still fit? What jewelry will you wear with it? Many women waste precious time on the day of the party trying to make up their minds about what to wear. These decisions should all be made down to the last detail well in advance—shoes, hose, accessories, undergarments, belts, jewelry. You should know exactly what you're going to wear at least a *week before* the party. This applies to men too. Host or hostess should have everything in the party wardrobe in order and laid out the night before the party. And of course you'll leave room in your Flo chart for the beauty salon and barber shop; I recommend doing this on the day of the party.

One Day Before: You should eliminate day-of-party shopping for anything unless absolutely necessary. In the menus and recipes in this book I have eliminated day-of-party shopping except in a few special cases.

I haven't gone into menu planning in this chapter; the menus and recipes will be dealt with separately in detail. However, I'm sure you'll be happy to know that the major part of all the work required for the menus in this party book can be done well in advance. Nearly all the recipes, from hors-d'oeuvre to desserts, can be cooked or baked ahead of time, and put in the freezer or refrigerator, so that all you have to do is get them out and assembled either the day of the party or the day before.

Remember to double-check your refrigerator space, as well as your oven capacity and auxiliary heating equipment. These will make a difference in your schedules.

You should know, for example, whether you can put several casseroles in your oven at one time or if they have to be staggered. If your fruit or vegetable platter won't fit in your refrigerator with everything else, then this arrangement will have to be done just before serving, but all the fruits and vegetables should be sliced and ready for the arrangement. Most of this can be done the night before the party.

All decorations and table settings should be finished the night *before* the party, except fresh-cut flowers.

The Day of the Party: Relax as much as possible. Don't wear yourself out chasing around on last-minute errands. If you've organized your Flo charts properly this won't be necessary. You should save time for an afternoon nap. Finish your fresh-flower arrangements. Make a final check of everything from bar to bath to see if there's anything you've forgotten. There shouldn't be. Double-check your menu and timetable on the refrigerator door to see if everything is on target. Now you're ready to dress and relax again and then greet your guests, looking as fresh as if you hadn't lifted a finger all week! That's what the Flo chart does for you.

Coping: What do you do if your guests are about to arrive, or have already arrived, and a fuse blows?

What if the lights go out and the stove doesn't work?

What do you say to those invited guests who have unexpected company from out of town? Sure, bring them along? Or those who show up anyway, uninvited?

As a professional caterer, and especially in Palm Springs with its celebrity-oriented ambience of unpredictability, I had to learn to adjust quickly to unpredictables. Though I probably encountered more of these in a week or a month of one Social Season than I might otherwise have experienced in a lifetime, they are by no means uncommon.

Most important for you as the hostess: No matter what happens, don't panic; stay calm and cool. BE IN CONTROL OF THE SITUATION!

I know this is easier said than done. But try to remember, if you're angry, upset or nervous, your guests are going to know it. Your uneasiness will permeate the party. Maybe you're annoyed with the unexpected guests. Don't allow it to ruin your evening. Perhaps you're tense over somebody's inconsideration. Try not to show it. You may think everything's going wrong; party jitters are not uncommon even among experienced social hostesses. But its *your* party; at least pretend you're enjoying it. When it's over you'll wind up with great pride and satisfaction in knowing *you did it!* Even if you didn't like it. And none of your guests knew how you felt.

If there's an accident in the kitchen, no need to make a Federal case out of it. You can always make a little adjustment, improvise, think of some thing or some way to cope—*if your mind is clear.*

This is the key to coping with any party mishaps, and believe me, I've had some horrendous ones.

My most traumatic crisis occurred while I was catering a party for Magda Gabor for 385 people, more or less. It was a nightmarish experience. Magda's home is a Mediterranean-style villa on a small mountain peak known as Little Tuscany, with a magnificent view of Palm Springs and the whole desert area. For this particular party (one of her engagement parties) she had all of her furniture removed and put in storage to make room for her guests.

The place looked like a Hollywood movie set: high wrought-iron gate, 10-foot-tall Atlas-type statues with torches illuminating the entrance; formal Romanesque veranda and mammoth pool; a red-carpeted stairway and mirrored wall reflecting the entire panoramic view; white marble floors inside, a striking contrast to the engulfment of red—antique clocks and a grand piano painted red, a red bar and barstools; party tables with red tablecloths, napkins, and centerpieces of a dozen red carnations in a white vase on each table; and Magda in a magnificent red chiffon gown.

Magda's delightful little kitchen exudes opulence, right up to its elegant crystal chandeliers. But its postage-stamp size was not designed for heavy cooking. In this tiny space, one of my helpers put down a container of food, suddenly twirled around and flailed at me, narrowly missing my head as I ducked, and then fell to the floor with the most awful eerie scream I have ever heard. But apparently no one else heard it.

I had sense enough to go out and find two doctors I knew to be among the party guests. They called an ambulance and worked over the man in the kitchen as he lay sprawled on the floor a few feet in front of the oven and near the doorway. I had literally to step over him (and the mess he was making) to go on with the party—heating the hors-d'oeuvre, handing them on trays to waitresses through the half-open door so they couldn't see what was going on inside. The ambulance lost its way and took a whole hour to arrive, one of the most ghastly hours I've ever spent. Another helper went in the ambulance with him. I had just lost my two key people, the men whose jobs were to shuttle back and forth between my place and Magda's with containers of food and clean dishes!

Can you imagine what it's like to be faced with 385 dinner plates, 385 salad plates, 385 cups and saucers, 385 silver settings (knives, forks, spoons), especially when they're dirty?

I had three men stationed at Lowell Manor to load and unload the dishwashers as the dishes were brought in. But when two hours went by and no one came with the dishes to be washed, the dishwashers left! They thought they had made a mistake on the date. So now I had no dishwashers. That made minus five help.

But the party went on. Except for the two doctors, most of the guests, I'm sure, were not even aware that an ambulance came that night and took away my two right-hand helpers.

Everyone seemed to have a good time, especially Magda, who loves parties and who is really a stickler for details when she's the hostess. She complimented me on my efficiency and probably won't know until she reads this what went on behind the scenes at her party.

Don't ask me how I got through it. All I know is that I was left with an all-night cleanup job. But by noon the next day you wouldn't have known from the looks of my kitchen what a mess it had been only a few hours before. We had to get it in order to start preparing for a garden party that very night.

You should be ready by now to take over this role yourself. You've learned the most important tricks of the trade in throwing a successful party. You've learned the importance of pre-party planning and step-by-step organization with your Flo charts. You've learned short-cuts, time-savers, ways of improvising and coping with difficult or unexpected situations.

Most important, you've learned the *principles* of *being a guest at your own party,* which is what this book is all about. It is not just another cookbook of recipes. It is a *party* book with *special menus* for *special occasions.*

Perhaps many of you reading this book are already experienced, you enjoy parties, you *love* entertaining. I hope so. For you there will be a very special treat in trying all the new recipes and menus. You may already do so much entertaining that you're running out of ideas for your parties. You'll find new ideas here that will surprise and delight your friends.

For those of you who simply dread the thought of giving a party, I guarantee you're going to get over that nonsense. Your fears are all in your head.

I'm going to offer you specific plans for a number of parties you can choose from as a beginning; all you have to do is plunge right in and follow directions. It's that simple.

Your approach may not be as joyous as mine, for a while. Give yourself a little time. I assure you there's nothing more exhilarating than the glorious feeling you'll have when you know you've given a wonderful party.

My directions will help you do it successfully, I know.

My hope is you'll do it joyously, too!

PART II

....

SPECIAL OCCASIONS

....

CHAPTER III

. . . .

Brunch

. . . .

Brunch time is about the earliest hour of the day you should plan a party. People love the kind of food that is served for breakfast. However, I find that most brunches become lunches, since a good hour is spent in drinking Bloody Marys, Salty Dogs, and the like, and most guests find it difficult to get going much before noon. For timing brunch really falls heavier on the "unch" than the "br," but the taste emphasis should be on breakfast, on the pleasures and joys of savoring the delicious flavors of breakfast menus in a relaxed party-time setting.

Sunday is the ideal day for a Brunch Party, with 12 o'clock noon or 12:30 the best hour for "refreshments" and 1 o'clock or 1:30 for serving the food. I have found that a compromise between the two types of menus, breakfast and lunch, is the most successful.

Some hosts are old hands at brunches. If you're not one of them, I suggest that you start with my Simple Brunch for a few friends, work up to *My Favorite Brunch* and then *An Elegant*

41

Brunch when you feel you're ready *really* to put on the dog. If you do it in gradual stages, you'll find it as easy as falling off a log.

A SIMPLE BRUNCH

(For 10 to 12)

MENU

Orange juice, freshly squeezed, chilled
Bacon and Egg Casserole
Oven-Browned Potatoes (optional)
Cottage Cheese and Fruit Platter
Tomato and Asparagus Vinaigrette
Orange Streusel Coffee Cake
                        and/or
Dainty Brioches, Walnut Twists, Heavenly Sour-Cream
    Cake
Butter Curls
Strawberry or Blueberry Preserves
Coffee or Tea, or both

Let me forewarn you: though this menu looks simple, it's a little more elegant than the ordinary throw-it-together breakfast, and you're going to be introduced to a few furbelows that maybe you haven't done before. Don't let them throw you. Most of them can be prepared well in advance.

EQUIPMENT WORK SHEET FOR A SIMPLE BRUNCH

3-ounce juice glasses
pitcher for juice
3-quart ovenproof dish, about 5½ x 11½ inches, for Bacon-and-Egg Cas-
    serole
glass bowl for cottage cheese
round tray, 12 to 14 inches, for fruits
medium-size round tray (silver, glass or aluminum covered with foil) for
    Heavenly Sour-Cream Cake
silver or glass tray with doily for Walnut Twists
oblong trays with linen napkins for Dainty Brioches
large roasting pan for Oven-Browned Potatoes
chafing dish to serve potatoes
oblong tray, about 12 x 16 inches, for Tomato and Asparagus Vinaigrette
butter dish
bowls or jam pots for preserves
coffee maker
silver coffee and tea service
cocktail napkins; luncheon-size napkins
1 package 9-inch doilies
silverware (knives or butter spreaders, forks, teaspoons, salad or dessert
    forks for coffee cakes, butter server, jam spoons, buffet serving
    pieces)

This is the kind of brunch that can be served from a buffet and
eaten lap-style around the coffee table. If you choose to have separate tables don't forget:

tables and chairs
salt and pepper
sugar and creamer
ashtrays
centerpiece
tablecloth or place mats
                and provide a set of these for each table.

MARKETING WORK SHEET FOR A SIMPLE BRUNCH

1 quart milk
1 quart buttermilk
2 cups light cream
2 cups coffee cream
2 cups dairy sour cream
4 pounds small-curd cottage cheese
3½ pounds butter
1 pound margarine
3 dozen eggs
3 cakes compressed fresh yeast
1 pound regular sliced bacon (not thin or paper-thin)
2 dozen juice oranges
1 extra large orange
1 fresh pineapple
3 bananas
1 pint fresh strawberries, or 1-pound jar or can of crab apples
4 limes
2 lemons
4 medium-size fresh tomatoes
1 large head of romaine or Boston lettuce, or ½ pound endives
2 bunches of curly parsley
fresh chives or scallions
10 medium-size boiling potatoes
1 can (29 oz.) peach halves
1 can (29 oz.) pear halves
1 can (29 oz.) green-tipped white asparagus
1 can (4 oz.) pimientos
1 can (20 oz.) tomato juice
1 carton (1 qt.) grapefruit juice
1½ cups shelled pecans
1 cup shelled walnuts
1 package (4 oz.) shredded coconut
strawberry and/or blueberry preserves
1 bottle (3 oz.) rosewater (available in drugstores)
vodka
Cointreau
Margarita salt

STAPLES LIST FOR A SIMPLE BRUNCH

Check your kitchen for the staples that you assume are there, and be sure you have enough of anything that is used in large amounts.

salt
coarse (kosher) salt
black pepper
white pepper
paprika
ground cinnamon
grated nutmeg, or whole nutmeg if you have a grater
granulated sugar
brown sugar
powdered (confectioners') sugar
packages of active dry yeast, if you are not using fresh yeast
baking powder
baking soda
all-purpose flour
vanilla extract
garlic
dried chervil
capers
green olives
sweet gherkins
polyunsaturated oil
vinegar
coffee
tea or tea bags

BACON AND EGG CASSEROLE   10 to 12 Servings

1 pound bacon
1½ dozen eggs
⅓ cup light cream
¼ teaspoon salt

⅛ teaspoon freshly ground pepper
1 pinch of dried chervil

Recipe Continues . . .

Separate bacon slices and place them in bottom of an oblong 3-quart casserole. Place in preheated 400°F. oven. Precook for 12 minutes. (This can be done early on the day of the party or even the day before.) Remove from oven and pour off almost all the grease, leaving just enough to coat the bottom so that the eggs will not stick to the casserole. Keep the cooked bacon strips evenly distributed in the casserole.

At 1 hour before serving, beat eggs well and add cream and seasonings. Pour over bacon and place in preheated 350°F. oven. Bake for 1 hour.

Cut into squares approximately 4 x 3 inches.

I must add that this lovely, fluffy creation is more like a soufflé and must be served at its height of beauty before it falls flat on its casserole.

How to prepare in advance: This bacon and egg casserole is so simple and easy there's no reason it can't all be done on the day of the brunch, precooking bacon and beating eggs with cream in a mixing bowl in the morning, then putting it in the oven 1 hour before serving.

However, you can do both the bacon and eggs separately the day before if you wish. Precook the bacon as directed; leave in the casserole, covered, at room temperature. Crack eggs into mixing bowl; add seasonings. Do *not* add cream until ready to bake. Do *not* put in refrigerator, as this will change texture and timing of eggs. It's perfectly fine to keep the raw eggs at room temperature overnight in a *covered* mixing bowl. However, I suggest doing this as late as possible in the evening. When you are ready to bake the casserole, add the cream to the raw eggs, whip vigorously, then pour over the bacon and pop into preheated oven. If you are doing this in advance, it is most important to remember to leave the whipping of eggs and cream until the last minute; do *not* let them set; pour over bacon immediately and put in oven immediately for the 1 hour of baking. Serve immediately. You must adhere to this schedule to get the right degree of height, volume and fluffiness in your casserole.

OVEN-BROWNED
POTATOES
10 to 12 Servings

As noted in the menu, these are optional, but if you're having a brunch where men are included, let me tell you, they'll love them!

10 medium-size potatoes	½ teaspoon paprika
2 tablespoons butter or margarine	½ teaspoon pepper
	1 can (4 oz.) chopped pimientos
½ teaspoon salt	½ cup chopped fresh parsley

A day or two before the party, boil the potatoes *unpeeled* until fork tender, being careful not to overcook. Best to prick the skins so they don't explode. Cool and refrigerate. Early in the day of the party, peel and cube potatoes.

OPTION: Again, you can do this part of your preparations the day or evening before the party. The peeled and cubed potatoes will keep overnight in the refrigerator without turning black, but be sure they are well covered.

TO HEAT: Melt butter or margarine in a large roasting pan or extralarge frying pan with heatproof handle; add potatoes and shake to coat. Sprinkle with chopped pimiento and place in 350°F. oven; stir occasionally with a long-handled spoon to keep potatoes from sticking to bottom of pan. Bake for one hour. Transfer to chafing dish. Scatter the chopped pimiento on top. Serve while hot.

You can do your Bacon and Egg Casserole and Oven-Browned Potatoes ahead of time; then bake them in the oven together.

COTTAGE CHEESE AND FRUIT PLATTER

12 to 16 Servings

1 fresh pineapple
1 can (29 oz.) peach halves
1 can (29 oz.) pear halves
1 pint fresh strawberries or crab
 apples
3 bananas
¼ cup fresh lemon juice
Few drops of green vegetable
 coloring
¼ cup shredded coconut

Romaine or Boston lettuce, or
 endive
4 pounds small-curd cottage
 cheese
Parsley sprigs
Tomato rose
Paprika
Turnip flowers
Grapefruit flowers

Cut off top and bottom of pineapple; slice lengthwise, then cut each part again into halves, yielding 4 quarters. (One large fresh pineapple should yield 5 or 6 slices per quarter.) Drain canned fruits. Wash strawberries, leaving stems on for color. If berries are not available, substitute canned crab apples. Pour lemon juice into a shallow pan and lay peeled bananas in juice to coat all over. (The purpose of this is to keep bananas from turning dark.) Blend a little of the juice with coloring, and mix with coconut. Roll bananas in coconut, then lay them on a cookie sheet until ready to use.

ARRANGEMENT: All fruit and fresh vegetable platters can be enhanced with feast-your-eyes appeal by proper color coordination and decorative touches in the arrangement, which is most important. For this one I suggest using a glass punch bowl if you have one, or any bowl with an interesting shape. Stand crisp, washed, and dried romaine, endive or Boston lettuce around border, stem ends upward. (The tops of the endive and lettuce are not as crisp and uniform as the bottoms.) Fill the bowl with cottage cheese. With the bottom of a small juice glass, make an indentation in the center and fill with parsley. Place a tomato rose* on the parsley and sprinkle cottage cheese with paprika. Place the decorated bowl

49

of cottage cheese in the center of a round 12- to 14-inch tray, or one large enough to leave ample space around base of bowl for your fruits. Put clumps of parsley in spokelike lines radiating from the base of the bowl in 4 evenly spaced sections. Decorate spokes of parsley with turnip* and grapefruit flowers.* Place the sliced pineapple in rows in one section, the peach halves, cavity side down, in the next section, the strawberries or crab apples in the third section, and the pears, cavity side down, in the fourth section.

Border the tray with the coconut-coated banana sections. Bananas should be cut into halves, then quartered lengthwise.

Now, can't you just picture how pretty this will look?

IMPORTANT: All the fruits in this recipe except the bananas can be prepared *the day before the party.* Likewise, the parsley, lettuce and endive can be cleaned the day before, wrapped in paper towels, then in plastic wrap and refrigerated. With everything prepared ahead of time, you'll only need to allow 12 or 15 minutes on the day of your party to make the arrangement for this cheese and fruit platter.

TOMATO AND ASPARAGUS VINAIGRETTE
10 to 12 Servings

This will serve as your vegetable dish.

8 medium-size tomatoes, peeled
and sliced
3 cans (13 oz. each) green-tipped
white asparagus, chilled

Parsley sprigs
Vinaigrette Dressing (recipe follows)

To make peeling tomatoes easier, either immerse them in boiling water for 15 seconds, or pierce through stem end with a long-pronged fork and rotate over direct heat until the skin pops.

*Tomato roses, turnip and grapefruit flowers all will be made in advance. See recipes in Chapter VI, pp. 181ff.

Recipe Continues . . .

ARRANGEMENT: Use an oblong tray; lay drained asparagus in 2 lengthwise rows, bottom ends touching each other. Then make a long row of parsley at tip ends of asparagus. On each side of parsley, put sliced tomatoes in equal rows on each side of platter. Moments before serving, dribble dressing lightly over tomatoes and asparagus.

This salad is no big deal to make; you should be able to do it in about 10 minutes in the morning on the day of your brunch. However, you could peel your tomatoes the evening before, wrap in plastic, and refrigerate. For that matter, if your refrigerator will hold the tray, you could make the whole arrangement the evening before but be sure you cover it tightly with foil or plastic wrap to preserve freshness.

The *pièce de résistance* for this salad is the vinaigrette dressing.

VINAIGRETTE DRESSING   1 Quart

1 cup vinegar
1 teaspoon salt
½ teaspoon white pepper
2¾ cups polyunsaturated oil
2 teaspoons minced capers
2 teaspoons minced green olives
1 teaspoon minced sweet gherkins

2 teaspoons chopped parsley
2 teaspoons chopped chives or
   scallions
1 tablespoon chopped hard-
   cooked egg
1 garlic clove, peeled

Pour vinegar into a large bowl and add salt and pepper. Beat well with a wire whip or electric beater and gradually add the oil, beating constantly until dressing thickens. Setting the bowl over another bowl filled with ice while beating will hasten the thickening process.

Stir in the next 6 ingredients until well blended. Pour into a bottle, then drop in the whole garlic clove. Refrigerate. Shake well before using. Keep garlic in the bottle until the last drop of dressing has been used. Make this dressing in advance and keep on hand for other salads as well.

•

Let me remind you, we're still on *A Simple Brunch* for a *special occasion*. The "meat and potatoes" of your menu happens to be one of the most popular all-time favorites with American taste buds. There's nothing at all wrong with good old American-style bacon and eggs and potatoes anytime, anywhere. But this is a party book and these menus are designed to help you dress up an ordinary casserole, take it out of the commonplace, and make it a gourmet delight.

Besides your salad, you'll need just the right kind of bread, roll, brioche, or coffee cake for the finishing touch. Those I have selected are especially suited to the Bacon and Egg Casserole, but they can be used with other dishes as well. All of the following recipes are given for large quantities because while you're at it, and in a baking mood, you'll want to make enough to put in the freezer and have on hand for future use.

•

HEAVENLY SOUR-CREAM CAKE   2 Cakes

¼ pound butter
¼ pound margarine
1½ cups sugar
1 teaspoon vanilla extract
1 teaspoon rosewater (this tastes
   like roses smell; available at
   most drugstores)

6 eggs
4 cups sifted flour
2 teaspoons baking powder
2 teaspoons baking soda
1 teaspoon salt
2 cups sour cream

Recipe Continues . . .

Filling and Topping

2 cups light brown sugar	½ teaspoon grated nutmeg
6 ounces butter	1½ cups shelled pecan halves
2 teaspoons ground cinnamon	

Preheat oven to 350°F. Prepare filling and topping: With fingertips, mix the brown sugar, butter, cinnamon and nutmeg. Set aside.

Butter well 2 bundt pans or angel-food pans or any 10-inch pans with a tube in center. Cream butter and margarine with sugar until light and fluffy. Add vanilla and rosewater, then add the eggs one at a time, beating well after each addition. Sift dry ingredients. Add alternately with sour cream, beginning and ending with flour. Beat for 2 minutes, frequently scraping down sides of bowl. Into each pan spread a quarter of the batter. Scatter a quarter of the pecans over batter, then a quarter of the filling and topping. Spoon over this the remainder of the batter, equally divided into the 2 pans. Spread remaining pecans, filling and topping over each cake.

Bake in the preheated oven for 1 hour. Remove from oven and let pans stand on cooling racks for 10 minutes; then invert pans to remove cakes. These will keep in refrigerator for several days. If frozen, allow to defrost at room temperature for 2 hours.

Have this recipe handy because you will receive many requests for it!

WALNUT TWISTS   36 Rolls

Make ahead and freeze. It's great to have some in the freezer at all times for the unexpected "kaffeeklatschers." Wonderful when served warm. Will defrost and be heated through in the same time it takes for the coffee to perk.

1 cake of compressed fresh yeast or package of active dry yeast

1 teaspoon and 2 cups granulated sugar

¼ cup warm water (80° to 90°F. for compressed yeast, 105° to 115°F. for dry yeast)

¼ pound margarine

½ teaspoon salt

½ cup milk, scalded

3 to 4 cups sifted flour

3 eggs, beaten

¾ cup melted butter

½ teaspoon ground cinnamon

1 cup finely chopped walnuts

In a small bowl, dissolve yeast and the 1 teaspoon sugar in warm water. Combine margarine, ½ cup sugar and the salt in a large bowl. Add scalded milk; stir until margarine is melted. Cool to lukewarm.

Add dissolved yeast and mix well. Pour in the 3 beaten eggs. Add 3½ cups of the flour gradually, beating after each addition to make a soft dough. Knead dough on lightly floured board or cloth for about 3 minutes. Grease a bowl well, put dough in, and flip over so that the top is now well greased. Cover lightly with plastic or damp towel. Let rise in warm place for about 1½ hours.

Punch down dough and divide into 3 parts. Shape each on lightly floured surface into a 12-inch roll. Divide each roll into 12 pieces. Shape each piece into a 7-inch rope. Dip each rope into melted butter, then into 1½ cups sugar and cinnamon mixed and the chopped nuts. Fold each rope in half and twist to make a braid. Place braids on greased baking sheet. Cover and let rise in a warm place until doubled in bulk, about 45 minutes. Bake in preheated 350°F. oven for 15 to 20 minutes.

Remove from pan while warm and place on a cooling rack. When cool, wrap well and freeze. To serve, remove from freezer; heat, covered with foil, in preheated 325°F. oven for 20 minutes. Serve warm.

DAINTY BRIOCHES

72 Small or 60 medium-size brioches

While these are time-consuming to make, the delicious results are well worth the effort. When you have many other details to occupy your time, the simplest way to have these delicious rolls at your brunch is to phone your favorite bakery and order them. If you prefer to do it yourself, remember that these rolls can be made in advance and frozen.

Butter
8 cups sifted flour
2 packages active dry yeast or 2 cakes of compressed fresh yeast
½ cup warm water (105° to 115° for dry yeast, 80° to 90°F. for compressed yeast)

½ cup margarine and 2 tablespoons milk
¾ cup sugar
1 teaspoon salt
6 whole eggs
10 extra egg yolks

Butter well 6 muffin tins each with 12 depressions, or 72 fluted tart pans. Sift flour, measure 8 cups, divide in half and set aside 4 cups each in 2 separate bowls. Soften yeast in warm water; let stand for 5 to 10 minutes. Scald 1 cup milk.

Put the margarine, sugar and salt into a large bowl. Pour scalded milk into the large bowl and stir to melt margarine. Set aside to cool to lukewarm. Add ½ cup flour from one of the bowls of flour and blend in until smooth. Stir in softened yeast and beat with a large wooden spoon. Gradually add remaining 3½ cups flour from the first bowl of flour, beating well after each addition. Add whole eggs one at a time, beating well after each addition, then add 8 egg yolks all at one time and beat very well. Gradually add remaining 4 cups flour, beating well for about 5 minutes. The purpose of dividing the flour into 2 separate bowls is to make sure that 4 cups are left for the last addition. Pour the batter into a buttered deep bowl and brush top with more melted butter. Cover with heavy plastic or foil, buttered on the inside. Set bowl aside in a warm place, about 80°F., and let dough rise until doubled, about 2 hours.

Punch down dough with fists. Butter surface of dough and cover again. Set in refrigerator overnight. Remove dough from refrigerator, punch down again (it will rise even in the refrigerator), and set aside, covered as before. Let rise until doubled, about 2 hours. Place dough on a lightly floured surface. Keep the portion not being shaped covered all the time.

Remove one fourth of dough from the large piece and set aside one third of this piece. Shape remaining two thirds into 18 two-inch balls. Place one ball into each muffin pan or tart pan. Form 18 small balls from remaining one third of dough. Gently roll each small ball into a cone shape between palm of hands. Cut a cross in the center of each ball and insert a cone, pointed end down. Continue until all dough is shaped. Cover and set aside in a warm place until doubled, about 30 minutes. Brush with the mixture of remaining 2 egg yolks beaten with remaining 2 tablespoons milk. Bake in a preheated 325°F. oven for 15 to 20 minutes.

(Store in refrigerator or freezer the egg whites left over from this recipe to use for the Snowballs on p. 180.)

Freeze rolls in airtight containers. To serve, defrost at room temperature for 2 hours, or cover with foil and place in preheated 325°F. oven for 20 minutes.

BUTTER CURLS

With butter curler (available in all housewares departments), using a firm grip and slight pressure, scrape sides of butter. Drop curls into a bowl of ice water until firm enough to handle. If made a few days ahead, store covered in refrigerator in a bowl free of water, or they will turn very pale. One pound of butter will make about 60 curls.

ORANGE STREUSEL COFFEE CAKE

1 Cake, about 24 pieces

The tantalizing odors of these cakes while being baked is surpassed only by their delicate flavor.

¼ pound butter	½ teaspoon salt
2 ounces margarine	2 tablespoons grated orange rind
1 cup sugar	1 tablespoon orange juice
2 cups flour	2 eggs
2 teaspoons baking powder	¾ cup cultured buttermilk
½ teaspoon baking soda	Orange Icing (recipe follows)

Preheat oven to 375°F. Cream together butter, margarine and sugar; add 1 cup of the flour and blend until mixture resembles crumbs. Remove ½ cup of this mixture and set aside. To the larger portion of mixture add baking powder, baking soda, salt, 1 tablespoon of the orange rind and the orange juice. Add eggs one at a time and beat well after each addition. Add remaining flour alternately with buttermilk, beginning and ending with flour. Do not overbeat; beat only enough to blend well. Spread batter in a well-greased baking pan 9 x 13 inches. With a fork or fingertips, work the mixture that was set aside until it resembles coarse crumbs. Add the remaining tablespoon of orange rind. Sprinkle this mixture over top of batter. Bake for 35 minutes, or until an inserted toothpick comes out clean.

While warm, dribble orange icing in thin streams over top of cake. Let cake cool. Wrap well and freeze. Remove from freezer 2 hours before serving. Allow to defrost at room temperature for 1½ to 2 hours, depending on the warmth of the room. Serving this type of coffee cake slightly warmed in oven will enhance its flavor; however, it is mighty good served at room temperature.

Orange Icing

½ cup sifted powdered sugar
1 tablespoon orange juice,
 heated

Blend sugar and juice until icing is smooth and satiny.

SALTY DOGS

**12 Drinks,
6 ounces each**

3 cups grapefruit juice
1 cup vodka
¼ cup Cointreau

1 lemon
Coarse (Kosher) salt
Crushed ice

In advance combine grapefruit juice, vodka and Cointreau; refrigerate.

Cut lemon into halves; rub rims of 6-ounce Champagne glasses with lemon halves and dip into coarse salt or Margarita salt.

When ready to serve, combine grapefruit and vodka mixture with 1 cup crushed ice. Shake well. Pour into salt-rimmed Champagne glasses.

A bowl of limes, each cut in 8 wedges, is a nice added touch for those who like the lime flavor in either Bloody Marys or Salty Dogs.

BLOODY MARY

7 Drinks

2½ cups tomato juice
2½ cups vodka
1 tablespoon lemon juice
½ teaspoon Worcestershire
 sauce

¼ teaspoon Tabasco
¼ teaspoon celery salt

This mixture can be made several days in advance, to be bottled and refrigerated.

Fill either 8- or 6-ounce glasses half full of ice. Pour in vodka mixture to fill glasses.

FLO CHART FOR A SIMPLE BRUNCH

TWO WEEKS BEFORE Decide on date. Phone invitations. Check equipment and marketing lists. Check kitchen for staples. Purchase canned and packaged items. Use this week to finish everything that can be done this far in advance. With the menu written in detail, those items prepared in advance should be checked off, and those which are yet to be prepared should be marked distinctly with red pencil as a reminder. Prepare and freeze baked goods.

ONE WEEK BEFORE Early in the week continue advance preparations. Check liquor supply, wardrobe, flowers, decorations. Cross-check with the general Flo Chart timetable in Chapter II.

TWO DAYS BEFORE Make turnip flowers, tomato roses, butter curls. Combine drink mixtures. Refrigerate.

ONE DAY BEFORE Finish marketing for fresh fruits, vegetables, salad greens, cottage cheese. Precook bacon, crack eggs, peel and cube potatoes, prepare fruits and tomatoes as instructed. Squeeze orange juice, put in refrigerator in tightly capped bottle. Assemble equipment items—trays, platters, dishes, glassware, silverware; check them off the list as they are set out. Set up tables, centerpieces, etc.

DAY OF THE PARTY Now, you see how little there's left for you to do?

In the morning, fix bananas for the fruit platter. Check the freezer; remove baked goods for defrosting. Make tomato and asparagus salad if you didn't make it the day before. Remove cottage cheese and prepared fruits from refrigerator and put them together according to instructions for the arrangement. If your refrigerator won't hold the fruit platter and bowl, it's fine to leave it out in a cool spot with a damp dish towel over it until time to serve. All of the above can be finished easily by 11:30, with lots of time to spare in between for dressing, decoration touch-ups, setting up the bar.

Your guests begin arriving at 12:30 and you should be at the door to greet them, instead of in the kitchen. About 10 minutes before they arrive, you should do the final putting together of potatoes in the roasting pan and the Bacon and Egg Casserole; leave the whipping of the eggs until last. Have the casserole ready to pop into the oven at 12:25, along with the potatoes. Plug in the coffee maker and heat water for tea.

Most of the baked goods will be fine served at room temperature; if you want to warm the brioches and walnut twists, this can be done in 5 to 10 minutes, and at the last minute while you're setting out the chilled orange juice in a pretty water pitcher, surrounded by juice glasses so guests can serve themselves.

This timetable will leave you a maximum amount of time to relax with your guests and enjoy your own party.

EGGS

Add a few drops of vinegar to the water in which eggs are poached. It will keep the eggs from running all over the pan.

Hard-cooked eggs, either shelled or unshelled, will keep well in the refrigerator for several days if stored in water-filled jars.

Cooked eggs do not freeze well; they get rubbery and watery. This is why I do not recommend making quiche far enough ahead to freeze it (see Chapter XI). Although it *can* be frozen and many people do it with relative success, the really great super-quiche depends mainly on the eggs, as do many other recipes that contain eggs.

How long will a fresh egg stay fresh in the refrigerator? Usually 2 to 3 weeks, though some people seem to keep them indefinitely. Eggs do not spoil unless they're really old; they won't make you sick if not fresh; but it isn't so much a matter of spoiling as the *degree of freshness* that makes the difference in taste as well as the tenderness of an egg. The fresher it is the better its flavor, and as it gets older, it gets tougher, because it loses its moisture and albumin.

How to test the freshness of an egg: Drop it into a glass of water. If it's fresh, it will sink to the bottom of the glass. The older it is, the higher it rises to the top. (As it loses moisture, it gets lighter.) Also when you break an egg, notice the yolk. The older it is, the darker the yolk, also sometimes runny. A fresh egg has a nice plump, pale lemon-yellow yolk.

PARSLEY
Parsley will stay beautifully fresh if you first rinse it, then shake off all the water and put it in a plastic bag; blow up the bag as you would a balloon. Close the top with a metal tie and refrigerate.

HEATING ROLLS AND BURNED BOTTOMS
Do not heat rolls until just before serving. Even covered with linen napkins, they cool quickly. The same applies to toast.

Have a fine grater handy just in case the buns, toast or pastries burn a little on the bottom. Rub them firmly across the grater and presto! No more burned bottoms.

PINEAPPLE
Many people make a mistake in buying pineapple only when it is soft and brown on the outside; this can mean it's almost rotten inside. It's best to buy pineapple when it is still somewhat green outside. It will be sweet and delicious inside. Don't be deceived into thinking that a pineapple isn't ripe if still green on the outside. Even if quite green, a pineapple will ripen *in the refrigerator* in 2 days. When purchased ahead of party time, pineapples should always be refrigerated, not left out to ripen and rot inside. There's nothing worse than an overripe and squishy-squashy glob of pineapple. Some recipes call for canned crushed pineapple but *fresh* pineapple should always be served in delectable bite-size chunks or slices.

Cut pineapple lengthwise into quarters. Cut away the center hard core. With a sharp paring knife, cut close to the shell, but not too close; you do not want to retain any of those prickly brown spots. Lift section out of shell. Slice into 5 or 6 long slices.

ENGLISH MUFFINS
I recommend using whole, unsplit English muffins and splitting them with a fork. This creates little ducts and valleys for the butter to seep in. The muffins taste much better when prepared this way than when halved with a knife, which leaves a smooth, flat surface.

COFFEE AND TEA
I recommend using decaffeinated coffee exclusively at large parties because it's less complicated and troublesome than having separate pots for decaffeinated and regular coffee. More people today are into health foods and abstain from coffee either by personal choice or on a doctor's advice. The decaffeinated coffee won't hurt them and the regular-coffee drinkers probably won't be able to tell the difference. One pound of coffee will make 60 cups of a rather mild brew. Allow 2 cups per person when serving coffee with dinner or breakfast, but only ½ cup when serving with tea at a tea party.

You will note that coffee and tea are on almost every menu and that in my Flo chart instructions, I remind you to PLUG THE COFFEE MAKER IN a few hours before serving. This is to prevent an overloading of your electrical circuits while you're using the oven, toaster, blender or other electrical appliances for the rest of your food preparations. The electric coffee maker automatically turns itself off when the coffee has perked enough but also automatically remains on WARM which uses less current. See page 128 for hints on making tea properly.

MY FAVORITE BRUNCH

(For 12)

MENU

Apple Juice with Frozen Lemon Cubes
Baked Canadian Bacon
Polka-Dot Egg Casserole
Rice Ring with Sherried Chicken Livers
Compote de fruits
Sesame Loops
Chocolate-Chip Coffee Cake
Walnut Butterhorns
Coffee or tea, or both

This is one of my all-time favorite brunch menus and a great favorite with everyone who has sampled it. With the exception of the chicken livers and the egg casserole, everything can be prepared in advance. Although these are to be cooked shortly before serving, the component parts can be made ready in advance so there need not be any last-minute pressure. They're among the few dishes requiring same-day preparation that I recommend because they're so yummy. Neither the egg casserole nor rice and chicken livers is difficult to prepare the same day of your brunch, if you have yourself well organized in all other departments.

EQUIPMENT WORK SHEET FOR MY FAVORITE BRUNCH

Champagne glasses for apple juice
water pitcher
roasting pan for Canadian bacon
tray, about 16 x 20 inches
small carving board
carving knife

ovenproof casserole, 11 x 7 x 2½ inches, for Polka-Dot Egg Casserole
chafing dish or warmer for casserole
2½-quart ring mold
large round tray, about 20 inches, for Rice Ring
large bowl for fruit compote
serving pieces
2 roll trays or baskets
small deep bowl for butter curls
oblong tray for coffee cake
cake platter or large glass tray
24-cup coffee maker
coffee urn for self-service
teapot
silver coffee/tea service and silverware
tables and chairs
tablecloths
luncheon-size napkins
dinner plates
sauce dishes for compote
dessert plates
cups and saucers
salt and pepper shakers
sugar and creamer for each table
ashtrays

MARKETING WORK SHEET FOR MY FAVORITE BRUNCH

1½ quarts milk
2 cups coffee cream
2 cups dairy sour cream
1 pound Cheddar cheese
1½ pounds butter, or 1 pound butter and ½ pound margarine
1 pound butter for butter curls
20 eggs
12 ounces chicken fat, or ¾ pound margarine
4 pounds fresh chicken livers

4 pounds Canadian bacon, in one piece
1 cake of compressed fresh yeast
3 lemons
1 green pepper
2 bunches of parsley, or 1 bunch of parsley and 1 bunch of watercress
1 pound long-grain rice
3 quarts apple juice
2 cans (6 oz. each) frozen lemonade
1 can (29 oz.) crushed pineapple
1 can (3 oz.) pimientos
1 box (2 oz.) sesame seeds
1 package (3 lbs.) frozen white bread dough (3 loaves)
1 box (8 oz.) quick-cooking tapioca
1½ pounds dried apricots
1½ pounds dried prunes
½ pound dried pears
½ pound dried apples
¼ pound dried peaches
10 ounces seeded white raisins
10 ounces dried currants
1 cup shelled walnuts
1 cup semisweet chocolate pieces
sherry

Most of these items can be purchased in advance, but chicken livers and parsley and/or watercress should be purchased at the last moment.

STAPLES LIST FOR MY FAVORITE BRUNCH

salt
white pepper
ground cinnamon
ground cloves
ground ginger
cinnamon sticks

dry mustard
granulated sugar
brown sugar
powdered (confectioners') sugar
packages of active dry yeast, if you are not using fresh yeast
all-purpose flour
Tabasco
Worcestershire sauce
curry seasoning
bottled gravy seasoning
soy sauce
dehydrated onion flakes
dried chervil
coffee
tea or tea bags

APPLE JUICE WITH FROZEN
LEMON CUBES 15 Servings

2 cans (6 oz. each) frozen lem-   3 quarts apple juice
onade, defrosted

Empty defrosted cans of lemonade into a mixing bowl. Add 2 cans of cold water and mix well. Pour into ice-cube trays and freeze. When frozen solid, remove from trays and store in freezer bags or containers.

To serve; chill the apple juice. Place a frozen lemon cube in a Champagne glass and pour in juice.

By adding the frozen lemon cubes to the apple juice, you take it out of a rather ordinary category and make it something very special. Also, serving it in Champagne glasses instead of juice glasses lends an elegance to this simple drink and to the party itself.

This juice course, as you can see, can be prepared well in advance of your party brunch.

BAKED CANADIAN BACON   12 Servings

Some markets do not carry Canadian bacon in rolls as large as 4 pounds. However, it is readily available when ordered in advance.

4 pounds precooked Canadian bacon
1 can (29 oz.) crushed pineapple
¾ cup light brown sugar
1½ tablespoons dry mustard
1½ tablespoons soy sauce
¼ cup lemon juice
1 teaspoon ground ginger
½ teaspoon ground cinnamon
¼ teaspoon ground cloves
Watercress or parsley sprigs
4 marshmallow flowers

Preheat oven to 350°F. Remove paper casing or other wrapping from the bacon and place in a rather deep roasting or baking pan. Combine other ingredients except garnishes and pour over bacon roll. Place in the preheated oven and bake for 50 minutes, basting every 10 to 15 minutes.

This can be prepared the day before the party, then reheated.

When ready to serve, the bacon should have a lovely glaze and tantalizing aroma. Place it on a small carving board in center of a tray; slice as thin as possible; pour over all the pineapple sauce from the pan in which it was baked. Decorate tray with well-dried watercress or parsley sprigs. Put a cluster of 4 marshmallow flowers on top of bacon roll, using parsley stems as stems for the flowers.

POLKA-DOT EGG CASSEROLE   12 Servings

Butter
2 cups shredded Cheddar cheese
1½ dozen eggs
1½ cups milk
½ teaspoon salt
¼ teaspoon crumbled dried chervil
¼ teaspoon white pepper
½ teaspoon Tabasco
1 can (3 oz.) pimientos, chopped
½ medium-size green pepper, chopped

Preheat oven to 350°F. Butter well a casserole 11 x 7 x 2½ inches. Scatter the shredded cheese on bottom. Beat together the eggs and milk. Add all remaining ingredients and carefully pour over the cheese. Bake for 50 minutes to 1 hour, or until set. Serve immediately.

Important note: You may want to bake your Canadian bacon at the same time. You can have it all ready to pop into the oven along with the egg casserole; or bake it earlier and reheat for 20 minutes while eggs are baking. Again, if you're ambitious, you may want to double or triple this recipe; then use 2 or 3 casseroles, but remember to double or triple all the other recipes in this brunch menu too!

As in the previous menu, the ingredients in this casserole can be assembled and prepared ahead of time: cheese shredded, eggs cracked, pimiento and green pepper chopped.

RICE RING WITH SHERRIED CHICKEN LIVERS

12 Generous servings

Rice Ring

Butter for mold	1 pound uncooked long-grain
1¼ quarts water	rice
1 teaspoon salt	Parsley
¼ teaspoon curry seasoning	Tomato Roses (p. 182)
2 ounces butter or margarine	

Butter a 2½-quart ring mold well. Combine water, seasoning and butter or margarine in a large cooking pan; bring to a boil. Stir rice into water, reduce heat to low, and cover tightly. Cook until all the water has been absorbed, 20 to 25 minutes. Remove from heat and let stand for 5 minutes. Fluff with a fork and pack into the buttered mold. Set in a pan with warm water three quarters up the sides of the mold until ready to serve. When ready to serve, remove mold from pan of water and let stand for a few minutes.

Put a serving tray 3 to 4 inches larger than the mold over the

Recipe Continues . . .

top of it; hold the mold firmly with your thumbs; quickly flip over the tray and mold. Tap gently on the surface of the table and carefully remove the mold. Fill center with sherried chicken livers, which you're preparing at same time rice is cooking, and surround the outer edge with tomato roses in beds of parsley. The roses can be made a day or two ahead and kept in a plastic refrigerator bag.

The rice ring can be made the day before the brunch, packed into the buttered mold, and refrigerated.

Sherried Chicken Livers

4 pounds fresh chicken livers
1½ cups milk
½ cup chicken fat or margarine
½ cup all-purpose flour
1 tablespoon dehydrated onion flakes
1 tablespoon Worcestershire sauce

1 tablespoon salt
½ tablespoon bottled gravy seasoning
2 cups water
2 cups dairy sour cream
1 cup sherry wine

Rinse chicken livers. Heat milk until warm; do not boil. Drop livers into milk, about one third at a time. Cook for 2 to 3 minutes, then remove with a slotted spoon onto paper towels and pat until dried. Repeat until all of the livers have been cooked. This process will insure against discoloration of the gravy. It also helps to bring out the sweet flavor of the livers. Melt fat or margarine in a heavy skillet. Sauté livers for 5 minutes, stirring gently. Remove them from skillet to a bowl or pan and set aside. Stir flour, onion flakes, Worcestershire sauce, salt and gravy seasoning into drippings in skillet. Gradually stir in 2 cups of water. Bring to a boil, stirring constantly. Boil gently for 1 minute. Remove skillet from heat.

Combine sour cream and wine. With a wire whip, stir into the gravy in the skillet, whipping to a smooth consistency. Add the chicken livers. Heat, but do *not* boil as this could curdle the sour cream. (It would also curdle if chilled and reheated, so can't be made in advance and refrigerated.) To serve, spoon into center of rice ring.

COMPOTE DE FRUITS   15 Servings

Because of its sweetness, this delicious Danish dish is usually served as a dessert. However, I enjoy serving it with this type of menu because it complements the other dishes and is always a favorite with guests. It can also be served warm as an accompaniment to beef, particularly pot roast of beef.

I have given this recipe in ample proportions because it's a dish that will be gobbled up. It can be made a week or so in advance and refrigerated if placed in plastic containers with tight-fitting lids. Many people, when they're going to so much trouble to make something special, prefer to make enough to have on hand for future use.

1½ pounds dried apricots	1½ cups seeded white raisins
1½ pounds dried prunes	1½ cups dried currants
½ pound dried pears	¾ cup quick-cooking tapioca
½ pound dried apples	1 lemon, sliced
¼ pound dried peaches	2 cinnamon sticks
5 quarts water	2 cups sugar

If you do not have a pot large enough to hold this much fruit and water, divide the ingredients into halves or thirds, and cook in batches. Bear in mind that the fruit will swell and the capacity of the saucepan (preferably stainless-steel or enamel) should be large enough to allow for the expansion of the fruit. Add enough of the water to cover completely all the fruits with the exception of the raisins and currants. Reserve the balance of the water. Allow fruits to soak in the water for at least 6 hours, or preferably overnight.

Add the raisins and currants and the rest of the water. Stir in the tapioca; add the lemon slices, cinnamon sticks and sugar. Bring slowly to the boiling point. Cover the pan or pans, reduce heat, and simmer very slowly for 2 hours, stirring occasionally

Recipe Continues . . .

with a wooden spoon to prevent the fruits sticking to the bottom of the pan. Let cool.

Remove and discard cinnamon sticks. Ladle compote into the bowl from which it is to be served, and cover with plastic wrap. Refrigerate if prepared a day or more in advance. However, allow to stand at room temperature before serving, allowing enough time to remove the chill.

To serve as a dessert, spoon into compote glasses or saucers and top with a dollop of sweetened whipped cream. But you don't need this when served with the egg casserole and rice and chicken livers. Best to keep it as a fruit complement.

SESAME LOOPS   24 Rolls

When you have a full day to devote to baking breads, rolls and coffee cakes, making your own dough is a bit more economical and undoubtedly more gratifying. However, with so many details to occupy your attention before a large party, I wholly recommend using prepared frozen dough as a short cut. Aside from the convenience, the results are very satisfactory and defy censure from the most discriminating devotee of homebaked rolls and coffee cakes.

1 package (3 lbs.) frozen white bread dough (3 loaves)	1 egg Sesame seeds

Remove frozen bread dough from freezer and allow to defrost at room temperature. This will take upwards of 5 hours. Or defrost dough in the refrigerator overnight and then stand at room temperature for about 3 hours. Separate the 3 loaves and cut one into halves. Set aside 1½ loaves for the Walnut Butterhorns (p. 71); cover with a plastic bag or double thick layer of wax paper.

Divide the full loaf into 4 pieces and the half loaf into 2 pieces. Roll each piece out on a lightly floured board into a rope about 8 inches long and 1 inch wide. Divide each rope into 4 pieces. With the palm of the hand, roll the pieces into strands about 4 inches long. Hold the left end of the strand between the left thumb and middle finger. Grasp the right end and loop around the forefinger. Slip the end through the loop like a dough knot. Brush the tops of the rolls with the egg that has been lightly beaten with 1 teaspoon water. Sprinkle sesame seeds on top. Let rise until doubled, about 1 hour.

Preheat oven to 360°F. Bake loops for 20 minutes. These baked rolls will keep well in the freezer for several weeks when well wrapped. To serve, remove from freezer at least 3 hours before serving. Heat in a preheated 350°F. oven for 5 minutes before serving.

WALNUT BUTTERHORNS   36 Rolls

Without a doubt, these are the lightest, flakiest, most delicate and melt-in-your mouth sweet rolls it will be your pleasure to devour! When time permits, prepare a batch made from all 3 loaves of frozen bread dough and freeze for future use. When that unexpected company arrives, you'll be delighted you did.

1½ loaves defrosted frozen bread (see Sesame Loops, p. 70)	¾ cup sugar
	1 teaspoon ground cinnamon
	½ cup chopped shelled walnuts
½ pound cold butter	Icing (recipe follows)
¼ cup melted butter	

When dough has defrosted and risen to double its volume, knead both pieces together to form one smooth ball. Cover and let rest for 10 minutes. Roll dough out on pastry cloth or lightly floured board to form a rectangle approximately 12 x 36 inches. Cut one third of the cold butter into small pieces and scatter over center third of dough. Fold the right third of the dough over the buttered section. Scatter another one third of the butter cut into small pieces over that surface. Fold the left third of the dough over the buttered section. Turn the dough one quarter turn (imagining the bottom of folded dough at 6 o'clock, turn to 3 o'clock). Roll it again into a rectangle about ½ inch thick. Scatter the center third of the rectan-

Recipe Continues . . .

gle with the remaining butter, cut into small pieces. Bring ends of the rectangle to meet in the center, then fold in half, bringing the edges together. Place on a greased pan, cover, and let rise until almost doubled, about 1 hour.

Punch dough down, wrap in a plastic bag, and refrigerate for at least 3 hours or overnight. When ready to bake, divide dough into 6 equal portions. Return 5 pieces to the refrigerator as you work on the first piece. Remove 1 piece at a time from the refrigerator as needed. Place dough on pastry cloth or lightly floured board and tap lightly with a rolling pin. Roll into a circle until the dough is about ¼ inch thick. Brush surface of dough with some of the melted butter. Sprinkle with some of the combined sugar and cinnamon and walnuts. With a sharp knife, cut dough into 6 pie-shaped wedges. Starting at wide end, roll toward the center, placing point end down on an ungreased cookie sheet. Continue until all dough is shaped. Let horns rise until about doubled, 50 minutes to 1 hour.

Preheat oven to 375°F. Bake horns for 20 to 25 minutes. Remove to cooling rack and spread tops with icing.

To make these several days or weeks in advance, wrap well and freeze *uniced*. To serve, remove from freezer at least 3 hours in advance; spread with icing. As with all rolls, heating them for just a few minutes before serving is an added bonus.

Icing

2 tablespoons lemon juice, heated	1 cup sifted powdered sugar

Stir heated juice into the sugar and beat until smooth. Spread on top of butterhorns.

CHOCOLATE-CHIP COFFEE CAKE
1 Cake

Some recipes do not do so well when doubled or tripled. This cake is best prepared one at a time. Its regal height and crowning shape is so attractive that it is worth the effort of making additional cakes. These can be frozen and kept for several weeks, if properly wrapped.

1 package active dry yeast or 1 cake of compressed fresh yeast	1 cup milk
	2 ounces butter or margarine
	1 teaspoon salt
¼ cup warm water (105° to 115°F. for dry yeast, 80° to 90°F. for compressed yeast)	3¼ cups all-purpose flour
	1 egg
1 teaspoon and ¼ cup sugar	Chocolate Topping (recipe follows)

Soften yeast in warm water with 1 teaspoon sugar sprinkled in the water. Set aside until mixture becomes foamy and light. Scald the milk. Add ¼ cup sugar, butter or margarine, and salt to milk. Cool to lukewarm. Add 1 cup flour and beat well. Beat in softened yeast and the egg. Work in remaining flour to form a soft dough. Cover and let rise in warm place until doubled in bulk, 1½ to 2 hours.

Grease a 10-inch tube pan. Punch dough down and turn out on lightly floured pastry cloth or board. Roll into a rectangle 1-inch thick.

Sprinkle three quarters of the chocolate topping over the entire surface of the dough. Roll tightly, lengthwise, and place in the greased tube pan, squeezing the ends together. Sprinkle remaining topping over top of dough and press lightly into the surface. Let rise at room temperature until almost doubled in bulk, about 1½ hours.

Preheart oven to 350°F. Bake the cake for 50 minutes. Remove to a cooling rack, and let stand for 10 minutes. Invert pan and remove cake. When cool, turn cake over to its upright position and enjoy the chocolate aroma. To enhance the already delicious flavor, serve warm.

If baked and frozen, keep well wrapped while defrosting at room temperature. Then warm just before serving.

Recipe Continues . . .

Chocolate Topping

½ cup packed brown sugar
2 tablespoons soft butter
1 cup semisweet chocolate
pieces

2 tablespoons flour
½ cup chopped shelled walnuts

Mix all ingredients with tips of the fingers until crumbly.

FLO CHART FOR MY FAVORITE BRUNCH

TWO TO THREE WEEKS BEFORE Decide on date. Phone invitations. Check equipment and marketing lists. Check kitchen for staples. Do advance marketing. Place order for Canadian bacon and chicken livers. Prepare and freeze sesame loops, butterhorns, chocolate-chip coffee cake, grapefruit and orange-rind flowers (if you're using these).

THREE DAYS BEFORE Prepare fruit compote. Refrigerate.

TWO DAYS BEFORE Pick up Canadian bacon and chicken livers; refrigerate apple juice. Prepare frozen lemon cubes and refrigerate.

ONE DAY BEFORE Prepare Canadian bacon and marshmallow flowers. Combine eggs with all ingredients except milk; let set out of refrigerator overnight. Prepare rice ring. Assemble all dry ingredients and seasonings for chicken livers on a small tray. Set up buffet.

DAY OF THE PARTY

9 A.M. Remove baked goods from freezer, fruit compote, rice ring and Canadian bacon from refrigerator. Place baked goods and fruit compote on the buffet table.

10 A.M. Plug in coffee maker; keep warm. Heat water for tea. Remove sour cream from refrigerator. Butter casserole; scatter on the shredded cheese, set aside. Preheat oven to 350°F.

11:30 A.M. Set rice ring in pan of hot water. Cover with foil. Heat on top burner.

11:35. Time to get dressed and have your second cup of coffee because there's nothing else to do.

12:00. Put Canadian bacon in oven. Cook chicken livers in milk, set aside. Beat eggs, milk and remaining ingredients; pour over cheese; bake. Set out butter or margarine on buffet. Put frozen lemon cubes in glasses (it's good if they melt a little).

12:30. Guests arrive. Say "Hello." Pour chilled apple juice into glasses; serve.

12:45. Slip quietly into the kitchen. Fix the sherried chicken livers.

12:50. While livers are cooking, remove rice ring from mold onto serving tray. Set bacon on buffet.

12:55. Remove egg casserole from oven, set on buffet table. Spoon chicken livers in center of rice ring. Place on buffet.

1 P.M. Voila! Brunch is ready.

You will note that for this brunch I have allowed only half an hour between guests' arrival and serving time, since the menu calls for apple juice rather than bar service. Not everyone serves drinks (liquor) before brunch! However, if you prefer to serve Bloody Marys and Salty Dogs with this brunch, simply move your guests' arrival time up to 12 noon or your serving time to 1:30, and adjust your timetable accordingly. My Flo charts cannot apply to everyone individually; they are intended as guides to help you with your own timetables.

CANADIAN BACON

While at first glance Canadian bacon may seem to be much more expensive than regular bacon, when you consider that there is no loss in cooking, it really isn't an extravagant item. Furthermore, it has the best of two worlds, bacon and ham, the nice tender texture of ham and the delicious flavor of bacon. A delightful treat for either breakfast or brunch.

AN ELEGANT BRUNCH

(For 30)

MENU

Chilled Spinach Soup
Savory Dilled Fresh Salmon
Poached Eggs in Artichoke Bottoms, Hollandaise Sauce
California Fruit Platter
Hearts of Palm and Sliced Tomatoes
Thin-sliced rye and pumpernickle bread
Tiny Bagels, whipped cream cheese
Strawberry Crème Crêpes
   (served with fresh or frozen sliced strawberries and sour
   cream)
Coffee or tea, or both

There you have it. Looks formidable, doesn't it? We'll take it a step at a time and you'll see how simple everything is.

The proportions in these recipes are all for 30 people because a truly elegant brunch deserves an elegant assemblage of guests to oooh and aaah and admire. As the hostess with the most chutzpah, your brunch party will be a conversation piece. If you prefer to cut the recipes down to half or a third, it's up to you, but you'll have to do your own arithmetic. (There is one complication: it's hard to get one third of an 8- to 9-pound salmon. You'll have to buy it sliced.)

Note: While the food in this menu will be served buffet-style, remember, this is *An Elegant Brunch,* and therefore elegantly set tables should be used. Don't treat your guests inelegantly by making them eat this brunch lap-style.

EQUIPMENT WORK SHEET FOR AN ELEGANT BRUNCH

30 punch cups
10-quart punch bowl for Chilled Spinach Soup
punch ladle
large oval tray for salmon
small glass bowl for capers
tiny spoons for capers
peppermill
long narrow tray for Hearts of Palm and Tomatoes
small bowl for Hollandaise Sauce
large round or oblong platter, or large cookie sheet covered with foil, for
    fruits
2 bread trays
servings pieces
small bowl and ladle for fruit dressing
chafing dish for Poached Eggs in Artichoke Bottoms
tray and electric warmer for filled crêpes
bowl and ladle or large serving spoon for fresh strawberries
bowl and serving spoon for sour cream
75-cup coffee maker
coffee urn for self-service
teapot
silver coffee and tea service
tables and chairs (preferably 5 round tables to seat 6 each)
tablecloths
luncheon-size napkins
dinner plates
dessert plates
cups and saucers
silverware (place settings)
salt and pepper shakers
sugar and creamer for each table
ashtrays

MARKETING WORK SHEET FOR AN ELEGANT BRUNCH

1 quart milk
5 cups coffee cream
2 quarts dairy sour cream
2 pounds cream cheese
1 pound whipped cream cheese, for bagels
1 pound butter
5 dozen eggs
1 whole fresh salmon, 8 to 9 pounds, or 5 pounds thin-sliced smoked
    salmon
12 slicing oranges
1 large orange (for grated rind)
8 large grapefruits
18 lemons (12 for juice)
10 tomatoes
6 avocados
4 large onions
8 pounds fresh spinach
1 head of lettuce
3 bunches of parsley
2 bunches of watercress
1 large bunch of fresh dill
fresh chives
4 pints fresh strawberries, or 6 packages (10 oz. each) frozen strawberries
6 cans (15 oz. each) hearts of palm
6 cans (8 oz. each) artichoke bottoms
2 cans (16 oz. each) large ripe olives
1 jar (3 oz.) capers
1 can (6 oz.) frozen orange juice
1 can (3 oz.) frozen daiquiri mix
1 can (12 oz.) peach nectar
1 jar (12 oz.) strawberry preserves
2 loaves of thin-sliced rye bread
1 pound thin-sliced pumpernickel bread
pink and green food coloring

STAPLES LIST FOR AN ELEGANT BRUNCH

salt
coarse (kosher) salt
white peppercorns
cayenne pepper
paprika
dry mustard
prepared mustard
granulated sugar
active dry yeast
flour
vanilla extract
salad oil
wine vinegar
ketchup
coffee
tea or tea bags

CHILLED SPINACH SOUP   8 to 10 Quarts

8 pounds fresh spinach   2 cups lemon juice
8 quarts water   16 eggs
4 large onions   1 quart dairy sour cream
8 tablespoons salt   Thin lemon slices
2 cups sugar

Cut thoroughly washed spinach into small pieces. Place in large
kettle with water; add peeled whole onions and salt. Cook for 30
minutes. Add sugar and lemon juice; cook for 10 minutes longer.
Remove from heat. Discard onions. Beat eggs until foamy. Very
slowly pour one quarter of the hot soup into eggs while beating
constantly until soup has been added. Then reverse this by pouring
the egg-soup mixture slowly into remaining soup. Chill.

When soup is thoroughly chilled, strain 4 cups of it into the
quart of sour cream and beat until well blended. Whirl the remain-

Recipe Continues . . .

ing soup in a blender. Combine with the sour cream-soup mixture. Stir until well blended. Chill.

To serve, pour soup into a glass punch bowl and float thin lemon slices on top. Ladle into punch cups for guests to drink, and cheer. Can be made days in advance and kept chilled.

SAVORY DILLED FRESH SALMON
30 Servings

This superb treatment of fresh salmon should not be confused with the commercially prepared lox or smoked Nova Scotia salmon. Rather it is like the traditional Scandinavian *gravlax*, salt-and-sugar-cured raw salmon. Your fish supplier can obtain the whole salmon (two sides) all ready to serve, but I encourage you to prepare your own fish. You will not only save about one fourth of the cost of the prepared fish but you'll learn the difference between "good" and "exceptionally good."

1 fresh salmon, 8 to 9 pounds
¼ cup coarse salt
½ cup sugar
1 large bunch of fresh dill (if not available, substitute 3 tablespoons dried dill)
2 tablespoons crushed white peppercorns (if not available,

substitute ground white pepper)
Parsley sprigs
Lemon slices
Large ripe olives
Capers
Dill sprigs

Remove the head and tail of fish and save them to use in arrangement of the platter. Cut the salmon lengthwise into halves. Remove the large backbone and all smaller bones. Place one half of the salmon, bone side up, on a cookie sheet or pan with sides. Mix salt and sugar and scatter over surface of fish. Lay the bunch of dill on fish and grind peppercorns over all. If using dried dill and ground pepper, mix them together and sprinkle over fish. Lay other half of fish on top, skin side up. Cover with a double-thick layer of wax paper or aluminum foil and place another cookie sheet or pan on top. Weight this with heavy objects, such as large cans of food or foil-covered bricks. Refrigerate for at least 48 hours. Turn the fish over every 10 to 12 hours and baste with the liquids that will accumulate. Force some of the liquid with the baster between the halves, and each time replace the pan and weights.

On the day before your brunch, remove fish from pan. Separate the halves and clean the surface of each with a damp towel, brushing off the dill and seasoning. Place one half at a time on carving board or ordinary bread board. With a very sharp knife, starting at the tail end of the fish, slice very thin on the diagonal. Place slices as you go along on sheets of wax paper until all the fish is so carved. Then follow the suggested platter arrangement and refrigerate until just before serving.

If you should prefer to use a ready-to-serve whole smoked Nova Scotia salmon, slice and arrange it exactly as described above; or if you buy it already sliced, follow the directions for the platter arrangement.

ARRANGEMENT: On a large oval tray, shape a mound of chopped lettuce to resemble the form of the salmon before it was sliced.

Place the head in position and lay the outside skin over the chopped lettuce; then place the tail in its proper place. Overlap the slices of salmon to cover the skin completely, building slices up a bit higher in the middle. Roll the remaining slices into spirals and border the entire tray with them.

Lay clumps of parsley between the fish and spirals. Cut thin slices of lemon halfway from the center to outer edge and twist. Lay these lemon twists on the parsley, alternating them with large ripe olives.

Should you receive the fish with its head removed, fill in that space with parsley or watercress, topped with a bouquet of small turnip flowers (p. 183).

Surround the platter with a small bowl of capers, a peppermill, and a small bowl of minced fresh dill.

POACHED EGGS IN
ARTICHOKE BOTTOMS   36 Servings

This really is the *pièce de résistance* of this menu. I didn't believe
it until I tried it. I had read that you could poach eggs a day or so
before serving, and when reheated they would taste as though they
had just been poached. Well, they do! Until I discovered this
method I didn't use eggs on menus for large groups, only for small
groups. But now I find it's no problem at all to prepare and serve
these poached eggs to large groups, and I trust neither will you.

36 medium-size fresh eggs   Hollandaise Sauce (recipe fol-
6 cans (8 oz. each) artichoke   lows)
  bottoms   6 tablespoons chopped fresh
Salt and pepper   parsley

To poach eggs, break them one at a time into a cup and slip each
egg into a shallow pan filled with simmering water. Simmer, and
baste often with the water. Cook for 4 to 5 minutes, until set.
Drain. Remove with a slotted spoon to a lightly greased cookie
sheet until cool enough to handle. Using a round cookie cutter, or
perhaps a jar top, cut eggs to fit cavity of artichoke bottoms. Pour
cold water into large jars to half-fill them and gently slip eggs into
the water. Refrigerate until shortly before using.

    To serve, reheat eggs by sliding them into slowly simmering
water in a shallow pan, such as a large frying pan, until warmed
through. Heat the artichoke bottoms in the liquid of the can until
warmed. Do not cook, as they are fully prepared and need only to
be heated. When ready to serve, first transfer the artichoke bottoms to a chafing dish; then spoon a poached egg into cavity of
each artichoke. Season eggs lightly with salt and pepper.

    Spoon hollandaise sauce over eggs. Sprinkle chopped parsley
over sauce.

HOLLANDAISE SAUCE   4 Cups

6 egg yolks, at room temperature
¼ cup lemon juice
¾ pound butter

2 tablespoons hot water
1 teaspoon salt
1 teaspoon prepared mustard
Pinch of cayenne pepper

Combine egg yolks and lemon juice in a blender. Melt butter, being careful that it does not brown. Add the hot water to the egg yolks and lemon juice and turn blender to highest speed as you very slowly pour in the hot butter in a steady stream. Add remaining ingredients and whirl until all ingredients are well blended, about 1 minute.

To keep sauce warm, pour into top part of double boiler over hot water. It will stay warm for quite a while. It may be necessary to stir again before serving.

If sauce is made a day or more ahead, warm it in a double boiler over hot, not boiling, water; stir until smooth and warm.

Save the 6 egg whites to make a Coconut Meringue Shell for a Chocolate Melt-away Pie (see Sweet Tooth Party, p. 144).

CALIFORNIA FRUIT PLATTER   30 Servings

8 large grapefruits
12 slicing oranges
6 ripe avocados

Fruit Dressing (recipe follows)
2 bunches of watercress

Here is an opportunity to make your decorative flowers from orange and grapefruit rinds. Your accomplishments will be two-fold as you will use the fruit itself and also use the flowers to decorate this and other arrangements.

Recipe Continues . . .

Grapefruit and Orange Roses

To make "roses" you will need a small very sharp paring knife. Starting at the stem end, make a slight cut at about a 90-degree angle, approximately ½ inch wide. Peel the fruit in a spiral fashion, keeping the width as uniform as possible. Cut away a piece about 1 inch long from the end and begin to re-wind spiral peeling, starting with the stem-end peel. Wind in a circle. Continue until all the rind has been wound and secure with a toothpick. Peeling will fall into the shape of a rose. Drop into jar or container with water colored with vegetable dye. Store in the refrigerator. When ready to use, drain well on paper towels.

ARRANGEMENT: Slice the peeled grapefruits and oranges into round slices, making certain that when you peel the fruits you remove all the white pulp. Peel avocados and cut into vertical slices with the knife striking the large pit. Grapefruits and oranges can be sliced a day in advance. Avocados should not be sliced more than a few hours before serving, to prevent them turning black.

Place a small bowl for dressing in the center of a round tray. Starting at outer edge, alternate slices of fruit in a circular fashion. (Grapefruit, orange, avocado.) Make 2 circular rows, separating them with sprigs of watercress. Place 4 or 5 "roses" on the watercress, using a variety of colors. Refrigerate until serving time. Fill bowl with dressing which has been stirred well.

FRUIT DRESSING   3 Cups

1 can (6 oz.) frozen orange
  juice
1 can (3 oz.) frozen daiquiri
  mix
1 can (12 oz.) peach nectar
½ cup salad oil

¼ cup wine vinegar
¼ cup ketchup
½ teaspoon salt
⅛ teaspoon paprika
½ teaspoon dry mustard

Defrost orange juice and daiquiri mix; combine with nectar. Beat in remaining ingredients until all are well blended. Shake well before using. Keep under refrigeration.

HEARTS OF PALM AND SLICED TOMATOES

30 Servings

6 cans (15 oz. each) hearts of palm
10 slicing tomatoes, peeled

Parsley sprigs
2 tablespoons chopped chives

Drain hearts of palm and cut into crosswise slices. Using a long and narrow tray, lay the hearts of palm in crosswise rows on both ends of the tray. Slice tomatoes and place them in lengthwise rows, separated with parsley sprigs. Sprinkle chopped chives over tomatoes.

For added color and beauty, remove some of the hearts of palm from one corner of the tray and in its place put a large clump of parsley. Lay on it some of the flowers made from the orange and grapefruit rinds (p. 84), or those made from turnips (p. 183), or a combination of both. Arrange as you would a bouquet.

Note: If you think you don't need two salads, take your choice. But some of your guests might like a choice.

TINY BAGELS

24 Bagels

Those tiny delicious rolls known as bagels are now available in most markets. They are packaged in miniature size, one dozen to the package. I prefer this size to the larger standard size for this menu, which also includes rye and pumpernickel breads.

It is said that making bagels is an ancient art. Perhaps it is, because there are days when I feel absolutely "ancient" that I find making bagels quite simple. I'm sure you'll find it simple, too, though you needn't consider yourself antique, just unique.

Recipe Continues . . .

3 cups flour
1¼ teaspoons salt
2 tablespoons sugar
1 package active dry yeast
⅔ cup lukewarm water (105° to 115°F.)

3 tablespoons salad oil
1 egg, slightly beaten
4 quarts boiling water with 2 tablespoons sugar

Sift dry ingredients into a large mixing bowl. Dissolve yeast in ⅓ cup water. Set aside for a few minutes. Add remaining water to the oil, then add to the dissolved yeast. Make a well in the center of the flour mixture and stir in half the liquid mixture. To the remaining liquid add the egg. Then all at once add the liquid to the flour mixture. Stir briskly for about 2 minutes. Transfer to a lightly floured board and knead gently for 2 to 3 minutes. Wash mixing bowl; grease bottom of bowl. Put ball of dough into bowl, then flip over; thus what was the bottom of the dough becomes the top and is lightly greased. Punch dough in 3 places (to make certain all the air is removed), cover with a damp towel, and let rise at room temperature for 25 to 30 minutes, or until dough has risen to top of bowl.

Preheat oven to 375°F. Transfer dough to a lightly floured board and knead until it feels smooth and elastic. Divide dough into 24 equal portions. With ball of hand, roll into equal lengths about ½ inch thick; pinch ends together as for a doughnut. Place on lightly floured pie tins or small cookie sheets and broil 5 to 6 inches from source of heat for 3 to 4 minutes.

When all bagels have been broiled, drop them into the rapidly boiling 4 quarts water to which 2 tablespoons sugar has been added. Cook for 15 to 20 minutes. Lift out with slotted spoon onto a tea towel to drain. Transfer to a lightly greased cookie sheet and bake in 375°F. oven for 10 minutes, then increase heat to 400°F. and bake for 5 to 6 minutes, or until bagels are golden brown and crisp.

Note: This recipe does not do well if doubled or increased for larger quantities. It is advisable instead to make a second or third batch to increase the amounts desired.

STRAWBERRY CRÈME CRÊPES

Making crêpes is an art in itself which you'll need to master before serving them as a dessert with this elegant brunch. But once you've mastered it, you'll be glad you did, for nothing can top Strawberry Crème Crêpes as the finishing touch for this menu, and for many others as well.

The crêpes can be made and frozen well in advance of a party. Simply defrost by placing the well-wrapped bundle of crêpes in a 200°F. oven for 15 to 20 minutes. The batter itself will keep for several days if refrigerated.

Crêpes   **65 Crêpes**

6 eggs	2 cups milk
1½ cups flour	1 tablespoon melted butter
½ teaspoon salt	Grated rind of 1 orange

Break eggs into a blender container or, if using rotary beater, use a medium-size bowl. Combine flour and salt. Add dry ingredients to eggs with milk, beating continuously. Add melted butter and orange rind. Let rest in refrigerator for 4 hours or longer. Stir just before using.

If the batter stands longer than four hours even overnight—it will thicken slightly. A small amount of cold water—about ¼ cup should be stirred into the batter so that it is no heavier than thick cream.

Use a nonstick skillet to eliminate the necessity of greasing the pan after each crêpe is made. Heat a 6-inch skillet until it is so hot that when water is sprinkled on it the drops will dance about. Using a measuring cup, cream pitcher, or other container with a "lip," pour into the skillet about 2 tablespoons of the batter, tilting the pan as you pour so the batter forms a thin film covering the entire bottom of the pan. If there are any holes where the batter missed the pan, add a few drops of batter to patch.

Recipe Continues . . .

Cook crêpe for 15 to 20 seconds, or until the edges turn slightly brown. Loosen crêpe from the sides of the skillet and slide it out of skillet, brown side up, onto a wooden board; continue. Stack crêpes onto platter as you go along. (They will not stick to one another.) (For the strawberry crème filling and for cheese blintzes, it is not necessary to brown crêpes on both sides. Be sure to read complete details on crêpes in Chapter IX.)

Strawberry Crème Filling   About 6 Cups

1 jar (12 oz.) strawberry pre-	2 eggs
serves	¼ teaspoon salt
2 pounds cream cheese	1 teaspoon vanilla extract
¼ pound butter, softened	

Combine all ingredients in a medium-size bowl. Using an electric beater, blend together until it is of a creamy consistency.

To assemble crêpes: Lay out 10 to 12 crêpes at a time, brown side up. Put 1 rounded tablespoon of filling on front edge of crêpe and roll over once. Then tuck in sides and continue to roll.

Place filled crêpes seam side down, laying them close together, on very well-buttered 4-sided cookie sheets. At this point, crêpes can be refrigerated for a few days, or frozen for several months to be defrosted before baking.

To serve, preheat oven to 375°F. Place cookie sheet of crêpes on center shelf of oven for 15 minutes, then raise to top shelf for 10 minutes, or until golden brown. Lift crêpes out of pan with wide spatula onto serving tray. Set tray on electric warmer. Surround with bowl of sugared strawberries (or defrosted frozen berries) and the quart of sour cream.

By baking half of the crêpes first, the rest 15 minutes later, you will be ready with hot crêpes when the line forms again for seconds, which I guarantee will happen.

Note: It is best to wash and hull strawberries only a few hours before serving. You should save time for this on the morning of your brunch, unless you're using frozen berries, or do it late the night before. *Never hull strawberries before washing,* as the water will soak into the berries, making them spongy.

FLO CHART FOR AN ELEGANT BRUNCH

THREE WEEKS BEFORE Decide on date. Send invitations. Check equipment list; arrange for rental equipment if necessary. Arrange for hired help. Check marketing list. Purchase staples.

TWO WEEKS BEFORE Start making, baking and freezing. Make grapefruit and orange flowers, strawberry crêpes, bagels. Order salmon.

FOUR DAYS BEFORE Prepare salmon.

THREE DAYS BEFORE Prepare spinach soup; refrigerate.

TWO DAYS BEFORE Finish marketing (fresh fruits and vegetables, etc.). Refrigerate salmon. Make poached eggs, fruit dressing. Take crêpes out of freezer and refrigerate.

ONE DAY BEFORE Follow directions for slicing salmon; refrigerate. Make hollandaise sauce. Cut up fruits except avocados. Put cans of hearts of palm in refrigerator so they will be nice and cold. Prepare whipped cream cheese. Arrange buffet table with trays, platters, etc. Set tables and chairs in place; set tables. Don't forget decorations, centerpieces.

DAY OF THE PARTY

10 A.M. *Plug in coffee maker.* When coffee is brewed, set on warm. Remove eggs from refrigerator to pan of water to be heated later. Place hollandaise sauce in top part of double boiler. Wash and drain strawberries.

11 A.M. Remove bagels and bread from freezer. Arrange fruit platter, hearts of palm and tomatoes. Refrigerate if possible, or keep in cool place.

11:30. Transfer spinach soup to punch bowl and set on buffet table.

12:00. Guests arrive. Start serving chilled soup.

12:45. Put poached eggs over low heat for warming. Set out fruit and vegetable platters.

12:55. Remove poached eggs from water and place in artichoke bottoms. Transfer hollandaise sauce to serving bowl.

1 o'clock. Invite your guests to a lovely buffet!

CHAPTER IV

. . . .

Luncheons

. . . .

Luncheons are usually a little fancier than brunches, perhaps because they're often given in the middle of a day that for many guests might also be a working day, in contrast to the more leisurely Sunday Brunch.

In general, people aren't as inclined toward rounding up a few friends for a luncheon party as they might be for a brunch or for cocktails. There's more often a *raison d'être* for a luncheon: an out-of-town guest, an event, or a "cause." Jillions of luncheons are given as fund-raisers for various charity and political causes (I think I've catered at least half a jillion!); then there are all those bridge club luncheons, businessmen's luncheons, planning-committee-for-this-or-that luncheons.

Whatever the reason, most women occasionally find themselves in the position of having to plan a luncheon, or maybe even wanting to. Or maybe it's your bridge club turn again and you'd like to serve something different for a change.

I have selected three menus that have proved most popular at the luncheon parties I've catered over the years, menus easily adaptable to smaller groups. The first, featuring my Bird of Paradise Salad with chicken-and-ham filling, was a great favorite of Mamie Eisenhower's and Nancy Reagan's. The Seafood and Rice Casserole menu always made a hit with the men. My Turkey Buffet specialty is one of the easiest for a hostess to handle for large groups.

MAMIE'S BIRD OF PARADISE LUNCHEON

(For 12)

MENU

Bird of Paradise Salad
Broiled Cheese Muffins
Flower Garden Dessert
Coffee and tea
Assorted bonbons
Sherry Punch

Now, I must warn you that the Bird of Paradise Salad isn't as simple as it may seem at first glance. It is a combination salad-and-meat main dish made of fresh pineapple, chicken and ham. It requires considerable time and a great deal of patience. But when it's all finished, be sure to have your camera handy because it makes a spectacular picture. Practically all of the preparations can be done the day before the party.

EQUIPMENT WORK SHEET FOR MAMIE'S BIRD OF PARADISE LUNCHEON

Champagne glasses or other wineglasses for Sherry Punch
punch bowl (optional)

cocktail napkins
serving tray
bowl and ladle for salad dressing
coffee maker and servers
water pitchers
tables and chairs
tablecloths
linen napkins
water glasses
dinner plates
paper doilies
bread and butter plates
12 clay flowerpots, 3 inches across
cups and saucers
silverware: salad forks, butter spreaders, demitasse spoons or teaspoons,
    teaspoons for coffee
salt and pepper shakers for each table
sugar and creamer for each table
bonbon or candy dish for each table
ashtrays
1 box drinking straws
pointed toothpicks
sheet of cardboard

MARKETING WORK SHEET FOR MAMIE'S BIRD OF PARADISE LUNCHEON

1 quart whipping cream
2 cups coffee cream
½ pound butter
1 pound American or Cheddar cheese
1 pound mozzarella cheese (enough for 24 small slices)
½ pound Roquefort cheese
1½ dozen eggs
6 whole chicken breasts, 10 to 14 ounces each
2 pounds precooked ham
6 medium-size pineapples

8 lemons, for juice
3 tomatoes
2 heads of lettuce
1 head of Boston lettuce or curly endive
2 bunches of parsley
1 onion
2 cans (8 oz. each) artichoke hearts
2 cans (20 oz. each) white asparagus spears
1 can (16 oz.) colossal ripe olives
1 can (2 oz.) slivered pimientos
3 cans (6 oz. each) frozen lemonade
12 English muffins
1 angel-food cake, 9 inches
3 bottles (23 oz. each) dry sherry

STAPLES LIST FOR MAMIE'S BIRD OF PARADISE LUNCHEON

salt
white pepper
bay leaf
paprika
whole cloves
granulated sugar
envelopes of unflavored gelatin
red maraschino cherries
olive or salad oil
coffee
tea or tea bags
bonbons or other candy

BIRD OF PARADISE SALAD

12 Generous servings

6 medium-size pineapples
24 maraschino cherry halves
12 whole cloves
3 hard-cooked eggs, sliced into rounds
1 head of curly endive or Boston lettuce
24 canned white asparagus spears
12 small artichoke hearts
6 whole chicken breasts, 10 to 14 ounces each
1 teaspoon salt
¼ teaspoon white pepper
1 bay leaf

1 medium-size onion
½ bunch of parsley
2 pounds precooked ham
1 pound American or Cheddar cheese
2 heads of lettuce
1 can (2 oz.) pimientos, cut into strips
3 tomatoes, peeled and quartered
12 colossal ripe olives
Paprika
Mousseline Roquefort Dressing (recipe follows)

This can all be done in advance.

Choose pineapples with firm green tops and slightly green skins. Cut lengthwise into halves, including the tops. With a grapefruit knife or other sharp serrated knife, remove the fruit from each half shell in one piece by bearing down and pressing firmly against the sides as you cut the fruit. Leave at least ½-inch edge at base of pineapple to which you will attach the bird's head. It may be necessary to go around the border several times until the fruit can be lifted out in one piece; but it is important that this be done in order to have a slice from which you can cut the shape of the bird's head.

When all pineapples have been cut and their fruit removed, place the shells upside down on paper towels or on a cookie sheet to drain. Store in refrigerator. Place the pineapple fruit halves with flat side down and cut a slice ½ inch thick from the bottom. Set aside rounded pieces for use in the salad.

To make heads of the birds, draw or trace a head to resemble

Recipe Continues . . .

the bird of paradise (or any bird you prefer) on cardboard. The total size of the head should be 3½ inches high by 2½ inches wide at the base of the neck. Lay cardboard head on top of center core of pineapple and cut with a very sharp pointed paring knife, tracing around the cardboard. Store the heads in covered dish in the refrigerator.

Discard the core section of slice that is left after the head has been removed. Cut the remaining edible portion of fruit into small chunks, for use in the salad. Store in refrigerator.

ASSEMBLING THE BIRDS OF PARADISE: Pierce pineapple bird heads with toothpicks in the position of the eyes, so the toothpick protrudes from both sides. Insert cherries on toothpicks, pushing them close to head. Place cloves in position of beak. Insert toothpick in edge opposite the top of the pineapple shell, which now becomes the feathery tail, and set head firmly on toothpick with the head facing outward. Line the cavities of the pineapple shells with curly endive or Boston lettuce leaves, allowing some to protrude from the sides, thus giving a rather lacy effect.

Now you're ready to fill the shells with the chicken and ham mixture (recipe follows). Insert 1 asparagus spear on each side of the front to emulate wings. Imbed a well-drained artichoke heart in center of salad, place alternate strips of pimiento, chicken and ham around it like spokes of a wheel. Place a tomato quarter directly behind the neck of the bird, and a ripe olive on the opposite end. Set an egg slice on the portion where the top and shell are joined. Sprinkle with paprika.

Now, stand back and take a look. Wasn't it worth all that trouble?

To serve, place birds on doily-lined dinner plates with halves of broiled cheese muffins (p. 97) on each side.

Chicken and Ham Salad

This must be done on the day of the party.

Place chicken breasts in a large pot. Add enough water to cover. Add salt, pepper, bay leaf, onion and parsley. Cook until tender, 30 to 40 minutes. Remove chicken from broth. Strain and save the broth. Remove meat from bones and chill. When cold, cut part of the chicken into small julienne strips, 40 to 45 strips, and set aside. Cut remaining chicken into fairly large dice. Lightly salt and set aside in a large mixing bowl.

Cut the ham into medium-size julienne strips and set aside. Dice cheese. Add to bowl with the chicken. Cut the remaining fruit of the pineapple into chunks. Add to the bowl of chicken, ham and cheese.

Trim lettuce and cut into small chunks; add to bowl. Toss together with a bit more than half of dressing, just enough to moisten. Store in refrigerator until ready to use. (Additional dressing is to be served during the luncheon.)

Mousseline Roquefort Dressing　　　　　　6 Cups

6 egg yolks	1 cup crumbled Roquefort
½ cup olive or salad oil	cheese
¼ cup lemon juice	2 cups whipping cream
½ teaspoon salt	

Beat egg yolks until thick and lemon-colored. Slowly add oil, beating constantly until mixture thickens. Gradually add lemon juice, ½ teaspoon at a time, beating constantly. Blend in the salt and cheese. Whip cream until stiff; add to cheese mixture. Chill. Dressing will keep well in refrigerator for 4 to 5 days.

BROILED CHEESE MUFFINS　　　　　　24 Pieces

12 English muffins, unsplit	24 round slices of mozzarella
2 ounces butter, or more	cheese

The muffins, of course, must be done the day of the luncheon.
Split muffins into halves with a fork. Spread with butter. Place

Recipe Continues . . .

under broiler until lightly toasted. This can be done an hour or so before serving. Place a slice of cheese on each muffin half. When ready to serve, broil until cheese melts and turns brown and bubbly.

Important: Do not leave the oven while muffins are broiling for they will brown in a few minutes and burn quickly.

To serve with Bird of Paradise Salad: Brown the exact amount necessary to allow ½ muffin per serving. Cut each half into 2 pieces, placing one on each side of pineapple . . . When all salads have been served, broil remaining muffins and offer guests these second helpings hot from broiler.

FLOWER GARDEN DESSERT   12 Servings

As long as you're going all out with the pineapple Birds of Paradise, you should have a really dramatic and grand finale for dessert. And what better for your birds than a flower garden? All of this, too, can be prepared ahead of time, so all you have to do on the day of your luncheon is to make your grand entrance with a tray of flowerpots, bedecked with fresh garden flowers, drinking straws, and filled with a yummy whipped-cream-cake dessert. (If you're a calorie counter, this is a day you should forget to count.)

12 clay flowerpots, 3 inches across	6 eggs
12 drinking straws, with large holes	1½ cups granulated sugar
12 or 24 fresh garden flowers	½ cup lemon juice
1 angel-food cake, 9 inches	¼ teaspoon salt
1 envelope unflavored gelatin	Grated rind of 1 lemon
¼ cup cold water	¼ cup sugar (for topping)
	1 cup whipping cream

PREPARATION OF FLOWERPOTS: You can buy the flowerpots, with saucers, at most dime stores, hardware stores and flower shops. They come in assorted colors and in the natural clay color, which you may want to spray in colors that best fit your color scheme; or they can be left in their natural state. Before using pots for the first time, wash them well in soapy water, rinse in hot water, and dry well. To insure complete dryness so they won't turn moldy, heat the oven to 400°F., turn heat off, and set pots on shelves to dry overnight. Repeat this process each time the pots are used. If you buy the natural clay pots, you might want to have them lacquered inside. I bought mine at the nursery and my husband lacquered them for me. This should be done days or weeks in advance of your party.

Whipped-Cream Cake Dessert: The Filling

There's a time and a place for everything, as the saying goes, and the time and place for store-bought angel food cake is now. Generally I'd say there is no substitute for baking a cake yourself, but for this dessert the cake is only a part, though an integral part, of the whole, and so an already-baked cake will be most satisfactory.

Tear the cake into small chunks, put in large mixing bowl, and set aside. Soften gelatin in ¼ cup cold water; set aside.

Separate eggs, dropping yolks in top part of a double boiler. Set whites aside. Beat yolks until thick and lemon-colored; gradually beat in 1½ cups sugar. Set over hot water in the bottom pan and beat continuously as you add the lemon juice, salt and lemon rind. Stir with a wooden spoon and cook until mixture thickens and coats the spoon. Remove from heat, and stir in softened gelatin until dissolved. Chill.

Beat egg whites until frothy; add remaining ¼ cup sugar very gradually; continue beating until stiff peaks form. Fold stiffly beaten whites into the chilled lemon mixture and pour over the chunks of cake. Toss together lightly. Fill flower pots three-fourths full. Cover with plastic wrap. Chill overnight.

To serve, cut drinking straws into halves. Push straw through cake mixture to bottom of pot. Then insert a fresh garden flower into the straw; if stems are small, you may want to use 2 flowers. Place pots on doily-lined dessert plates. Now you're ready for your

Recipe Continues . . .

grand entrance, carrying in your entire "garden" at one time on an elegant serving tray; or at least as many of the pots as you and the tray can handle. You may prefer to have someone help you, and carry in a second flower-garden tray. It is far more dramatic and effective to have the flower-bedecked pots carried in at one time than to serve them individually. The whole scene gives a charming, walk-in garden ambience to the party. Moreover, you will find, as I have, that your guests will enjoy and join in the spirit of the occasion by bedecking themselves with the flowers. Placing flowers in straws as containers also keeps the flower stems free of food particles.

SHERRY PUNCH   20 Servings

3 bottles (23 oz.) dry sherry
3 cans (6 oz. each) frozen lem-
    onade, defrosted

½ cup freshly squeezed lemon
    juice

Combine sherry with defrosted, undiluted lemonade and freshly squeezed lemon juice. Pour into freezer containers or empty cans, cover, and freeze for at least 24 hours before serving.

To serve, remove from freezer about 30 minutes before serving. This punch will have a slushy consistency at first, but will liquify as it stands and while being sipped. If you have a helper, it's a nice touch to pass the punch in glasses on trays. However, it can be poured into a punch bowl and placed where the guests can serve themselves. For an extra note of elegance, bring out your Champagne glasses for the punch.

FLO CHART FOR MAMIE'S BIRD OF PARADISE LUNCHEON

TWO WEEKS BEFORE It's more appropriate to phone invitations for this type of luncheon. Check tables and chairs, particularly if your guests are staying on for a meeting or to play bridge. You won't need extra help in the kitchen for this unless you decide to double or triple the recipes.

TWO DAYS BEFORE Finish marketing. Make Sherry Punch.

ONE DAY BEFORE Prepare the Birds of Paradise, filling, dressing, and refrigerate. Do all preparations for Flower Garden Dessert except whipped cream; pick up flowers, cut straws into halves. Place bonbons in candy dishes. Set up tables, centerpieces, decorations.

DAY OF THE PARTY

10:00 A.M. Whip cream. Spoon over tops of cake in the flower pots. Insert stems and flowers in each pot. Cream—whipped by hand, not sprayed from a can—will hold up for several hours in the refrigerator.

10:30 A.M. *Plug in coffee maker* (This is the easiest thing in the world to forget). Prepare English muffins according to directions.

11 A.M. Remove punch from freezer and pour into bowl.

11:15. Arrange birds and salads in the pineapples. This will take about 45 minutes. (You can do this earlier if you prefer and cover loosely with damp towels to keep salads cool and moist.)

WAY-TO-A-MAN'S-HEART LUNCHEON

(For 30)

MENU

Filled Avocado Salad
Sherry French Dressing
Parmesan Cheese Bread
Seafood 'n Rice Casserole
Pineapple Parfait
Three-Layered Yummies
Coffee and tea

I have found that men generally prefer a limited selection of solid, satisfying foods rather than a great variety. This menu is one I served to the same group of men five years in a row at their annual gathering in Palm Springs, each time by special request. That's how much they liked it. Ladies love it too. It's a great menu for buffet luncheons, so I'm giving the recipes here for 30 people. All the party arrangements, decorations, table settings, and so on of course can be done well in advance.

With most of the details out of the way, the preparation of the casseroles early on the morning of the luncheon should not be too great a chore. I prefer to prepare seafood dishes on the day of the party, even if it means getting up an hour or two earlier, but there's nothing wrong with doing it the night before. At least most of the ingredients in these casseroles can be prepared the night before and even partially precooked if you wish. The avocados, though, *must* be done on the morning of the luncheon (see recipe). The parfaits are better when prepared the day before to assure their chilled and thickened state. The layered yummies are so moist that they can be made as far as 3 or 4 days in advance.

Note: If you can do simple arithmetic, this is an easy menu to double for 60 or cut down for 10 or 20. Hint: At luncheons, men feel more comfortable in large groups.

EQUIPMENT WORK SHEET FOR WAY-TO-A-MAN'S-HEART LUNCHEON

salad plates
small glass bowl and ladle for dressing
2 bread trays
3 deep 3-quart casseroles
dinner plates
cups and saucers
parfait glasses

medium-size glass or silver tray
60- to 75-cup coffee maker
coffee and tea service
tables and chairs
tablecloths
dinner napkins
silverware (fork, knife, 2 teaspoons, parfait spoon for each place)
serving pieces
water glasses
water pitcher
salt and pepper shaker for each table
sugar and creamer for each table
ashtrays

MARKETING WORK SHEET FOR WAY-TO-A-MAN'S-HEART LUNCHEON

2 quarts low-fat milk
5 cups coffee cream
2 pounds butter
¼ pound Parmesan cheese
3 eggs
3 pounds South African lobster tails, 15 tails (if frozen, 5 packages, 10 oz. each)
5 pounds fillet of sole
15 avocados
8 lemons
2 heads of romaine or bronze-leaf lettuce
1 whole celery stalk
1½ pounds onions
3½ pounds long-grain rice
4 cans (20 oz. each) peeled whole tomatoes
6 cans (11 oz. each) mandarin orange sections
2 cans (20 oz. each) sliced pineapple
1 can (16 oz.) pitted large ripe olives
5 cans (11 oz. each) minced clams
5 bottles (1 cup each) clam juice

3 packages (20 oz. each) frozen peas
1 jar (4 oz.) red maraschino cherries
8 packages (3 oz. each) low-calorie dessert whip
1 pound marshmallows
4 ounces shelled pecan halves
½ cup chopped shelled walnuts
1 package (4 oz.) flaked coconut
6 ounces semisweet chocolate pieces
1½ quarts olive or salad oil
½ cup pear or wine vinegar
½ cup sherry
4 loaves of French or sourdough bread
⅛ ounce whole saffron (This flavoring, from India, is very expensive but
    it is well worth it; it will enhance this dish as nothing else can.)

STAPLES LIST FOR WAY-TO-A-MAN'S-HEART LUNCHEON

salt
pepper
paprika
granulated sugar
confectioners' sugar
unsweetened cocoa powder
vegetable bouillon cubes
garlic
graham crackers
vanilla extract
instant vanilla pudding mix
coffee
tea or tea bags

FILLED AVOCADO SALAD   30 Servings

Since avocados are very perishable, most markets stock them before they are ripened. It is therefore wise to anticipate the time you wish to use them and purchase them several days in advance. They ripen readily when left in a paper sack in the pantry, or on a shelf. Once they have ripened, they should be refrigerated, where they will keep for several days.

15 ripe avocados
6 cans (11 oz. each) mandarin
   orange sections
1 whole celery stalk, heart only
10 pitted large ripe olives

2 heads of romaine or bronze-
   leaf lettuce
8 lemons, quartered
Sherry French Dressing (recipe
   follows)

Cut ripe avocados lengthwise into halves; do not peel; lift out large seeds. Drain mandarin oranges. Slice the celery heart and olives. Toss oranges, celery and olives together. Chill well.

At serving time, fill hollows of avocados with orange and celery mixture. Place a washed leaf of romaine or bronze-leaf lettuce on each place, set a filled avocado on the left, and lay a lemon wedge along the right side. Pass sherry French dressing.

Because avocados have a tendency to turn black after cutting or peeling, I suggest you leave this chore until the morning of the luncheon. However, the filling can be made on the day before.

Sherry French Dressing   5 Cups

2 eggs
1 tablespoon sugar
½ teaspoon salt
½ teaspoon paprika
4 cups olive or salad oil, or a
   mixture of both

½ cup pear or wine vinegar
½ cup sherry
Garlic clove, peeled

Blend together the eggs and seasonings. Beat in the oil, vinegar

Recipe Continues . . .

and sherry. Pour into a container and drop in the garlic clove. Let stand for a few hours or preferably overnight.
Chill. Remove garlic and shake well before serving.

PARMESAN CHEESE BREAD

There is no absolute must as to which type of bread or brand of cheese should be used. However, it is an absolute must that the bread be served piping hot.

4 loaves of French or sourdough
  bread
½ pound butter, softened

¼ pound Parmesan cheese,
  freshly grated (1 cup)

Slice bread diagonally through the bottom crust, keeping the bread in its original shape. Blend together the butter and cheese. Spread each bread slice generously with the mixture. Wrap the buttered bread in its original shape in heavy foil.

This preparation of the bread can be done the day before and refrigerated overnight. (Can be made 4 days ahead.)

To serve, place in a 350°F. oven for 15 to 20 minutes.

SEAFOOD 'N RICE CASSEROLE   30 Servings

3 pounds South African lobster
  tails, fresh or frozen (5 packages frozen, about 10 oz.
  each)
1½ pounds onions, chopped
3 garlic cloves, minced
1¼ cups olive oil
7½ cups uncooked long-grain
  rice
⅛ ounce whole saffron
5 vegetable bouillon cubes
2 tablespoons salt

5 pounds canned peeled whole
  tomatoes (four 20-oz. cans)
5 cups bottled clam juice
5 cups water
5 pounds fillet of sole
5 cans (11 oz. each) minced
  clams
¼ pound butter or margarine,
  melted
3 packages (20 oz. each) frozen
  peas

Cook lobster tails according to directions on package. When cooked, set aside and cool. If you are lucky enough to find fresh lobster tails, drop them into boiling water and cook for 4 minutes after water has returned to boiling. Preheat oven to 350°F.

In the meantime, sauté the onions and garlic in the oil in a very large pan, until onions become soft and transparent. Remove from pan with a slotted spoon; set aside.

Rinse rice in cold water until water runs clear; drain well. Stir into the oil remaining in pan and add saffron. Cook, stirring constantly, until rice is golden. Put the onions and garlic back in pan along with the bouillon cubes, salt, tomatoes, clam juice and water. Heat until liquid just comes to a boil. Remove from heat.

Cut 15 medium-size slices of the sole; set the slices aside. Cut remaining sole into small pieces; add with minced clams to the rice mixture. Toss together, then transfer to 3 buttered deep 3-quart casserole dishes. Cover them well and bake for 30 minutes.

While casseroles are baking, prepare the cooked lobster: using scissors, cut through the thick membrane on underside of shell and remove. Take out lobster meat by peeling the hard shell back with fingers of one hand and pulling meat toward you with the other. Cut the tails lengthwise into halves; thus you will have 30 pieces.

When the casseroles have baked for 30 minutes, remove from oven and remove covers. Cut the 15 slices of sole lengthwise into halves, thus giving you 30 slices. Roll slices into spirals and place on top of rice alternating with lobster tails (10 portions of each fish for each casserole), arranging them like the spokes of a wheel. Brush tops of fish with melted butter. Cover and refrigerate.

Important: All of this up to this stage can be done the day before.

Remove from refrigerator 1 hour before serving. Bake covered at 350°F. for an additional 45 minutes. Meanwhile, cook peas for 6 minutes and drain. Keep warm over hot water.

To serve, remove covers of casseroles and spoon peas around the border. Serve immediately.

PINEAPPLE PARFAIT   30 Servings

This light, refreshing dessert tastes far more fattening than it really is. Of course, one could add unnecessary calories and a richer taste by using whipping cream instead of the low-calorie dessert whip. However, the results are so minimal that it would be hardly worth the indulgence. Save those calories for the yummies that accompany the parfait.

2 cans (20 oz. each) sliced pineapple (16 slices)	8 packages (4 cups) low-calorie dessert whip
1 pound marshmallows	8 cups low-fat milk
1 jar (4 oz.) maraschino cherries	30 pecan halves

Drain the pineapple; pour ¾ cup of the juice into a heavy-bottom kettle. Add the marshmallows and heat slowly until all marshmallows have melted. Stir constantly and watch carefully since this mixture burns quickly. Set aside to cool.

Cut the pineapple slices into fairly small pieces. Drain cherries, chop, and add to the melted marshmallows along with pineapple pieces. Beat dessert whip with the milk until stiff; it should have the consistency of whipped cream. Fold in the pineapple-marshmallow mixture until well mixed. Spoon into parfait glasses and refrigerate. Serve when cold and firm. Top each parfait with a pecan half.

Remember, this tastes better when prepared a day or two in advance.

THREE-LAYERED YUMMIES   36 Squares

How could anything so good be so easy to prepare? They don't even require baking! Keeping a pan of these on hand at all times could provide an accompaniment to ice cream, canned fruit, or other quick dessert for the unexpected guest and bring raves whenever served. There is no reason why these confections cannot be served by themselves, as I have often done.

First Layer

¼ pound butter or margarine
¼ cup sugar
¼ cup cocoa powder
1 teaspoon vanilla extract
1 egg, beaten

2 cups fine graham-cracker
  crumbs
1 cup flaked coconut
½ cup chopped walnuts

Combine butter, sugar, cocoa and vanilla in the top part of a double boiler. Cook over boiling water until blended. Carefully stir in egg and cook for 3 minutes longer, stirring constantly. Stir in crumbs, coconut and walnuts. Press into a buttered 9-inch-square pan. Cool.

Second Layer

¼ pound butter
2 cups sifted confectioners'
  sugar

3 tablespoons milk
2 tablespoons instant vanilla
  pudding mix

Cream butter and sugar until light and fluffy. Beat in milk and pudding mix. Spread over cooled first layer and let stand until firm.

Third Layer

6 ounces semisweet chocolate
  pieces

1 tablespoon butter

Melt chocolate and butter together in the top part of a double boiler over hot, not boiling, water. When melted, spread over second layer. Chill until firm.

Cut into 1½-inch squares. Store in refrigerator.

FLO CHART FOR WAY-TO-A-MAN'S-HEART LUNCHEON

ONE TO TWO WEEKS BEFORE No need to send formal invitations. Men are usually *notified* of business luncheons, conventions, etc. Decide on tables and chairs, seating arrangement, etc.

FOUR DAYS BEFORE Buy avocados; if already ripe enough to use, refrigerate. If still green, let ripen in brown grocery bag at room temperature. Make sherry dressing, refrigerate.

THREE DAYS BEFORE Finish marketing. Make yummies, cover with plastic, and refrigerate; do not cut until day of party.

TWO DAYS BEFORE Check bar, liquor supply, tomato juice, Tabasco, lemons and limes, mixes. Check out seafoods, frozen or fresh. (Some people turn up their noses at frozen seafoods.)

ONE DAY BEFORE Prepare cheese bread, seafood casserole (except for frozen peas, to be sprinkled on top later), pineapple parfait. Make orange/celery mixture for avocados, wrap in plastic, and refrigerate. Wash, wrap in plastic, and refrigerate romaine or bronze-leaf lettuce.

DAY OF THE PARTY

10:00 A.M. Plug in coffee maker. Remove seafood casserole from refrigerator.

12:15. Put casserole in oven.

12:30. Put avocado salad at each place setting.

12:45. Put wrapped Parmesan bread in oven.

1 o'clock. Turn off oven, sit down, and have your avocado salad. The rest of the food is passed. Allow casserole to stay in oven until ready to serve.

Bon appétit!

BUYING SEAFOOD

1. Be prepared to spend a king's ransom if you're buying it on today's market. Fish is no longer a budget item, but if you're having a party, why not have a fling?

2. Find yourself a really good, reliable seafood market, if you do not already have one, and one that you can trust implicitly to sell you *only* fresh fish, not last week's. I do not recommend looking for bargains in just any old meat market's fish-food counters. It is worthwhile to find someone you can trust, especially when you're buying fresh oysters and lobsters. You should be able to tell if seafood is not fresh by the unpleasant odor, but some folks don't smell too well and some fish-counter clerks don't give them the chance to sniff their products. In any case, where fresh fish is concerned, my advice is not to depend solely on your own sense of smell but to find an experienced and trustworthy seafood expert to guide you in what and when to buy. It's the safest way.

3. An important consideration is which seafoods will be available at the time you plan your party. Fresh oysters and lobsters are particularly hard to get, at any price, in certain areas and seasons. Also, remember that some people simply can't stand raw oysters, so don't overbuy. Two medium-size oysters per person should be ample. The guests who love them will gobble up the turndowns.

BUFFET LUNCHEON

(For 30)

MENU

Breast of Turkey Salad
Cranberry Cottage Ring
Curried Peas and Parsnips
Baked Noodles and Cream
Stuffed Prunes and Rosy Peaches
Relishes on Ice
Potato Parker House Rolls, Butter Curls
Apple Torte
Coffee and Tea

I'll never forget how shocked I was the first time I saw "chicken" salad being prepared in a restaurant kitchen and discovered it was being made with boiled turkey. I later learned this is a rather common practice, for good reason. A 15-pound turkey provides more meat with less waste and a lot less bother than cleaning and cooking three 5-pound chickens. And the flavor of the meats is similar. Still, I think a lot of people would resent having their "chicken" salad made of turkey, and I see no reason to be deceitful about it. What's wrong with turkey salad anyway? At one time turkey was snubbed because it was considered a "cheap" dish. That was in pre-inflation days. Moreover, the production and packaging of turkeys and turkey breasts have improved considerably in recent years.

The recipes are for 30 people, a good all-around average number for a luncheon buffet. They are easy to double or halve if you wish. This is another menu that can be prepared mostly in advance, so why not make it a gala and festive occasion? It's especially appropriate during the holidays when you're bound to have more guests in and out, and when you're thinking maybe you really *ought* to throw a big whiz-bang party, and when people generally let their calorie counts down and are more apt to eat your Apple Torte. But don't forget, it's a good menu in *all* seasons.

EQUIPMENT WORK SHEET FOR BUFFET LUNCHEON

large bowl or tray for turkey salad
2 three-quart ring molds of equal depth
round platter for Cranberry Cottage Ring
2 ovenproof casserole dishes, 11½ x 5½ x 2½ inches, for noodles
glass tray for prunes
deep bowl for peaches
glass bowl for relishes
2 bread trays
compote, bonbon dish or bowl for butter curls
9-inch springform pan
dessert plates and forks

60-cup coffee maker and servers
teapot
tables and chairs
tablecloths
luncheon napkins
dinner plates
silverware (complete place settings)
cups and saucers
serving pieces
water glasses
water pitcher
salt and pepper shakers for each table
sugar and creamer for each table
ashtrays

MARKETING WORK SHEET FOR BUFFET LUNCHEON

1 quart milk
5 cups coffee cream
3 quarts dairy sour cream
2 pounds butter
2½ dozen eggs
2 pounds creamed cottage cheese
½ pound cream cheese
2 turkeys, 10 to 12 pounds each
8 parsnips
3 onions
½ pound shallots
3 pint boxes cherry tomatoes
7 large or 9 medium-size cooking or baking apples
1 orange (for rind)
3 lemons (for rind and juice)
1 pound seedless grapes, or 2 cans (11 oz. each) grapes
1 large tomato
1 large bunch of celery
2 or 3 heads of romaine lettuce
1 head of curly endive or soft-leaf lettuce
2 bunches of watercress

5 cans (29 oz. each) peach halves
3 cans (1 lb. each) whole-cranberry sauce
1 can (29 oz.) pineapple chunks
1 quart cranberry juice
3 cans (1 lb. each) large ripe olives
2 jars (9 to 11 oz. each) stuffed green olives
1 quart tiny dill pickles
1 jar (4 oz.) capers
4 jars (4 oz. each) red maraschino cherries
4 dozen pieces of angelica or citron
2 quarts mayonnaise
4 packages (1 lb. each) frozen peas
3 pounds wide egg noodles
5 pounds all-purpose flour
3 packages (6 oz. each) raspberry-flavored gelatin
3 pounds large prunes (48 prunes)
2 jars (12 oz. each) red currant jelly
½ pound blanched whole almonds
1 box (5 oz.) instant potato flakes, or 3 medium-size potatoes
1 cake of compressed fresh yeast
1 package (6 oz.) zwieback
1 bottle rosé wine
lemon leaves or other greens

STAPLES LIST FOR BUFFET LUNCHEON

salt
white pepper
paprika
onion salt
dry mustard
ground cinnamon
ground ginger
grated nutmeg
whole cloves
curry seasoning
chicken stock base seasoning

granulated sugar
Worcestershire sauce
vegetable oil
envelopes of unflavored gelatin (be sure you have 4 envelopes)
lemon extract
vanilla extract
package of active dry yeast, if you are not using fresh yeast
all-purpose flour
coffee
tea or tea bags

BREAST OF TURKEY SALAD   30 Servings

2 turkeys, 10 to 12 pounds each	1 ounce butter
5 tablespoons salt	4 cups mayonnaise
1 can (29 oz.) pineapple chunks	2 teaspoons dry mustard
1 bottle (4 oz.) capers	1½ tablespoons chicken stock
1 pound seedless grapes, or 2 cans	base seasoning
(11 oz. each) grapes	Romaine lettuce
1 large bunch of celery	Cherry tomatoes
14 hard-cooked eggs	Ripe olives
½ pound whole almonds,	Parsley sprigs
blanched	Paprika

Dress turkeys, then cook them together with the necks and giblets, but excluding hearts and livers, by immersing them in water with 3 tablespoons of the salt in a covered large pot, or 2 pots. With breast side up, cook over moderate heat for 1½ hours. Grasping the legs, flip turkeys over onto their breasts, and cook for an additional 30 to 40 minutes, or until fork tender. Remove from broth and cool until comfortable enough to handle. You will find it easier to remove the meat from the bones and cartilages while turkey is warm rather than chilled.

Strain the broth and set aside to make stock or soup later by adding to it some vegetables and the carcass of the turkeys. Cut the turkey meat into bite-size pieces and drop into a large bowl. (I

Recipe Continues . . .

hope you, too, have an aversion to mashed-up salads and will cut good-size chunks of the meat.) Sprinkle on remaining 2 tablespoons salt.

Drain the pineapple chunks, capers and grapes. Chop celery rather coarsely; grate 12 hard-cooked eggs on a coarse grater (save 2 eggs for the arrangement). Add all to the turkey.

Sauté the almonds in the butter in a frying pan; cool.

In a separate bowl, mix together until well blended the mayonnaise, dry mustard and chicken stock base. Pour over the turkey mixture and toss all together, scraping bottom and sides of bowl as you toss. Add the cooled almonds, along with whatever butter remains in the pan. Toss once again to distribute the nuts. Taste for salt; add more if your taste directs you to do so. Chill well before serving.

This salad can be made the day before serving if refrigerated in a well-covered bowl. It will then be ready for the arrangement.

ARRANGEMENT: Line the border of a large platter with romaine lettuce, extending the romaine beyond the edge. Mound salad on the platter to within an inch or two of platter's edge. Decorate border with cherry tomatoes, ripe olives and parsley. Lay slices of remaining 2 hard-cooked eggs cascading from the top. Sprinkle yolks with paprika.

CRANBERRY COTTAGE RING

This molded salad is particularly colorful with the contrasting color of the peas and parsnips in the center. The alternating red and white colors in the arrangement make a spectacular dish. The molds and vegetables can be prepared in advance, thus leaving only the arrangement of the platter as a last minute detail.

To insure removing the molds without any melting, which can happen when molds are immersed in hot water, brush the bottom and sides of the molds well with vegetable oil. Never use olive oil or the gelatin will not congeal. After the mold has been well oiled, tap upside down on the table so that any excess oil will drip down the sides. To remove the gelatin salads, use a rounded knife, such as a dinner knife, and cut around inner and outer edges, pressing firmly against the mold as you go around. Place a serving tray larger than the mold over the top of the mold. Holding both tray and mold firmly in both hands, quickly flip them over. Let stand a few minutes to release the suction. Voila!

Cranberry Mold   3 Quarts

3 packages (6 oz. each) rasp-   1 quart cranberry juice
  berry flavored gelatin   3 cans (1 lb. each) whole cran
6 cups boiling water   berry sauce

Dissolve gelatin in the boiling water. Stir in the cranberry juice, then the cranberry sauce. When well mixed, pour into an oiled 3-quart ring mold. Refrigerate until solid. Remove from mold according to above directions at the same time as the cottage mold is removed.

Cottage Mold   3 Quarts

4 envelopes unflavored gelatin   2 teaspoons onion salt
1 cup cold water   3 cups dairy sour cream
2 cups hot milk   1 teaspoon lemon extract
1 quart creamed cottage cheese

Soak gelatin in cold water for 10 minutes. Stir in the hot milk. Mix well until gelatin is thoroughly dissolved. Add the cottage cheese, onion salt, sour cream and lemon extract. Mix well and pour into an oiled 3-quart ring mold.

The cranberry and cottage molds must be exactly the same in depth to accomplish a perfect ring for the arrangement.

ARRANGEMENT: Unmold the cranberry and cottage molds fol-

Recipe Continues . . .

lowing directions on page 125. On the back side of 2 cookie sheets or other flat pans, cut each mold into 6 equal parts by first cutting each into halves and then each half into 3 equal parts. Using a large round tray twice the size of one mold, assemble the ring into a perfect round shape by alternating the red and white sections. Lift the molded sections with a wide spatula until all 6 portions of each mold have been used to make a large ring. Fill center with curried peas and parsnips. Border ring with clumps of watercress alongside the cottage mold sections and uncolored turnip roses next to the cranberry mold sections.

To serve, cut each section into 5 portions but only as the serving is performed in order to keep the ring intact.

When you've figured out your arithmetic on this one, you'll find you have 60 servings, but the 3-quart ring mold is pretty standard and a smaller size would not be as effective. Besides, you can count on a lot of second helpings for this. If you have any left over, have yourself some cottage-cranberry mold for breakfast next morning. (You won't need dinner after this luncheon!)

CURRIED PEAS AND PARSNIPS   30 Servings

8 parsnips, pared and cut ju-
    lienne
4 pounds frozen peas

2 teaspoons salt
1½ teaspoons curry seasoning
1¼ cups mayonnaise

Put parsnips and peas in separate pots, cover with water and add 1 teaspoon salt to each. Bring to a boil and cook gently for 6 to 8 minutes, leaving vegetables slightly undercooked so they remain firm and crisp. Drain and cool. Cut parsnips crosswise into small pieces. Combine with peas. Blend the curry seasoning and mayonnaise. Toss together with peas and parsnips. Adjust for salt if necessary. Chill. Spoon into the cranberry cottage ring.

BAKED NOODLES AND CREAM
30 Servings

3 pounds wide egg noodles
1 tablespoon vegetable oil
3 tablespoons salt
3 onions, finely chopped
½ pound shallots, finely chopped
¼ pound butter or margarine

6 tablespoons Worcestershire sauce
2 teaspoons white pepper
6 cups dairy sour cream
6 eggs
½ cup melted butter

In a large pot bring 2 gallons of water to a boil with the oil and 1 tablespoon salt. Add the noodles gradually so the water continues to boil. Cook uncovered, stirring occasionally, until tender, about 10 minutes. Drain thoroughly. Preheat oven to 350°F.

While noodles are cooking, sauté the finely chopped onions and shallots in ¼ pound butter or margarine until lightly browned. Add to the drained noodles. Blend the Worcestershire sauce, 2 tablespoons salt and the pepper with the sour cream. Combine with the noodles. Beat eggs well and add to noodle sour-cream mixture. Mix all together. Divide mixture into 2 buttered casseroles 11½ x 5½ x 2½ inches. Brush tops of each with melted butter. Bake in the preheated oven for 35 minutes, or until tops are golden brown and crisp.

STUFFED PRUNES AND ROSY PEACHES

You will note throughout this book that the number of servings often exceeds the number of persons served. This is to allow for "seconds," which are often served. While prunes are not particularly classified in the category of gourmet or extraordinary foods, I have never served these stuffed prunes without guests exclaiming, "Oh, prunes, I love them!" Apparently not many people think to serve them so I'm glad when I do.

Recipe Continues . . .

Stuffed Prunes   30 Servings

48 large prunes
5 whole cloves
½ teaspoon ground ginger
grated rind of 1 large orange
grated rind of 1 lemon

½ pound cream cheese
48 maraschino cherry halves
48 pieces of angelica or candied
citron

Drop prunes into water about 1 inch deep. Cover pot and simmer gently for about 1 hour. Drain, saving ½ cup of the liquid. Cool and pit prunes.

While prunes are cooling, cook the saved liquid with the cloves, ginger and grated rinds. Bring to a boil, then lower heat to simmer for 12 to 15 minutes. Strain and cool.

Combine spiced mixture with the cream cheese and beat to a smooth consistency. Put cheese in a pastry bag or cookie press and pipe into cavity of prunes. Allow cream cheese to extend above surface in a rippled design. Place a cherry half on center of cream cheese, using small pieces of angelica or candied citron to emulate leaves.

Rosy Peaches   30 Servings

5 cans (29 oz. each) peach
halves (approximately 38
halves)

1 cup rosé wine
2 jars (12 oz. each) red currant
jelly

Drain peaches, reserving 1 cup of the juice. In a rather deep pot, beat together the wine and jelly. Stir in the reserved peach juice and bring to a boil. Simmer slowly for about 10 minutes, or until sauce thickens very slightly. Cool. Pour over peach halves in a large bowl, turning them every so often to coat all sides. Chill and transfer to a serving bowl to center the tray on which the stuffed prunes will be placed.

ARRANGEMENT: Place bowl of peach halves in center of tray

and surround with circular rows of the stuffed prunes. Border rim edge of tray with curly endive or lacy soft lettuce leaves.

RELISHES ON ICE 30 Servings

2 pint boxes cherry tomatoes
2 cans (16 oz. each) large ripe
olives
2 jars (9 to 11 oz. each) stuffed
green olives

1 quart tiny dill pickles
1 large tomato
Lemon leaves or other greenery

ARRANGEMENT: Wash cherry tomatoes, leaving stems on for handles and color contrast.

Fill a large glass bowl with crushed or shaved ice. Border edge of bowl with the cherry tomatoes. Lay the olives and pickles all over the ice except for the center top on which you now set a tomato rose (p. 182), and lemon leaves or other greenery.

POTATO PARKER HOUSE ROLLS 50 Rolls

This basic refrigerator dough, which keeps well from 3 to 5 days, produces light, airy rolls, with a unique flavor. (An especially nice and different roll to serve at lunch as an accompaniment to a fruit salad is made by following the directions below, and in addition laying on each round of cut out dough a segment of sugared orange.) Bake according to directions. Then spread a thin powder-sugar icing over tops and serve warm.

1 cup mashed potatoes (instant
or fresh)
1 cake of compressed fresh yeast
or 1 package active dry yeast
2 teaspoons and ½ cup sugar
½ cup water (80° to 90°F. for
compressed, 105° to 115°F.
for dry yeast)

1 cup milk, scalded
¼ pound margarine or butter
3 eggs
1½ teaspoons salt
6 to 7 cups flour

Recipe Continues . . .

Prepare potatoes, saving water if fresh potatoes have been cooked. Set potatoes aside. Mix yeast with 2 teaspoons sugar to thin consistency. Pour in ½ cup water, using saved water from cooked fresh potatoes or tap water if the instant potatoes are used, but be sure water is at correct temperature. Pour scalded milk over margarine or butter in a rather large bowl. Add ½ cup sugar. Cool. Add eggs one at a time; beat well after each addition. Add dissolved yeast to the milk-egg mixture and stir well. Add the salt and mashed potatoes. Sift flour into the mixture, beating until smooth and stiff. Turn out on a floured board and knead lightly. Grease bottom of a bowl. Put dough into it and immediately flip it over, thus greasing the top evenly. Cover with plastic or foil covering. Set in the refrigerator overnight.

Roll out dough ¼-inch thick. Cut rounds with a floured 2½-inch biscuit cutter. Flour the handle of a wooden spoon. Make a crease to one side of center in each round. Roll handle of spoon toward edge, flattening half of round slightly. Brush lightly with melted butter or margarine. Fold thicker half over thinner half, pressing edges together. Transfer to lightly greased cookie sheets, placing the rolls about 1 inch apart. Cover with a dampened towel and set in a warm place to rise.

Preheat oven to 425°F.When rolls are doubled in size, set in oven and bake for 15 to 20 minutes, or until golden brown.

Butter Curls

(See directions, p. 55.)

APPLE TORTE   16 Servings

(Dinah's Apple-Tennis Torte, Chapter X, is an alternative to this delicious recipe.)

Crumb Crust

1 package (6 oz.) zwieback rolled into crumbs	¼ pound butter, melted
	½ teaspoon ground cinnamon
¾ cup granulated sugar	¼ teaspoon grated nutmeg

Preheat oven to 350°F. Butter a 9-inch springform pan with removable sides. Combine crust ingredients. Press half onto bottom and sides of springform pan. Reserve other half of crumbs for top of torte.

Apple Filling

7 large or 9 medium-size cooking or baking apples	½ teaspoon ground cinnamon
	¼ teaspoon ground nutmeg
4 tablespoons lemon juice	5 eggs, well beaten
⅔ cup sugar	2 cups dairy sour cream
1½ ounces butter	½ teaspoon vanilla extract

Peel and core apples. Cut into chunks, sprinkling lemon juice over apples as you proceed. Add the butter and spices and cook over moderate heat until apples are slightly cooked and glossy in appearance. Do not overcook. Remove from heat and cool.

Add eggs, sour cream and vanilla to cooled apples. Cook over moderate heat until slightly thickened, about 20 minutes. Stir occasionally to prevent scorching. Remove from heat and cool slightly. Pour filling into crumb-lined pan. Sprinkle remaining crumbs on top. Place springform pan on a cookie sheet. Bake for 1 hour. Cool on a rack. *Do not* remove sides of pan until torte is completely cooled. Refrigerate. Will keep in refrigerator for several days. Can be served with or without a whipped cream topping.

FLO CHART FOR BUFFET LUNCHEON

THREE WEEKS BEFORE Decide on date. Send invitations. Call help to be hired, etc.

TWO WEEKS BEFORE Do all marketing except for fresh fruits and vegetables, dairy products and turkey.

ONE WEEK BEFORE Bake Parker House rolls and freeze.

FOUR DAYS BEFORE Pick up turkey.

THREE DAYS BEFORE Prepare the two molds.

TWO DAYS BEFORE Prepare butter curls, apple torte, noodle casseroles; cook the prunes, prepare peaches. Finish marketing.

ONE DAY BEFORE Prepare the turkey salad, parsnips and peas, and refrigerate; also assemble the relishes. Bake noodle casseroles and refrigerate.

DAY OF THE PARTY

4 hours before serving. Remove rolls from freezer and noodles from refrigerator. Put rolls on serving trays.

3 hours before. Plug in coffee maker; keep warm.

2 hours before. Prepare stuffed prunes and arrange on platter with peaches.

1½ hours before. Arrange cranberry cottage ring and fill center with peas and parsnips. Allow 45 minutes for this arrangement. Remove butter curls from refrigerator. Arrange turkey salad on platter. Put noodle casseroles in a 325°F. oven. Arrange relishes on ice. Put everything on buffet table. Your luncheon is ready to be served.

BUYING AND PREPARING TURKEY

I've been asked what makes my turkey salad different.

First, I cut it into nice chunky pieces, big enough to bite into. Most people have a tendency to make a gooey mish-mash of turkey salad.

Second, the pineapple chunks, capers and almonds give it

more consistency and flavor than your everyday, run-of-the-mill turkey salad served in most restaurants, which so often is mixed mundanely with only celery, hard-cooked eggs and much too much salad dressing masquerading as mayonnaise.

Third, and *most* important, I use only *real* mayonnaise, not ersatz salad dressing that looks like mayonnaise but isn't. There's a big difference in price but there's a good reason for it. Whole eggs are used in mayonnaise, but not in those look-alike salad dressings. It's the eggs that give the bona fide mayonnaise more consistency and firmness. I not only recommend but urge *you* to stick to the real McCoy that sticks to your ingredients and holds them together. You'll find a difference in your own salads.

Finally, I take special care in the *kind of seasoning* I use and the way I mix it. The chicken stock base seasoning and dry mustard give it a special flavor. You will note that I have specified mixing the dry mustard and chicken base into the mayonnaise until it is *well blended*. Any time a dry seasoning is used, it should be mixed into the mayonnaise instead of into the salad itself, and stirred until it is evenly distributed. Don't just toss it in and let it settle in one spot. Stir it vigorously or whip in a blender so that the mayonnaise is evenly and thoroughly seasoned. Then, when you pour it over your turkey mixture and toss it all together, you'll find every bite of your salad equally and deliciously seasoned.

A general rule of thumb for buying fresh or frozen turkeys: For *roasting* a fresh turkey is preferable. For *boiling* (to make a salad) a frozen turkey is okay but I still prefer to boil a fresh turkey. Frozen turkey now comes in parts (breasts, legs) in meat markets, which is a definite advantage for those who don't want to prepare a big holiday bird, but the best flavor, of course, comes from cooking the whole turkey, bones and all.

When using frozen turkey, allow 3 days to defrost in the refrigerator.

ON REMOVING JELLIED SALADS WITHOUT MELTING
The old-fashioned way to remove gelatin salads is to dip the mold

into hot water, but this isn't always successful because it often causes melting. A better way is to oil the mold very well. Then, simply loosening the mold should make the salad slide right out intact, with no melted edges.

A word of caution: Use corn or other vegetable oil for brushing the gelatin pan or mold. Do *not* brush with olive oil. If olive oil is used, the gelatin will not set well; it only gets semihard, will not solidify as it does with vegetable oil. The best kind is almond oil.

HINT: Do not use fresh pineapple in gelatin. The enzyme in the pineapple dissolves the gelatin so that it will never become firm.

CHAPTER V

. . . .

Tea Parties and Receptions

. . . .

Tea parties and receptions afford the opportunity of entertaining large numbers of people during a period of a few hours.

The main distinction between a tea and a reception is in the kind of occasion rather than the type of food served. A reception is usually held in someone's honor—a distinguished guest, a bride and groom, a special achievement, an anniversary. A tea party is most often a for women only affair, sometimes a get-acquainted introduction to a house guest, a bride-to-be, a new daughter-in-law; but more frequently used by various kinds of groups, clubs or organizations to gain membership.

Afternoon, between 2 and 4 or 5 o'clock is the customary time for coming and going on these special occasions, though it may vary according to geographic location. In Boston, for instance, 3 o'clock sharp is the traditional High Tea Time.

Whatever the time, the table service follows similar guidelines: your silver coffee and tea services are placed one at each end of the table; silver or crystal candlesticks on either side, with a lovely

127

fresh floral centerpiece. All of this sets the stage for your dainty and pretty assortment of sandwiches, mints, nuts and sweets.

While the other sections in this book have menus and recipes planned specifically for a certain number of people (10, 20, 30), teas and receptions vary too much in numbers—from 20 to 200 or more—to suggest precise menus to please everyone. More importantly, the time of day—after lunch and before cocktails and dinner—eliminates the necessity of having anything more than a basic menu of finger sandwiches, sweets, nuts, relishes, etc.

I have chosen an ample assortment of recipes for two basic menus, one for a tea party, the other for a "Sweet Tooth" dessert party menu appropriate for after concert, theater, lecture, or special occasion, or to add to your other buffet or dinner party menus if you wish.

All the recipes in this chapter give the exact proportions, so you can plan the number of guests you wish to invite. With the following suggestions, plus your own ingenuity, even a proper Bostonian will be delighted with your Tea Party.

Important priorities: Here's where you must know your tea and coffee formulas. One pound of coffee will make 60 cups of a rather mild brew. Allow 2 cups per person when serving coffee with dinner but only about ½ cup per person when serving it along with tea at a tea party.

Allow 1 teaspoon of tea or 1 tea bag per cup. The most important factor in brewing good tea is the use of rapidly boiling water, not merely hot water. Be sure your serving teapot is warm before pouring boiling water into it. One pound of tea will make 200 cups.

BASIC TEA PARTY

MENU

Assorted Finger Sandwiches
  Chicken and Cranberry Ribbons
  Tuna Pinwheels
  Watercress Sandwiches
  Asparagus Diplomas
  Orange-Date Triangles
  Ham Circles
Bonbons in pastel shades
Salted Pecan Halves
Petits-fours
Clove-studded Lemon Slices
Tea   Coffee
Cubed sugar   Cream

EQUIPMENT WORK SHEET FOR BASIC TEA PARTY

assorted sizes and types of trays and platters for sandwiches
paper doilies for use on other than glass trays
one or two silver tea services (depending on number of guests)
small glass plate and lemon fork
2 compotes for bonbons
2 nut dishes
cake plates and trays for petits-fours and cookies
sugar tongs
dessert plates (luncheon size) and cups
teaspoons
napkins (nice quality paper)
pair of candelabra and candles
floral centerpiece
tablecloth
coffee maker
large teakettle

MARKETING WORK SHEET FOR BASIC TEA PARTY

1 pullman loaf of unsliced white bread
1 pullman loaf of unsliced whole-wheat bread
3 two-pound loaves of sliced white sandwich bread
1 pint milk
1 quart buttermilk
½ pound butter
1 pound soft-spread margarine
3 pounds cream cheese
1 dozen eggs
1 frying chicken, 3 to 3½ pounds
1½ pounds sliced cooked ham
1 whole celery stalk
1 onion
2 bunches of watercress
2 large oranges (for peel)
3 lemons
2 cans (20 oz. each) green asparagus spears
2 cans (1 lb. each) jellied cranberry sauce
1 can (8 oz.) chopped ripe olives
2 cans (3 oz. each) sliced pimientos
1 small jar of sweet pickles
1 can (7 oz.) white meat tuna
1 pint mayonnaise
1 pound pitted dates
½ pound dried apricots
3 ounces almond paste
8 ounces thin spaghetti
1 small box cornflake crumbs
2 pounds salted shelled pecans
6 ounces chopped shelled walnuts
3 ounces blanched shelled almonds
1 jar (4 oz.) red maraschino cherries
2 pounds assorted bonbons
A candy thermometer

STAPLES LIST FOR BASIC TEA PARTY

salt
whole cloves
chicken stock base seasoning
Worcestershire sauce
prepared mustard
prepared horseradish
red and green and yellow food coloring
salad oil
all-purpose flour
cake flour
granulated sugar
confectioners' sugar
baking soda
cream of tartar
vanilla extract
coffee
tea or tea bags

FINGER SANDWICHES

It isn't necessary to prepare all 6 or 7 kinds of finger sandwiches for one tea party. Select those that appeal to you most, or perhaps eliminate one kind and make more of another. You can halve or double a recipe according to your needs.

The general rule of thumb, or finger, is 5 finger sandwiches per person at a tea party or reception.

How much bread to purchase? A 2-pound loaf generally has about 28 slices, a 3-pound loaf 44 slices. One pound of soft-spreading margarine, or butter, will spread 96 slices of bread, allowing 1 teaspoon per slice. One quart of sandwich filling will spread about 20 slices of bread, thus making 80 triangles.

While the preparation of finger sandwiches is quite time-consuming, they can be done in stages, such as making the filling one day, preparing the sandwiches the next day, and finally slicing,

Recipe Continues . . .

decorating, and arranging on the following day when the party is held.

The sandwiches should be rolled and wrapped in dampened towels as fast as possible, so the bread won't become dry during the preparation.

On the day of the party, an extra pair of hands will be of invaluable help so that one person can do the slicing while the other places the sliced sandwiches on the platters for final arranging and decorating. This cannot be done more than a few hours before the guests arrive; therefore it is advisable to have all other items ready so this remains the only project yet to be completed.

Save the trimmed crusts and ends for they can be used to make an accompaniment for soups and salads by spreading them with a mixture of butter or margarine and grated Parmesan cheese, placing them on buttered cookie sheets and toasting in the oven. Store in covered containers.

CHICKEN AND CRANBERRY RIBBONS

32 to 34 Sandwiches

1 pullman loaf of unsliced white bread
1 pullman load of unsliced whole-wheat bread
Soft-spreading margarine
1 cup finely chopped, cooked and seasoned chicken
⅓ cup finely chopped celery
⅓ cup finely ground, toasted blanched almonds
¼ teaspoon salt
½ teaspoon chicken stock base seasoning
½ cup mayonnaise
2 cans (1 lb. each) jellied cranberry sauce
½ pound cream cheese, softened, for decorating
Vegetable coloring

Order the pullman loaves in advance from your bakery and have them sliced horizontally into 5 slices, not counting the crusts.

Prepare the chicken salad filling by combining the chopped chicken and celery with the almonds, seasonings and mayonnaise.

Trim all crusts from the slices, covering the bread with a dampened towel as you work.

For one ribbon loaf, lay a long slice of white bread on a board, then above it lay one of whole-wheat, and then another of white. Spread margarine over first slice and spread chicken salad about ¼ inch thick over it. Cover with the slice of whole-wheat bread. Spread with margarine. Lay ⅛-inch slices of cranberry sauce all over, patching empty spaces with dabs of the sauce. Spread the last slice of white bread with margarine and lay this side down on cranberry sauce slices. Wrap this long loaf in wax paper. Transfer to a cookie sheet or pan and cover with a well-dampened tea towel.

Prepare another ribbon loaf in the same manner, however, start with a slice of whole-wheat bread, resulting in a combination opposite to the other loaf. Refrigerate overnight. This loaf can be sliced if set for 6 to 8 hours, but for easier slicing let it set overnight.

ARRANGEMENT: With a sharp serrated knife, slice across into ¼-inch slices, thus yielding 16 slices. Lay in rows with filling in a vertical pattern. Place a small bowl in center of tray and fill with clumps of parsley. Arrange a few turnip roses (p. 183), which have been tinted a delicate pink, on the parsley. Tint half of the cream cheese pink, the other half pale green. With the star decorating tip, make pink-colored cream-cheese rosettes in the center of each slice and complete with a green leaf, using green-tinted cream cheese and the leaf tip on the decorating bag.

TUNA PINWHEELS

40 Pinwheels

1 can (7 oz.) white meat tuna or albacore
2 hard-cooked eggs, chopped fine
½ cup minced celery
¼ cup finely chopped sweet pickles
2 teaspoons finely chopped onion
½ teaspoon salt

½ cup mayonnaire
Butter or margarine, softened
Remaining slices of bread from the pullman loaves
1 can (3 oz.) sliced pimientos
1 can (8 oz.) chopped ripe olives
Watercress or parsley sprigs
Turnip flowers (p. 183)

Open can of tuna, leaving top intact. Pour scalding water over top and squeeze to release all the water and oil. Chop tuna rather fine and combine with next 6 ingredients.

Cut the long slices of bread remaining from chicken and cranberry ribbons (2 white and 2 whole-wheat) crosswise into halves, yielding 8 slices. Roll thin with rolling pin and spread with softened butter or margarine. Place strips of pimiento at front edge of each slice of bread and a row of finely chopped ripe olives across the center. Spread with tuna salad ¼ inch thick and roll tightly. Place seam side down in a pan. Repeat until all 8 rolls have been made. Cover with wax paper and a dampened tea towel. Refrigerate overnight.

ARRANGEMENT: Cut each roll into 5 slices. Arrange in circular rows on a round tray, placing a cluster of watercress or parsley in center of tray. Set a bouquet of carved turnip flowers, tinted yellow and orange on the parsley.

WATERCRESS SANDWICHES

56 Small sandwiches

Prepare enough of these dainty sandwiches for they require little time and are most popular.

1 flat-top 2-pound loaf of sliced white sandwich bread (28 slices)
1 cup finely chopped watercress
½ pound butter or margarine, softened

1 tablespoon grated onion
1 tablespoon Worcestershire sauce
½ teaspoon salt
Sprigs of watercress
Tomato roses (p. 182)

Trim crusts from slices of bread. Roll them slightly with a rolling pin. Blend watercress with butter or margarine, grated onion and seasonings, and spread over bread. Roll slices and place seam side down in a pan. Cover with wax paper and a dampened tea towel. Refrigerate.

ARRANGEMENT: Cut each roll into halves; tuck a sprig of watercress into each end. Arrange on a doily-lined tray in even rows, leaving upper corners free to decorate with tomato roses set on sprigs of watercress.

ASPARAGUS DIPLOMAS 28 Sandwiches

You will graduate with honors when you serve these delicious rolled sandwiches. By placing them in pyramiding rows, they will resemble little diplomas.

1 flat-top 2-pound loaf of sliced white sandwich bread (28 slices)
½ pound cream cheese, softened

1 tablespoon chopped pimiento
2 cans (20 oz. each) thin green asparagus spears
1 cup cooked thin spaghetti
5 drops of red food coloring

Trim crusts from all sides of bread slices. Set them aside covered with a damp towel.

Combine cream cheese and pimiento. Drain asparagus. Cook spaghetti in boiling water to which food coloring has been added. When cooked, drain; do not rinse, lay out on cookie sheet, separating strands and cover to keep them pliable. Lay out about one

Recipe Continues . . .

third of bread slices at a time to keep others from drying. Spread bread all over with cream-cheese pimiento mixture. Lay an asparagus spear on the front end of slice with the tip extending about ½ inch on one side of bread. Roll tightly and place on serving tray with seam side down. Using a strand of spaghetti, tie around center of each roll, making a bow; cut off any extra length not needed for a neat bow.

ARRANGEMENT: Stack in a pyramid by using 12 rolls on the bottom, 8 rolls on the next layer, then 5 rolls, ending with 3 rolls on top.

ORANGE DATE TRIANGLES

These unusual tea sandwiches are made of 2 delicious breads which can be baked and frozen far in advance. Either of the breads could be served other than in sandwich form, i.e., by using slices cut from the loaf, or spread with cream cheese and cut into triangles.

Orange Bread   1 Loaf

2½ cups sifted flour	1 cup buttermilk
¾ cup sugar	2 eggs, beaten
1 tablespoon baking powder	¼ cup salad oil
1½ teaspoons salt	1 cup cornflake crumbs
¾ teaspoon baking soda	
½ cup finely chopped orange peel	

Preheat oven to 350°F. Sift together flour, sugar, baking powder, salt and baking soda into a mixing bowl. Stir in orange peel. Add buttermilk, eggs and oil. Stir only until mixture is moistened. Fold in cornflake crumbs. Turn into a well greased loaf pan 9 x 5 x 3 inches. Bake for 1 hour.

When a toothpick inserted in center comes out dry, remove

pan to cooking rack. Let stand for 5 minutes, then turn loaf out onto rack and cool completely. Bread should be at least a day old before slicing. If freezing bread for future use, wrap well in foil. Remove from freezer about 2 hours before using.

Orange Date Triangles

128 Small triangle sandwiches

1 loaf of Orange Bread
1 loaf of Date-Nut Bread
¾ pound cream cheese

1 jar (4 oz.) red maraschino
   cherries

Lay the loaves on their sides and with a very sharp knife slice off the rounded tops only enough to make each loaf flat and both loaves the same height. Anyone lucky enough to be around at the time can nibble these tops.

With a very sharp serrated knife, slice each loaf into ¼-inch slices, yielding 24 even slices, not including the ends.

Chop cherries (not too small) and combine cherries and the juice in the bottle with cream cheese. Lay the slices of the orange bread on a board and spread with the cheese and cherry mixture. Top each slice with a slice of date-nut bread. Cover and store in refrigerator.

ARRANGEMENT: Cut diagonally from opposite corners to give 4 pieces—2 rather elongated triangles and 2 equal triangles from each large sandwich. When all sandwiches have been cut, arrange them on serving tray, point side up, making alternate circular rows of the elongated triangles and the equal ones.

Date and Nut Bread

1 Loaf

1 cup pitted dates
1½ teaspoons soda
½ teaspoon salt
1½ ounces butter or margarine
¾ cup boiling water

2 eggs
1 teaspoon vanilla extract
1 cup granulated sugar
1½ cups sifted flour
¾ cup chopped walnuts

Recipe Continues . . .

Cut pitted dates into small pieces and drop into a mixing bowl. Sprinkle on the baking soda and salt. Cut the butter or margarine into chunks and scatter over the dates. Pour the boiling water over dates and stir until mixture resembles a thick paste. Cool. Preheat oven to 350°F.

Beat the 2 eggs; add vanilla and sugar. Remove 2 teaspoons of the flour and toss with the walnuts. Alternately add the flour and date mixture, beginning and ending with the flour, to the beaten eggs. Fold in the floured nuts. Turn into a well-greased loaf pan 9 x 5 x 3 inches. Bake for 60 to 65 minutes. Test with a toothpick or straw after 60 minutes. When either feels dry, remove bread to a cooling rack. Let stand for 5 to 10 minutes. Turn out onto a rack and cool completely. The same storage and slicing principles apply here as in the Orange Bread.

HAM CIRCLES

80 Small sandwiches

20 slices of white bread	¼ pound cream cheese, softened
½ pound cream cheese	
1 tablespoon prepared mustard	Yellow and green food coloring
1 teaspoon prepared horseradish	Parsley sprigs
20 slices of ham	

Trim crusts from slices of bread. Roll with rolling pin on both sides of each slice to make certain the bread is rolled very thin. Combine ½ pound cream cheese with mustard and horseradish. Completely cover each slice with this mixture. Trim ham slices to fit bread, cutting the ham about ½ inch shorter than the bread. Roll tightly, jelly-roll fashion, and place seam side down in a pan. Cover with wax paper and dampened towel. Refrigerate.

ARRANGEMENT: When ready to serve, slice each roll into 4 pieces. Arrange on a round tray in circular rows radiating from the center. Color more than half of the ¼ pound cream cheese yellow and the remainder green. Spoon the yellow cream cheese into a pastry bag with a decorating tip with a small hole. Make a design in the shape of capital letter S. Spoon green cream cheese into pastry bag and place a dot of green cream cheese in the open curves of the S. Lay a row of parsley sprigs around outer border of tray and scatter amongst the sandwiches.

PETITS-FOURS

There is no doubt that preparing petits-fours requires time and patience; surely it is much easier to purchase them already made, which I wholeheartedly recommend if your time is limited. However, since they can be prepared as far as 3 days in advance, the challenge and pride of accomplishment make the effort worthwhile and gratifying. At first glance the project may seem overwhelming but taken step by step it isn't too bad, even for the neophyte. Think of how great you'll feel when your guests ask you where you bought the pretty little cakes and you reply, "I made them myself!"

Petits-Fours Cake (Step 1)   1 Cake, 7 x 11 inches

1 cup sifted cake flour	¼ cup almond paste
¼ teaspoon salt	2 tablespoons milk
2 whole eggs	½ teaspoon vanilla extract
2 extra egg yolks	⅓ cup melted butter
1 cup sugar	

Preheat oven to 350°F. Add salt to flour, sift together, and set aside. Put the whole eggs and extra egg yolks in the top part of a double boiler over hot, not boiling, water. Beat until light and lemon-colored; add sugar gradually while beating. Remove from heat. Beat until mixture is lukewarm.

Combine almond paste, milk and vanilla. Beat until smooth. Add a small amount of egg mixture and mix well. Then add this almond paste mixture to the cooled egg mixture. Fold in the dry

Recipe Continues . . .

ingredients. Blend in the melted butter. Pour into a well-greased and floured pan, 7 x 11 inches. Bake for 30 to 35 minutes.

Glazing the Petits-Fours (Step 2)

Apricot Glaze   1¾ Cups

½ pound dried apricots   1 cup sugar

Soak apricots overnight in water to cover. Drain and force through a food mill or strainer. Add the sugar and place over low heat. Bring to a boil. Cook gently for 5 minutes, stirring constantly to keep from scorching.

When cake is cool, cut into 35 small squares with a sharp knife; brush away the crumbs from the sides and bottom of each piece. Place the cake squares on a rack which has been set upon a sheet of wax paper to catch the drippings. Drippings of glaze can be reused, as is also the case when frosting the cakes. Using a spatula, spread the glaze over the top and sides of each cake square. Let stand for 10 minutes to allow the glaze to harden slightly. Application of the frosting is easier on this smooth surface.

Frosting the Petits-Fours (Step 3)

Glossy Frosting

2¼ cups granulated sugar   3¾ to 4 cups confectioners'
¼ teaspoon cream of tartar   sugar, sifted
1 cup plus 1 tablespoon water

Combine granulated sugar, cream of tartar and water in a deep saucepan. Stir until sugar is dissolved. Place over low heat, bring to a slow boil without stirring, and cook until syrup reaches 226°F. on a candy thermometer. Remove from heat. Cool to 110°F. Add the sifted confectioners' sugar, beating continuously to make a smooth shiny frosting, thin enough to pour but not too thin to be effective.

In decorating the cakes you can use your ingenuity and let your imagination accept the challenge. Tint the frosting if you wish. Top the cakes with tiny ornaments, chopped nuts, glazed cherries, tiny gumdrops, grated chocolate, tinted coconut or anything that strikes your fancy.

FLO CHART FOR TEA PARTY

You're on your own for Flo charts in this chapter, using the recipes of your choice and timetables for the individual recipes. Since, as I have mentioned, teas and receptions are mostly coming-and-going, in-and-out affairs, this eliminates the pressure of serving everything all at once. Also, more often than not teas and receptions are organized by a "planning committee," whose members share the various responsibilities of preparing the sandwiches, serving them, keeping trays and platters replenished, pouring tea or coffee, and so on. If you're planning your own private tea or reception without benefit of an affiliated group, club or organization, then I suggest that you form your own "planning committee" with recruits among friends and neighbors.

CLOVE-STUDDED LEMON SLICES
For an attractive lemon plate to go with your tea table, slice lemons very thin in whole round circles. Place them in an overlapping circular arrangement around the plate, like flower petals. Insert a whole clove in each lemon slice. This not only enhances the plate with eye appeal in the color contrast between the dark clove and yellow lemon, but it also adds a spicy flavor to the tea.

SWEET TOOTH PARTY

MENU

Chocolate Melt-Away Pie
Cherry-Nut Strudel
Viennese Fruit Kuchen
Walnut Crescents
Lemon Angel Freeze
Miniature Chocolate Éclairs
Holiday Squares

Remember when you were a child standing with a nickel in your pocket, in tiptoed wonder and wide-eyed, in a penny candy store? And surveying all of those delicious, delectable, mouth-watering sweets-and-treats that you could simply die for?

Well, it's not so much different for grown-ups. All of us once were awe-struck kids in a penny candy store. And grown-up people become children again at certain times, in certain places. Among the most memorable of these could be a "Sweet Tooth" party where guests recapture the glow of childhood at a buffet table laden with luscious loverlies such as chocolate melt-away pie, cherry-nut strudel, chocolate éclairs.

Don't stick your nose up at these fanny fatteners. You can put off your dieting until tomorrow. There's a time and place for them and believe me, you'll be glad to know when, where, and how to use them.

When and Where: At after-theater or after-concert parties for coffee and dessert; at one of those "progressive" roundelays (you-come-to-my-house-for-this and we'll-come-to-your-house-for-that sort of thing); at a special dinner party or buffet that appropriately lends itself to a bountiful buffet dessert table, as in my Bountiful Buffet (Chapter VII).

The beauty of these "Sweet Tooth" recipes is that they can be adapted to many types of party menus or forms of entertaining.

Among my catering clients for many years were Mr. and Mrs.

Howard Ahmanson, social and cultural leaders of Los Angeles, whose fabulous desert home at LaQuinta was perfect for party entertaining. Their Saturday-Before-Easter parties became a tradition and one of the highlights of the social season. Guests always included a number of distinguished VIPs such as the Eisenhowers, the Walter Annenbergs (former Ambassador to the Court of St. James's), California's former Governor Ed Brown, Dolores and Bob Hope, and a bank president whose name I don't recall but who always created quite a stir by landing on the front lawn in his private helicopter.

Mrs. Ahmanson, one of the most gracious hostesses I've ever known, had a knack of turning formalities into instant conviviality among such assorted dignitaries by serving menus that were conversation pieces. Instead of the traditional Easter ham, for instance, she would spring a surprise, like a Mexican feast topped by Sweet Tooth buffet. No matter what menu she planned, she always insisted on having her "sweet table," as she called it. The men loved it! Most of my Sweet Tooth recipes were planned or revised and refined especially for the Ahmanson parties.

How to Serve: If you're doing a whole buffet of all or several of the Sweet Tooth desserts, I suggest displaying them on doily-lined trays and platters of various shapes and sizes and at different heights as well. This can be done by placing the trays on pastry stands or pedestals of varying heights. It will make a much more attractive arrangement for your Sweet Tooth buffet table than putting the pastry trays down flat on the table. A more dramatic display can be created by using a garden flower cart for the goodies. Put your imagination to work and you can create an indoor garden of goodies-on-wheels.

You will need to make out your own Marketing List for the individual recipes, depending on how and when you want to use them—whether you plan a Sweet Tooth Party per se, or intend to incorporate some of the recipes into other menus.

Most of them can be prepared well in advance of a party and either refrigerated or frozen. If incorporated into other menus, you will need to adjust your Flo chart accordingly.

CHOCOLATE MELT-AWAY PIE

One 9-inch pie

Coconut Meringue Shell

⅔ cup shredded coconut
¼ cup powdered sugar
3 egg whites, at room temperature
¼ teaspoon cream of tartar

⅛ teaspoon salt
⅔ cup granulated sugar, sifted
¼ teaspoon almond extract
¼ teaspoon vanilla extract

Coat coconut with powdered sugar; set aside.

Beat egg whites until foamy, add cream of tartar and salt, and beat until stiff. Add granulated sugar, 1 tablespoon at a time, continuing to beat until stiff peaks are formed. Fold in the flavorings and the coated coconut. Spread on bottom and sides of a lightly greased 9-inch pie plate. Bake in a preheated 325°F. oven for 35 to 40 minutes, or until meringue feels dry.

Chocolate Filling

6 ounces sweet cooking chocolate
3 tablespoons milk

2 tablespoons sugar
4 eggs
1 teaspoon vanilla extract

Melt chocolate in the milk over low heat; stir frequently to prevent scorching. Add the sugar, remove from heat, and stir well. Separate eggs. Add the yolks slowly to the melted chocolate, stirring vigorously with each addition. Beat egg whites until stiff. Fold into the chocolate mixture. Fold in the vanilla. Pour into the baked coconut meringue pie shell. Chill.

Topping

1 cup whipping cream

Unsweetened chocolate, shaved

Whip cream until stiff. Spread over chocolate filling. Top with curls of shaved chocolate.

CHERRY-NUT STRUDEL

60 Slices, 1 inch wide

Although I use only butter in my apple strudel, I find that I always use oil in preparing this strudel. I'm not sure why, except that my mother did this, and nobody has ever prepared strudel as great as my mother's. I hope in a little way I emulate her talents.

This type of strudel improves with age and should be kept in the pan in which it was baked, in a dry cool place, but not necessarily refrigerated. After several days, the strudel will absorb most of the oil in the pan. That is, if "thieves in the night" haven't nibbled most of it by that time.

Prepare strudel dough, following the directions as for Apple Strudel (p. 267), and stretch dough. While dough is resting, assemble the filling.

Cherry Filling

1 quart cherry preserves
1 cup vegetable oil
½ pound vanilla wafers, rolled
   into fine crumbs
¾ cup sugar

1½ teaspoons ground cinnamon
3 tablespoons grated lemon rind
3 cups chopped (not fine)
   shelled walnuts

Preheat oven to 350°F. Empty the preserves into a colander placed over a bowl to remove some of the jelly which might cause the filling to run. Brush entire surface of stretched dough with ½ cup of oil.

Place cherry preserves along the edge of dough nearest you on the width of the table. Scatter crumbs over entire surface. Combine sugar and cinnamon, and sprinkle over all, also sprinkle on the grated lemon rind.

Lay 2¼ cups of the chopped walnuts in a row just above the cherries. Scatter the remainder all over. Roll as directed for apple strudel. Using ¼ cup of oil, generously grease baking pan. Brush top with remaining oil. Bake for 20 minutes. Brush top of strudel

Recipe Continues . . .

with oil that has accumulated in bottom of pan. Bake for 10 minutes longer.

VIENNESE FRUIT KUCHEN

1 Cake, 9 inches square

This recipe cost me a pair of nylon stockings, a bribe to one of the bakers in a famous Konditorei in Vienna. The rather odd measurements are the result of my translating the German recipe into English. I have prepared this many times with great success, so apparently I haven't completely forgotten the German language I learned in high school.

Crust

½ pound less 2 tablespoons butter
½ pound less 2 tablespoons sugar
½ pound less 1 tablespoon flour

1½ teaspoons baking powder
½ teaspoon salt
2 teaspoons cocoa powder
4 egg yolks

Fruit Filling

3 fresh peaches or pears
3 tablespoons plus 1 teaspoon sugar

⅛ teaspoon almond extract

Topping

3 egg whites

½ cup plus 1 tablespoon sugar

Preheat oven to 350°F. Butter a 9-inch-square pan that is 2 inches deep. Cream together the butter and the sugar. Sift the dry ingredients together, and blend them into the creamed butter. Add egg yolks one at a time, and mix together well after each addition.

Press crust into pan, pushing mixture 1 inch up the sides.

Peel and slice the peaches or pears into a bowl. Add the sugar and almond extract; toss together. Lay fruit in rows on unbaked crust. Bake for 35 minutes. Cool for 15 minutes or longer.

Preheat oven to 400°F. Beat egg whites until stiff enough to stand in peaks. Add sugar, 1 teaspoon at a time, beating continuously until stiff and glossy. Spoon meringue into a pastry bag with large star tip, and press over top of fruit in a crisscross design, allowing fruit to show through the empty spaces. Return Kuchen to oven for 5 minutes.

As one of a variety of desserts, this can be cut into fairly small squares. To serve as a dessert by itself, cut the Kuchen into 3-inch squares.

WALNUT CRESCENTS   32 Crescents

1 cake of compressed fresh yeast
or 1 package active dry yeast
¼ cup lukewarm water (80° to
90°F. for fresh yeast, 105° to
115°F. for dry yeast)
2 tablespoons sugar
2 cups flour
½ teaspoon salt

¼ pound butter
¼ pound margarine
2 eggs
½ cup sugar
½ teaspoon ground cinnamon
½ cup finely chopped shelled
walnuts
Icing (p. 72)

Dissolve yeast in water. Sprinkle in 2 tablespoons sugar and let stand for 5 minutes, stir. Sift flour and salt into a mixing bowl. Cut in butter and margarine, as for pie dough, until small lumps are formed. Add the dissolved yeast. Separate eggs. Beat yolks well and add to flour mixture; mix well.

Let dough rise in a warm place for 1 hour.

Transfer dough to workboard and divide into 4 parts. Set 3 parts aside keeping them well covered. Roll each piece into a circle approximately 8 inches in diameter.

Beat the 2 egg whites until stiff. Fold in ½ cup sugar, the cinnamon and walnuts. Spread a thin layer of the meringue over rolled-out dough. Cut the round of dough into 8 pie-shaped

Recipe Continues . . .

wedges. Roll each wedge from wide end to the point, and curve slightly. Place crescents on buttered cookie sheets, point end down. Repeat with other 3 portions. Let the crescents rise for 45 to 50 minutes.

Preheat oven to 350°F. Bake crescents for 16 to 18 minutes. Let cool, then brush tops with icing.

LEMON ANGEL FREEZE   One 10-inch torte

This refreshing dessert can be made in loaf-shaped pans or round springform pans. The loaf shape will yield more servings since it is not as high as the cake form, while the latter looks more elegant when displayed on a buffet table. In either case, you will find that this easy-to-prepare torte is a delightful dessert with any dinner or as one of a variety of desserts. Since it must be frozen, it can be prepared many days in advance of serving.

1 baked angel-food cake, 14 ounces	4 cups whipping cream
3 packages (3¾ oz. each) lemon pudding and pie filling	1 jar (4 oz.) red maraschino cherries, drained
	½ cup chopped shelled walnuts

Tear angel-food cake into medium-size pieces and put into a large mixing bowl. Prepare lemon pie filling according to the directions on packages; cool. Fold into broken cake pieces. Whip 2 cups of the cream until stiff. Fold into cake mixture until well blended. Turn into a 10-inch springform pan. Cover top with aluminum foil. Freeze.

To serve; remove from freezer shortly before serving. Run spatula around outside edge of cake; remove sides of pan. Whip remaining cream until stiff. Spread over top and sides of torte. Chop drained cherries and walnuts, and scatter over whipped cream on the top and sides of torte. Keep refrigerated until serving time.

MINIATURE CHOCOLATE ÉCLAIRS

7 Dozen tiny éclairs

Pastry

1 cup sifted all purpose flour
¼ teaspoon salt
½ cup butter

1 cup boiling water
4 eggs

Sift flour with salt. Add butter to boiling water, simmer until all the butter has been melted. Keep over low heat and add the flour all at once stirring vigorously until mixture, resembling mashed potatoes, forms a ball and leaves the sides of the pan. Remove from heat. Add unbeaten eggs one at a time beating thoroughly after each addition. Beat until a thick dough is formed. Spoon batter into a pastry bag filled with a large O tip. Press batter out in lengths of 2½ to 3 inches on ungreased cookie sheets. Bake in a preheated 425°F. oven for 20 minutes.

If the entire batch is not used at one time, the balance can be stored in a cool, dry place—not refrigerated.

Custard Filling

3 Cups

½ cup sifted flour
¼ teaspoon salt
¾ cup sugar

2 cups milk
4 egg yolks
½ teaspoon vanilla extract

Sift flour, salt and ½ cup sugar together. Heat milk, do not boil; add to the flour mixture, stirring until well blended. Place in the top part of a double boiler over simmering water. Cook for 5 minutes, stirring occasionally. Beat egg yolks slightly; add remaining ¼ cup sugar and beat well. Pour hot milk mixture slowly into the sugar and egg-yolk mixture; stir well. Return to the double boiler and cook for 3 minutes. Add vanilla and cool.

Recipe Continues . . .

Chocolate Frosting   2 Cups

1½ ounces unsweetened chocolate
¼ cup cream
1 teaspoon melted butter

1 egg yolk
⅛ teaspoon salt
½ teaspoon vanilla extract
1½ cups sifted powdered sugar

Place chocolate, cream and butter in a saucepan; heat slowly until chocolate is melted. Stir to avoid burning. Cool. Beat egg yolk slightly. Add salt, melted chocolate and vanilla. Beat in the powdered sugar until frosting is smooth and stiff. Should the mixture be too thin to spread, add a bit more powdered sugar to attain spreading consistency.

To fill the éclair shells, use a serrated paring knife to cut off the top, a little above half. Lay the tops in rows above the bottoms from which they were cut. Use a cocktail (two prong) fork and scrape out the insides of the shells.

Spoon the cooled filling into the shells. Replace the tops.

Spread the tops with chocolate frosting. Refrigerate. When frosting is hardened, cover the éclairs with plastic wrap. Keep stored in the refrigerator, but no longer than one day ahead to insure against becoming soggy.

The shells can be made as far as two weeks ahead. When cool, store in plastic bags in the refrigerator.

The filling and frosting can be made several days ahead—also refrigerated. If the frosting hardens, place it in a double-boiler over hot water until it returns to a spreading consistency.

HOLIDAY SQUARES

16 Squares

¼ pound butter
1 cup sugar
3 eggs
1 cup flour
½ teaspoon salt
½ teaspoon baking powder
½ cup mixed glazed fruits

1 ounce unsweetened chocolate
¼ cup chopped shelled walnuts
Powdered sugar, or Mocha
 Frosting (recipe follows)
Glazed cherries
Sliced angelica or glazed pine-
 apple

Preheat oven to 350°F. Cream together the butter and sugar. Add the eggs one at a time, mixing well after each addition. Sift together the dry ingredients. Beat into the butter sugar mixture. Remove half of the batter to another bowl. Chop the glazed fruits; stir into one portion of batter. Melt chocolate over hot water; stir into second half of batter. Add chopped walnuts to chocolate batter.

Alternately drop teaspoons of each batter into a greased 8-inch-square baking pan. Zigzag a spatula through the batter several times for a marbelized effect. Bake for 30 minutes. Cool.

Cut into 2-inch squares. Sprinkle tops with powdered sugar or spread with mocha frosting. Decorate each square with ½ glazed cherry and a leaf of sliced angelica or a wedge of glazed pineapple.

Mocha Frosting

1 tablespoon cocoa powder
1 cup powdered sugar
2 tablespoons prepared hot strong
 coffee

½ teaspoon vanilla extract

Sift cocoa and powdered sugar together. Stir in the hot coffee and blend until smooth; add vanilla.

CHAPTER VI

· · · · · · · · · · · · · · · ·

Cocktail Parties and Suppers

· · · · · · · · · · · · · · · ·

The cocktail hour is a ritual in many homes. The national anthem of the martini set is like a chant that is sung not by the dawn's early light but by the twilight's last gleaming—*"Come over for cocktails!"*

The truth is, as we all know, there are a lot of cocktail parties that do not fall under the heading of *Special Occasions,* but the ones in this book do.

I recommend that you plan your cocktail party for 30. Cocktail parties lend themselves comfortably to larger goups. Many a host and hostess, in fact, feel it's the easiest way to entertain. It's also a popular and appropriate way to reciprocate, repay those who have invited *you* to *their* parties; do it in large numbers and get it over with. Some believe a large convivial cocktail party for 30, 40, 50, or even 100 is the perfect solution for "paying back" all those people they "owe." Don't let it bother you that they know this is what you're doing; it happens to everyone. They'll have a good time if you make it a good party.

152

Large cocktail parties are as varied as the colors of a rainbow. It is gracious and thoughtful, therefore, to specify the type of party you're having on your invitation, such as "Cocktails," "Cocktail Buffet," "Cocktail Supper," so your guests will know how to plan their evening. Also specify type of dress.

The *cocktail party* that is "Strictly for Cocktails" is really always a little more than that. It should have some hot and cold hors-d'oeuvre, plus pickup foods such as raw vegetables, a dip for the vegetables, nuts, cheeses, etc. The invitation is usually extended for a period of 2 hours, such as 5 to 7 P.M. or 6 to 8 P.M.

The *cocktail buffet* may have all the items on the cocktail party menu, but in addition should have more substantial food such as tiny beef sandwiches, platters of cold meats and cheeses, seafood and pâtés. Cookies or tea cakes with coffee should also be served. Invitations usually specify a period of three hours: 5 to 8, or 6 to 9.

The *cocktail supper* combines the above two menus with the addition of hot casseroles or "fork food" (no knives required). This eliminates the necessity of providing tables and chairs for dining.

Don't forget the ice! Nothing is more irritating to guests, particularly at a *cocktail* party, than to run out of ice for their drinks. No matter how many ice cubes you've been advised to buy, my advice is to *buy more*. You can figure a minimum of 300 to 400 cubes for each 25 guests. They melt rapidly. If you have facilities for storing ice, start freezing ahead. Otherwise, buy ice in bulk.

For 30 guests, you should have 1 bar and 1 hors-d'oeuvre table spaced far enough apart to keep the guests circulating. For 50 to 60 guests, plan on 2 bars, 2 hors-d'oeuvre tables. If you're inviting everyone you know, like 100 or so, you may want to add an extra bar and bartender, though I've catered many parties of 100-and-more where drinks were served from only one bar with 2 or 3 very fast and efficient bartenders.

STRICTLY FOR COCKTAILS

(For 30)

MENU

For the Buffet
Basket Full of Vegetables
Dilly of a Dip
Sweet 'n Sour Meatballs
Picklated Pups
Blushing Eggs
Tuna Pâté

To be passed
Stuffed Mushrooms
Mini Cheese Tarts
Onion Puffs
Crab Amandine

EQUIPMENT WORK SHEET FOR STRICTLY FOR COCKTAILS

wicker basket and bowl that fits inside it
2 glass bowls
4 ovenproof insert casseroles, 1½ quarts each
1 tray, 12 to 14 inches
2 spreaders
2 round or oblong trays, 10 to 12 inches, for passing canapés
cookie sheets or pie tins for heating canapés
cocktail glasses
cocktail napkins
paper crinkle cups
canapé trays or small plates
chafing dishes to hold meatballs, picklated pups
ovenproof inserts for chafing dishes

bucket for ice cubes
ashtrays
silent butler

MARKETING WORK SHEET FOR STRICTLY FOR COCKTAILS

1 pound butter
3 cups dairy sour cream
1½ pounds cream cheese
6 ounces grated mozzarella cheese
4 ounces Parmesan cheese
3 to 4 ounces Swiss cheese
3 ounces blue cheese
3 dozen small eggs
1 large egg
5 pounds beef chuck or shoulder, or a combination, ground
2 pounds cocktail hot dogs or 24 knackwurst
½ pound bacon
1 head of cauliflower
5 or 6 carrots
3 zucchini
3 whole celery stalks
2 turnips
1 large cucumber
1 pint box cherry tomatoes
45 medium-size mushrooms
15 white onions
1 large yellow onion
1 bunch of watercress
1 bunch of parsley
2 cans (7½ oz. each) crab meat
2 cans (6½ to 7 oz. each) white meat tuna
1 can (29 oz.) pineapple chunks
1 can (24 oz.) pineapple juice
4 cans (12 oz. each) apricot nectar
1 quart apple juice

1 can (29 oz.) tomato sauce
2 cans (16 oz. each) extra large ripe olives
1 can (29 oz.) sliced beets
1 jar (12 oz.) sweet pickles
1 jar (8 oz.) prepared Dijon mustard
1 jar (8 to 10 oz.) red currant jelly
2 loaves of white bread
1 quart mayonnaise
1 bottle (12 oz.) light molasses
4 ounces sliced unblanched almonds
liquor
mixers
ice

STAPLES LIST FOR STRICTLY FOR COCKTAILS

salt
cayenne pepper
nutmeg (whole, to be grated when used)
ground ginger
caraway seeds
garlic salt
dry mustard
bay leaves
pickling spices
pickle relish
dillweed
Worcestershire sauce
soy sauce
cider vinegar
wine vinegar
chili sauce
flour
baking powder
cornstarch or arrowroot
vegetable shortening
light brown sugar

fine dry bread crumbs
oatmeal
bar supplies

A BASKET FULL OF VEGETABLES

How welcome is the sight of an array of crisp vegetables—colorful and inviting to the hungry and particularly enjoyed by the calorie conscious guest! The market basket emphasizes the freshness of the vegetables and that freshness is insured by placing the vegetables in crushed ice.

1 pint cherry tomatoes	2 cups pitted extra large ripe
1 whole celery stalk	olives
5 or 6 carrots	Medium to large wicker or
1 head of cauliflower	straw basket with handle
3 zucchini	Bowl to fit in basket (few inches
1 large cucumber	shallower than basket)
2 turnips	Crushed ice to fill bowl

Wash vegetables well in cold water. Leave blossom ends on tomatoes for handles. Cut celery in spears 4 to 5 inches long, leaving tops on most of the spears. Peel carrots and cut into sticks by cutting them crosswise into halves, then cutting each half into 3 or 4 lengthwise sticks.

Break the cauliflower apart into small clumps; slice the unpeeled zucchini into circles ¼ to ½ inch thick. Peel the cucumber and slice like the zucchini. Cut peeled turnips into wedges. Refrigerate all vegetables in plastic bags until ready to use. This preparation can be done a day in advance.

ARRANGEMENT: Shortly before serving, fill bowl with crushed ice and set into basket. Insert vegetables into ice, pointing them in different directions. Arrange a row of cherry tomatoes, alternating

Recipe Continues . . .

with drained ripe olives, around the border of the bowl. Place vegetables all over the ice to cover it completely. Set basket on a tray large enough to hold a bowl of dip and a small bowl for discards of tomato blossoms and celery tops.

DILLY OF A DIP   About 3 cups

½ pound cream cheese
2 cups sour cream
1 tablespoon prepared mustard
½ teaspoon dillweed

½ teaspoon caraway seeds
2 teaspoons grated onion
½ teaspoon salt
Paprika

Blend cheese and sour cream. Add remaining ingredients except paprika and mix well. Chill in the bowl used to serve dip. When ready to serve, sprinkle top lightly with paprika.

When not using this as a dip, surround bowl with crackers and serve as a spread to accompany raw vegetables. Delicious either way.

SWEET 'n SOUR MEATBALLS   30 Servings,
(Fritzie's Favorite)   Two 1½-quart casseroles

5 pounds beef chuck or shoulder, or combination, ground
2 teaspoons salt
½ teaspoon garlic salt

1 cup uncooked oatmeal
¾ cup chili sauce
Sweet 'n Sour Sauce (recipe follows)

Mix all ingredients except sauce until well blended. Shape into 1-inch balls. Place on an ungreased cookie sheet. Bake in 400°F. oven for 15 to 18 minutes. Remove from pan with a slotted spoon to prevent the excess fat of the meatballs from blending into the sauce. Put 20 to 25 meatballs into each 1½-quart casserole. Pour sauce over them to cover; do not make casserole so full that it spills when placing into the oven. Reduce heat to 350°F. Heat casseroles for 30 minutes. Lower heat to 225°F. to keep refill casserole warm.

Sweet 'n Sour Sauce

About 3 quarts

1 can (29 oz.) pineapple chunks
1 can (24 oz.) pineapple juice
1 pound light brown sugar
1 can (29 oz.) tomato sauce
¼ cup soy sauce
1½ cups cider vinegar

1 cup light molasses
1½ tablespoons prepared mustard
6 tablespoons cornstarch or arrowroot

Drain pineapple chunks. Combine juice with the can of pineapple juice in a heavy saucepan. Stir in the next 6 ingredients. Beat well with hand whip or rotary beater until smooth and well blended. Heat slowly, stirring often to avoid scorching. Spoon the cornstarch or arrowroot into a cup or small bowl. Pour about ½ cup of hot sauce over it. Stir to a smooth paste. Blend into the sauce in the pot and continue to heat over low heat. Stir occasionally but watch closely as sauce may burn on the bottom of the pot due to the sugar and molasses. When sauce begins to thicken, beat until it glistens. Remove from heat and add pineapple chunks.

PICKLATED PUPS

2 pounds cocktail hot dogs,
about 60 to a pound, *or*
24 knackwurst, each cut into
5 crosswise slices

Mustardy Pickle Sauce (recipe
follows)

When using the tiny hot dogs, merely drop them into a pot of boiling water but do not cook. Remove from heat. Allow them to stay in water until cooled to room temperature. Remove from water. Divide between two 1½-quart casseroles, reserving extra if needed. This step can be done well in advance of the party.

When using the fat juicy knackwurst, drop them into a pot of boiling water and heat until water returns to a boil. Remove from water and when cool enough to handle, slice. Divide them into casseroles as directed for the pups.

Recipe Continues . . .

Pour the mustardy pickle sauce over the pups or knackwurst to cover. Heat in a preheated 350°F. oven for 30 minutes. Lower heat to 225°F. to keep refill casserole warm.

Mustardy Pickle Sauce   About 3 quarts

4 cans (12 oz. each) apricot
  nectar
1 quart apple juice
5 ounces prepared Dijon mustard
1 cup red currant jelly

1 jar (12 oz.) sweet pickles
6 tablespoons cornstarch or arrowroot
2 tablespoons dry mustard
2 teaspoons ground ginger

Mix the fruit juices with the Dijon mustard. Beat the jelly with a wire whip or beater until smooth and devoid of lumps. Pour in all the liquid from the jar of pickles. Chop pickles rather fine. Add to sauce. Remove 1 cup of sauce to a small bowl. Heat remaining sauce while adding the dry mustard and ginger to the cold sauce. When well blended add the 1 cup of sauce with added mustard and ginger to sauce in pot and stir until thoroughly mixed. When sauce begins to bubble and thicken, remove from heat.

Mmmmm, take a whiff! I venture to say that when your guests arrive and inquire as to the source of the tantalizing aroma, it will be this sauce tickling their nostrils.

BLUSHING EGGS   30 Servings

3 dozen small eggs, hard
  cooked
2 cups wine vinegar
2 cups water
3 bay leaves

2 teaspoons pickling spices
Beet juice from 29-ounce can of
  sliced beets
Watercress or parsley sprigs

Shell hard-cooked eggs. Set aside in a deep bowl or gallon jar. In a saucepan combine the vinegar, water, bay leaves and spices.

Bring to a boil, lower heat, and simmer for 20 minutes. Remove from heat and strain. Add beet juice. Let cool.

Pour pickle liquid over the eggs, making sure they are all immersed. Should there not be enough liquid to cover eggs, add water to cover. Cover container and refrigerate. This should be done at least 2 days before serving but preferably 4 days before. They will keep under refrigeration for several days. Stir eggs occasionally so the pretty pink color will be distributed evenly.

To serve, remove eggs from liquid. Place in a mound on a bed of watercress or parsley in a glass bowl or platter. Never put them on silver because the beet juice eats away the silver finish.

TUNA PÂTÉ

1 Mold, 30 servings

1 pound cream cheese
4 teaspoons grated onion
2 tablespoons pickle relish
1 teaspoon salt
10 large pitted ripe olives, chopped fine

6 tablespoons chili sauce
4 cans (6½ to 7 oz. each) white meat tuna
Parsley (for decorating platter)
Ripe olives (for decorating platter)

Put cream cheese into a mixing bowl. Add grated onion, pickle relish, salt, chopped olives and chili sauce. Mix with a rotary beater until all ingredients have been blended together. Drain tuna, chop fine, and add to cheese mixture. Beat all together until smooth. Pack into a lightly buttered 4-cup mold or small bowl. Refrigerate for at least 6 hours, preferably overnight.

To serve, turn mold out onto serving platter or tray. Put clumps of parsley around bottom of mold. Set olives in clusters on the parsley. Slice 2 olives and lay in circular fashion on top of mold together with a few sprigs of parsley. Surround pâté with crackers or water biscuits.

STUFFED MUSHROOMS   45 Mushrooms

45 medium-size mushrooms
6 slices of bacon
3 tablespoons finely chopped
   onion
3 celery ribs, finely chopped
½ cup grated mozzarella cheese

1 tablespoon Worcestershire
   sauce
1 tablespoon fine dry bread
   crumbs
1½ tablespoons grated Parmesan cheese

Wash mushrooms well. Remove stems by twisting them off. Reserve stems for use in gravies or dressings, or store in a closed container in refrigerator. Fry bacon until very crisp. Remove from pan and drain on paper towels. Sauté onion and celery in pan in which bacon was cooked until lightly browned. Remove from pan with slotted spoon to a mixing bowl. Crumble bacon into very small pieces and add to onion and celery. Add mozzarella cheese and Worcestershire sauce. Mix well.

Place mushrooms, stem side up, in pie tins or broiler pans and stuff with bacon filling. Combine bread crumbs and Parmesan cheese. Sprinkle over filling. Set aside until ready to serve. If made a day ahead, cover with plastic wrap and refrigerate.

Broil 4 to 5 inches from the source of heat for about 6 minutes, or until top browns and bubbles slightly.

To serve, put each mushroom in a small white crinkle cup that you have coaxed from your candy shop or bakery. Not only will they look most attractive but they will be easy to pick up while hot. The usual method of spearing them on a food pick from which they may fall soils many an attractive gown or necktie. Serve hot.

MINI CHEESE TARTS   60 Tiny tarts

Tart Pastry

2 cups sifted flour
½ teaspoon baking powder
¼ teaspoon salt
½ cup vegetable shortening

¼ pound butter
½ cup ice water
Cheese Filling (recipe follows)

Preheat oven to 375°F. Sift dry ingredients into a bowl. Cut shortening and butter into the dry ingredients, then add the cold water. Chill dough for easier handling. Roll dough to ⅛-inch thickness. Cut 3-inch rounds and fit them into ungreased small muffin cups 1 inch deep and 1¾ inches in diameter. Prick pastry with a fork. Bake in the preheated oven for 10 minutes. Cool tiny tart shells. Fill with Cheese Filling.

Cheese Filling

½ cup grated Swiss cheese
1 egg
½ teaspoon prepared mustard
⅓ cup dairy sour cream
⅛ teaspoon salt
⅛ teaspoon cayenne pepper

2 tablespoons melted butter
3 tablespoons finely chopped onion
½ teaspoon freshly grated nutmeg

Spoon grated cheese into a medium-size bowl. Beat egg slightly; add to it the mustard, sour cream and seasonings. Pour over cheese. Blend together. Reserve 1 tablespoon melted butter. In remaining tablespoon of butter, sauté the onion just until golden; add to the cheese mixture. Fill tiny tart shells. Brush tops with reserved melted butter, then sprinkle lightly with nutmeg. At this point these tarts can be frozen for future use or refrigerated for several days before using.

To serve, heat oven to 375°F. Place tarts on cookie sheets or pie tins. Heat for approximately 15 minutes, or until tops brown slightly. Place each tart in a small crinkle cup (as with the stuffed mushrooms on p. 162) and pass while warm and delicious.

ONION PUFFS

60 Canapés

15 slices of white bread
Butter or margarine, softened
12 to 15 small white onions, thinly sliced
1 cup mayonnaise

1 tablespoon crumbled blue cheese
2 tablespoons grated Parmesan cheese

Recipe Continues . . .

Using a 2-inch round cookie cutter, cut 4 rounds from each slice of bread. Place rounds on cookie sheets and toast lightly in oven. Remove and cool.

Spread each round with butter or margarine. Place a thin slice of onion on each. Blend together the mayonnaise and cheeses. Spoon onto onion, covering most of the surface of toast round. Sprinkle more Parmesan cheese over tops. Freeze or refrigerate for several hours before heating.

To serve, preheat oven to 450°F. Bake puffs for 8 to 10 minutes or until golden brown. Watch them puff! Pass while hot.

CRAB AMANDINE
60 Canapés

15 slices of white bread
½ pound cream cheese
1 cup mayonnaise
2 teaspoons grated onion
1 teaspoon cayenne pepper

2 cans (7½ oz. each) crab meat
1 ounce butter
½ cup sliced unblanched almonds

Using a 2-inch round cookie cutter, cut 4 rounds from each slice of bread. Place on buttered cookie sheets and toast lightly in a 375°F. oven for 15 to 20 minutes. Remove and cool. Blend together cream cheese and mayonnaise. Add onion and cayenne and mix well. Drain crab meat, squeeze out all liquid, and remove any cartilage. Add to cream-cheese mixture. Blend all together. Spread on toast rounds, mounding slightly in the center. Melt butter in small frying pan. Chop almonds slightly and sauté in melted butter only until lightly browned. Keep a watchful eye for they will burn rapidly. When almonds are cool enough to handle, sprinkle over tops of crab mixture. At this stage these canapés can be frozen or kept under refrigeration for 2 days.

To serve, preheat oven to 400°F. Place on a high shelf in the oven for 10 minutes. Pass while hot.

FLO CHART FOR STRICTLY COCKTAILS

All major preparations can be done during the week before the party, and the dishes can be either frozen or refrigerated, according to instructions.

ONE DAY BEFORE PARTY Prepare all fresh vegetables, tuna pâté, onion puff and crab amandine fillings. Wash mushrooms and prepare filling. Remove meatballs from freezer.

DAY OF THE PARTY In the morning, remove all items from freezer. Check bar supplies.

About 1½ hours before party, spread toast rounds for onion puffs and crab amandine, place on cookie sheets. Stuff mushrooms.

About 30 minutes before party, set out tuna pâté, blushing eggs, dip and vegetables on crushed ice.

Preheat oven to 450°F. Onion puffs and crab must be done after guests arrive; this takes only 8 to 10 minutes.

Serve onion puffs first after guests arrive; then turn oven down to 400°F., allow 15 minutes to reduce temperature, then heat crab amandine for 8 to 10 minutes.

Throughout the party, I find it best to rotate warm containers of food in the oven with those on the buffet; foods keep warmer in the container they have been heated in, and this method works more successfully than using candle warmers or canned heat.

BAR TIPS

Your invitation may specify 2 hours, but forget it. The average strictly cocktail party lasts 3 hours (5 to 8 or 6 to 9 are the preferred hours). In this time, 8 people will consume an average of 1 quart of liquor. You would therefore need about 4 quarts in the following percentages: 40% Scotch, 40% vodka, 10% bourbon, 10% other (gin or rum). Again, I remind you that these are general estimates that vary according to geographical location, custom, and other factors. In some areas the trend is toward almost 50% wine drinkers, mainly white wine.

Mixes for the bar to serve 30 guests should include:

3 quarts soda
2 quarts tonic water
4 cans diet soda (Fresca and
  Tab)
1 bottle vermouth
Lemons, limes

Ice If you'd rather figure it in pounds instead of ice cubes, allow 1 pound of ice per person.

Hint Have plenty of cocktail napkins, 3 or 4 per person.

Don't worry about seating accommodations because even when there are adequate places for people to sit, somehow everyone likes to stand at strictly cocktail parties.

Setting up the bar: Bartenders are not as essential today as they once were because so many more people are drinking wine and tonics rather than hard liquors. Also, helping yourself at the bar has become more fashionable.

There's a widespread belief that if you let your guests pour their own drinks, they'll guzzle all your booze. I think it is a misconception. Believe it or not, a lot of partygoers *don't* drink and they can mix their own beverage without embarrassment if there isn't a bartender.

The last person in the world who should serve as bartender at a party is the host or hostess.

Bartender or not, the ratios usually work out the same: You should count on 8 or 9 quarts for 40 people, or an average of 3 or 4 drinks per person. Some will drink more, some less, and they'll drink more at a cocktail party than at a dinner party.

A few pointers: Where is your bar located in relation to your kitchen? Is it a part of your kitchen? Adjoining it? On the other side of it? In or near the dining area? Is it easily accessible for guests without disrupting kitchen and food service? If not, do you have space in your home to set up a special party bar for guests?

Important: If you do not have space to set up a bar in your entertaining area and if drinks must be served from your bar in or adjacent to your kitchen, then you *will* need a bartender (whether you like it or not), *plus* helpers to circulate among guests and replenish drinks. The bartender will stay put at the bar and pour drinks; the waiters will carry them out and bring back refill orders. There is no other way. You can't have guests go barging through the kitchen for drinks while food dishes are being prepared and/or served.

VEGETABLES

Never store tomatoes and cucumbers in the same bag or, unwrapped, next to each other. The cucumbers will turn mushy within 24 hours.

Refrigeration temperatures for most produce should be between 38° and 40°F., except for tomatoes. If you're in a hurry to ripen mature, pink tomatoes, keep them at room temperatures of 68° to 72°F. Never store them below 55°F. since chilling will stop any further ripening and can result in decay or impaired flavor.

Set tomatoes stem end up to avoid pressure on their most delicate part, the shoulders around the stems.

Do not wash fruits or vegetables before storing them in the refrigerator. Wash them just before using, *unless you're giving a party.* This may seem like a contradiction to all my pre-preparation timetables. Actually the never-wash-before-storing rule should be followed as much as possible and generally can be in your everyday needs and for small parties, *if* you can fit the wash-before-using into your timetable. But like most rules, this one can be broken for special occasions and therefore I've broken it in order to help you be a guest at your own party by doing many of your fruits and vegetables the day before the party. The point of this party book is to make it as easy as possible for you, the hostess, on the day of your party.

PASS-AROUNDS
At a party that is strictly for cocktails, it is important to have a variety of canapés, or pass-around foods, one- or two-bite food concoctions that are easy to pick up with your fingers and not messy. The stuffed mushrooms, mini cheese tarts, onion puffs and crab amandine in this chapter are ideal pass-around foods. They should be served while hot; trays should be replenished frequently.

A COCKTAIL SUPPER

(For 30)

MENU

Seafood Glacé
   Formal Shrimps
   Ladder-back Lobster
   Fresh Oysters
Complementary Companions
   Cheesecake Mousse
   Celery and Carrot Sticks
   Cherry Tomatoes
   Colossal Ripe Olives; Large Stuffed Olives
Sauces
   Standard Seafood Sauce
   Cocktail Sauce for Oysters
Creamy Crab Casserole
Turkey Tetrazzini
Honey Ring and Fruit
Bread: **French or Sourdough Roll Slices**
Desserts:
   Snowballs
   Miniature Chocloate Éclairs
   Ike's Favorites
Coffee, Tea

Everything in this menu can either be prepared far in advance and frozen, or made a few days ahead and refrigerated. The final presentation will require more time than the average buffet, but it's worth it.

I have planned this rather elaborate menu so there should be no interruption in the food service. The main casseroles, fruit mold, coffee and dessert are to be served an hour or so after the guests arrive, and there will be plenty to nibble on during the cocktail hour.

There should be no reason for the hostess to be running into the kitchen during the party, except to pop her already prepared casseroles into the oven and bring out later additions to the buffet.

Important Arrangement: Center a large bowl or punch bowl on a very large tray or pan and fill bowl with crushed ice, bringing ice high in the center to form something of a peak. Distribute remaining crushed ice over all the surface of the large tray or pan, packing rather tightly around the base of the bowl. This will serve as "center stage" or focal point for your *Seafood Glacé* and its complementary companions and sauces.

EQUIPMENT WORK SHEET FOR A COCKTAIL SUPPER

large bowl or punch bowl
extralarge tray or baker's full sheet pan with affixed sides of plywood 6 to
    8 inches high. Foil-covered protective plastic covering should be
    placed under this tray, which is for the seafood.
30 pounds crushed ice
3 medium-size bowls for olives, tomatoes
2 small bowls for seafood sauce
1 medium-size bowl for oyster sauce
1 large or 2 medium-size bowls for oysters
1 small bowl for discards (shrimp shells, etc.)
2-quart casserole and warmer
medium-size chafing dish
9-inch springform pan

large round platter for Cheesecake Mousse
cocktail picks
canned heat
2 three-quart casseroles for turkey
5-quart ring mold for Honey Ring
cake stand
serving spoons and spreaders
roll tray or basket
large round tray for Honey Ring and Fruit
3-tiered stand or 3 medium-size glass or silver trays for desserts
50-cup coffee maker
coffee and tea service
30 seashells or small canapé plates
30 seafood or cocktail forks
30 dinner plates
30 cups and saucers
12 teaspoons (Most people don't use them for tea or coffee.)
paper dinner napkins
cocktail napkins
highball and cocktail glasses
ice cubes for cocktails
bartending supplies
ashtrays

MARKETING WORK SHEET FOR A COCKTAIL SUPPER

1 quart milk
3 cups light cream
5 cups coffee cream
2 quarts dairy sour cream
2 pounds butter
½ pound soft-spread margarine
12 large eggs
2 pounds dry cottage cheese
1½ pounds cream cheese
1 pound Cheddar cheese
1 pound Parmesan cheese

6 ounces blue cheese
5 pounds raw shrimps, 16 to 18 to the pound
5 lobster tails, 1 to 1½ pounds each
5 dozen medium-size fresh raw oysters
1 turkey, 16 to 18 pounds
2 fresh pineapples
4 oranges
3 grapefruits
20 lemons, plus lemons for bar
2 pints fresh strawberries
mint leaves or watercress
2 bunches of parsley
6 pints cherry tomatoes
1 large bunch of celery
2 pounds carrots
2 onions
2 pounds spaghetti
2 packages (4 oz. each) rye toast Melbas
6 ounces cheese crackers
2 packages (12 to 16 oz. each) butter crackers
15 French or sourdough rolls
3 cans (10½ oz. each) chicken broth
2 cans (7 oz. each) crab meat
2 cans (29 oz. each) pear halves
1 can (24 oz.) mandarin orange sections
1 can (22 oz.) seedless grapes
2 cans (16 oz. each) stuffed green olives
2 cans (16 oz. each) pitted ripe olives
2 large truffles (optional)
1 jar (4 oz.) red maraschino cherries
10 ounces shelled filberts or hazelnuts
4 ounces sliced blanched almonds
12 ounces Angel Flake coconut
2 jars (3 oz. each) prepared horseradish
1 cup honey
3 ounces unsweetened chocolate
liquor
mixers

STAPLES LIST FOR A COCKTAIL SUPPER

salt
black pepper
white pepper
peppercorns
cayenne pepper
bay leaves
caraway seeds
garlic salt
ground cardamom
white vinegar
cider vinegar
chili sauce (be sure you have at least 1½ cups)
ketchup (be sure you have at least 3½ cups)
Worcestershire sauce
Tabasco
unflavored gelatin (be sure your box contains at least 6 envelopes of gelatin)
granulated sugar
powdered (confectioners') sugar
flour
cake flour
cream of tartar
vanilla extract
almond extract
coffee
tea or tea bags
bar supplies

SEAFOOD GLACÉ   30 Servings

Formal Shrimps (recipe follows)
Fresh oysters
Ladder-back Lobster (recipe follows)
Carrot sticks
Celery sticks
Cherry tomatoes
Black and stuffed green olives
Seafood sauces (recipes follow)
1 bunch of parsley
6 lemons, quartered
Paprika

FORMAL SHRIMPS   30 Servings

We call these "Formal Shrimps" because they are dressed in their
tails, thereby affording a "handle" with which guests can hold
the shrimps and dip them into a sauce.

5 pounds raw shrimps 16 to 18 to the pound, in shells	1 tablespoon salt
	2 bay leaves
2 lemons quartered	2 teaspoons caraway seeds
2 teaspoons whole black peppercorns	3 quarts water

Wash shrimps, set aside. Place next 5 ingredients in a large kettle.
Add the water and bring to a boil. Add the shrimps and cover.
When the water has returned to a boil, reduce heat and simmer for
5 minutes. Drain immediately and rinse under cold water until
shrimps are cool enough to handle. With fingers grasping the underside, and holding firmly to the tail, lift the shell upward. Break
off shell at the tail joint and discard the shell.

With a sharp pointed knife, cut a slit along back, which is the
curved surface, and remove the black vein. Rinse under cold water
to remove any particles adhering to the cut surface. Pat dry with
paper towels. Refrigerate shrimps in covered containers. Shrimps
will keep for several days when refrigerated or for many months if
frozen.

LADDER-BACK LOBSTER   30 Servings

3 quarts water	1 teaspoon black peppercorns
2 lemons, quartered	5 lobster tails, 1 to 1½ pounds
3 bay leaves	each
¼ cup white vinegar	Ripe olives or truffles, sliced

Into a large kettle pour the water and add the quartered lemons,
bay leaves, vinegar and peppercorns. Bring to a boil. Drop lobster
tails into the water and bring water back to a boil. Lower heat and

Recipe Continues . . .

simmer for 15 minutes. Remove from heat but allow lobster to remain in the liquid for another 15 minutes. Drain tails and run under cold water to cool.

With kitchen shears, cut along sides and down center of undershell and carefully lift out the meat in one piece. Rinse shells under cold water, pat dry, and store in refrigerator along with the lobster meat until serving time.

STANDARD SEAFOOD SAUCE
About 4 cups

1½ cups chili sauce
1½ cups ketchup
½ cup lemon juice
4 tablespoons Worcestershire sauce
4 tablespoons prepared horseradish

1 tablespoon grated onion
1 teaspoon salt
½ teaspoon pepper
½ teaspoon Tabasco

Mix all ingredients and refrigerate.

COCKTAIL SAUCE FOR OYSTERS
About 3 cups

2 cups ketchup
½ cup vinegar
3 tablespoons prepared horseradish

½ teaspoon salt
⅛ teaspoon cayenne pepper

Mix all ingredients and refrigerate.

ARRANGEMENT: With a spoon handle, make indentations in the ice around the rim of the prepared bowl about ½ inch apart and 1 inch deep. Insert shrimps in these indentations with the tails downward on the outside of the bowl. In irregular spiral rows, insert carrot and celery sticks into the ice, using the inner ribs of the celery with the leaves left on as a bouquet on the very top of the ice peak. Lay remaining shrimps horseshoe fashion around the carrot and celery sticks. If you are not able to place all the shrimps on at one time, reserve remaining for refilling the bowl. You will need them.

Lay the lobster tails on a cutting board. With a sharp knife slice crosswise into even ½-inch slices. Place the shells on the crushed ice, with ice mounded slightly under the shells. Lay the slices of lobster on the shells in overlapping fashion, like the steps of a ladder, keeping original shape of each tail. Place a slice of olive or truffle on alternate slices in even rows down the center.

Place the bowls of cherry tomatoes and varieties of olives around the bowl on the crushed ice in the extra large tray. Place the fresh oysters in 1 large or 2 medium-size bowls with the appropriate sauce close by. Set the bowls of seafood sauces in the crushed ice on opposite sides of tray. Divide the bunch of parsley into 4 portions and place a clump in each of the 4 corners. Dip center edge of the quartered lemons in paprika and lay on the parsley.

Place a small bowl for discarded tails in front of or alongside the seafood tray and indicate its use by putting a shrimp tail in it.

Place crab casserole and cheesecake mousse on one side of the seafood tray. The sea shells or small canapé plates, cocktail forks and napkins should be in several places, allowing room to add later the Turkey Tetrazzini casserole and the platter of the honey ring and fruit.

It might well be that in order to accommodate the dinner plates, napkins, coffee service and sweets, you will need to use a sideboard or extra buffet table. You will find this most expedient since this table can be arranged before your guests arrive.

CREAMY CRAB CASSEROLE   2 Quarts

1 pound cream cheese
2 cans (7 oz. each) crab meat
4 tablespoons grated onion
2 tablespoons light cream
1 heaping teaspoon cream-style
   horseradish

½ teaspoon salt
½ cup toasted sliced almonds
2 packages (4 oz. each) rye
   toast Melbas

Allow cheese to soften at room temperature. Drain crab meat. Tear into small pieces, discarding any pieces of cartilage. Blend crab into the cheese. Add remaining ingredients except almonds and toast. Mix well. Turn into a lightly buttered 2-quart casserole. Sprinkle top with toasted almonds. Bake in a preheated 375°F. oven for 18 to 20 minutes.

This casserole can be prepared a day in advance and refrigerated. When ready to use, allow to stand at room temperature at least 1 hour before placing in oven.

To serve, place on tray which fits on a warmer, a tray large enough to allow the casserole to be surrounded with the rye Melbas.

TURKEY TETRAZZINI   30 Servings

1 turkey, 16 to 18 pounds
Salt
2 pounds spaghetti
¾ pound butter or margarine
1½ cups flour
½ teaspoon salt

¼ teaspoon white pepper
3 cups chicken broth, heated
2 cups light cream
1 pound Cheddar cheese, grated
12 ounces Parmesan cheese,
   grated

Cook turkey in salted water for approximately 2 hours, or until tender. Cut up into fairly large chunks when cool. Sprinkle with salt to taste.

Cook spaghetti according to directions on package as length of time necessary varies with the brand you select. Drain and set aside. Melt butter. Combine flour and seasonings and gradually add to butter, stirring constantly. Cook for about 4 minutes to cook the flour; during this time the chicken broth can be heated. Slowly pour broth into flour mixture, beating constantly with a wire whip to keep the sauce smooth and satiny. Stir in the cream, beating to keep it smooth. Remove from heat. Stir in the grated Cheddar cheese. Beat until cheese is completely blended into the sauce. Add turkey to cheese sauce.

Butter two 3-quart casseroles. Spread cooked spaghetti over bottom of casseroles about ½ inch deep. Cover with a layer of the turkey mixture, then a layer of spaghetti, the turkey mixture, and top layer of spaghetti. Sprinkle half of the Parmesan cheese over the top of the 2 casseroles. Reserve remaining half of cheese for guests to sprinkle on their portions as they desire.

This casserole can be prepared completely and frozen for use within several months or can be prepared 4 to 5 days in advance and refrigerated. It is a most satisfying "fork food." Accompany it with slices of French or sourdough roll slices.

FRENCH OR SOURDOUGH ROLL SLICES   60 Slices

15 French or sourdough rolls   ½ cup soft-spreading margarine

Freeze rolls for at least 12 hours. This helps greatly in slicing them thin and evenly. Slice away a small piece of each end of the rolls. Cut on the bias, 4 slices to each roll. Butter slices and place on greased cookie sheets. Toast in a 400°F. oven for 10 to 12 minutes.

CHEESECAKE MOUSSE

One 9-inch
mousse

6 ounces cheese crackers
¼ pound butter, melted
2 envelopes unflavored gelatin
½ cup cold water
1 quart dairy sour cream

1 cup crumbled blue cheese
1 quart dry cottage cheese
½ teaspoon garlic salt
1 teaspoon minced fresh parsley

Roll crackers into very fine crumbs. Combine with melted butter; mix well. Press all but ⅔ cup on bottom and halfway up sides of a very well-buttered 9-inch springform pan. Soften gelatin in cold water. Let set for 5 minutes. Place over boiling water, stirring, until dissolved. Transfer to a larger bowl. Pour the sour cream into gelatin; stir well. Add the cheeses, garlic salt and parsley; mix well. Pour mixture into the crumb-lined pan. Sprinkle reserved ⅔ cup crumbs on top. Cover with plastic wrap. Refrigerate. This can be made several days in advance.

ARRANGEMENT: To serve, unmold on a round platter several inches larger than the mousse, by running blunt edge of knife around sides and releasing sides of pan. Allow mousse to remain on bottom of springform pan when setting it on the platter. Surround with butter crackers.

Note: Don't be deceived into thinking this Cheesecake Mousse is a dessert. It's an aspiclike side dish that makes a perfect complementary companion to an elegant seafood bowl.

HONEY RING AND FRUIT   30 Servings

1 cup cold water
4 envelopes unflavored gelatin
½ cup lemon juice
2 cans (29 oz. each) pear halves
1 cup juice from canned pears
1 jar (4 oz.) maraschino cherries, each cherry cut into halves
3 cups dairy sour cream
1 cup honey

1 can (24 oz.) mandarin oranges
1 can (22 oz.) seedless grapes
2 fresh pineapples
4 oranges
3 grapefruits
2 pints strawberries, if in season, or substitute colorful fruit of your choice
2 lemons
Fresh mint leaves or watercress

Pour cold water into a small bowl. Sprinkle in the gelatin and let stand for 5 minutes. Dissolve gelatin over hot water, stirring well. Transfer to a larger bowl. Add the lemon and pear juices; stir well. Chill gelatin until it is on the point of setting.

Oil a 5-quart ring mold well (do not use olive oil). Tap mold upside down to drain off excess oil. Coat mold with a thin layer of gelatin. Place pear halves cut side down all around ring. Insert 1 cherry half, rounded side down, in cavity of each pear. Chill until firm. Meanwhile blend the sour cream and honey into the remaining gelatin mixture.

Drain mandarin oranges and grapes. Add to the gelatin mixture. Mix all together. Pour over firm gelatin in mold. Chill until cold, but do not freeze. This can be prepared a few days in advance.

ARRANGEMENT: Unmold on a tray large enough to accommodate the mold and fruit. Peel and quarter the pineapples, cut away cores, and cut pineapple into long thin slices. Peel oranges and grapefruits and slice. Place around outer edge of mold, alternating citrus slices with the pineapple. Fill center cavity with washed strawberries with stems left on. Slice lemons into thin round slices. Slit each slice to the center and twist. Lay lemon twists on

Recipe Continues . . .

top of mold between pear halves. Place clumps of mint leaves or watercress on border of platter.

SNOWBALLS   30 Small cakes

1¼ cups sifted cake flour   1 teaspoon cream of tartar
1¾ cups sugar   ½ teaspoon vanilla extract
½ teaspoon salt   ½ teaspoon almond extract
1½ cups egg whites, at room   Fluffy Frosting (recipe follows)
    temperature   1½ cups Angel Flake Coconut

Sift together the flour, sugar and salt 3 times. Beat egg whites until frothy. Sprinkle the cream of tartar over egg whites. Continue beating until whites are stiff enough to form peaks. Gradually add both flavorings. Fold in sifted dry ingredients with a wire whip, a little at a time. Spoon batter into ungreased 1½-inch muffin tins. Bake in a preheated 325°F. oven for 20 minutes.

When cool, remove from pans with the aid of a spatula. Insert fork into side of each tiny cake and dip into Fluffy Frosting.

Fluffy Frosting   About 2 cups

1 egg white, chilled   ½ cup boiling water
1 cup sugar   ½ teaspoon vanilla extract
1 teaspoon cream of tartar

Combine egg white, sugar and cream of tartar. Add boiling water. Beat immediately with rotary or electric beater. Beat for 12 minutes, or until fluffy and thick. Add vanilla.

Spread coconut on a sheet of wax paper. Roll the tiny frosted cakes in the coconut and place in small white muffin cups or other fluted paper cups.

Can be frozen.

MINIATURE CHOCOLATE
ÉCLAIRS

Follow directions for Sweet Tooth Party menu (pp. 149–150).

IKE'S FAVORITES

At a luncheon at which Mamie Eisenhower was the guest of honor, I served a water ice accompanied by Filbert Squares. As she was leaving, the former first lady informed me that these cookies were the "General's" absolute favorite. She wondered if I would mind sending a few along with her for him. Would I mind! I was delighted to give her a box full. From that day on I have called these cookies "Ike's Favorites." For the recipe, see Chapter X, *Favorites of the Famous* (p. 275).

FLO CHART FOR COCKTAIL SUPPER

Here's your chance to make out your own Flo chart at your leisure, relying on the specific instructions with each individual recipe and on general guidelines in other Flo charts for your timing.

A word of caution on your *fresh seafood*, especially the lobster and oysters: order them at least a week ahead, to be picked up the day before the party. (The shrimps, you'll note, can be frozen.) About all you'll have left to do the day of the party is make your arrangements; you can have most trays, platters and bowls filled and set out in proper arrangements about 40 minutes before guests arrive. But cocktail suppers tend to be more casual and informal than buffet dinners, thus allowing for adjustable timetables. So be my guest on this one!

FANCIES AND FURBELOWS

In previous menus I have made frequent mention of the little "fancies and furbelows"—the tomato and turnip roses, the turnip, grapefruit- and orange-peel flowers that do so much to dress up a salad bowl, fruit platter, meat or fish dish, or just about anything on any menu, no matter how simple or elaborate. You can stick a tomato rose in the middle of a bowl of plain cottage cheese, for instance, and make it come alive with color. You can make a border of grapefruit- and orange-peel flowers around almost any food platter to try to create an artistic illusion that pleases the eye and whets the appetite.

Personally, I couldn't live without my little Fancies and Furbelows. I always have some in the freezer. They are particularly appropriate for cocktail parties when you're in the mood to add that little extra flourish and flair. But they're equally good to have on hand for any kind of party you're planning. They add eye appeal as well as taste appeal.

Here are the recipes and exact instructions for making my favorite Fancies and Furbelows which will come in handy at any party.

TOMATO ROSE

To make a tomato rose, use a small, very sharp paring knife. Starting at the stem of a small to medium-size tomato (not a cherry tomato), make a slit ¼ inch deep, cutting through skin and into the meat of the tomato. Cut in a circular manner and *peel* as you would an orange. Re-roll the resulting spiral of tomato peel into the shape of a flower and secure the end with a toothpick. Tomato roses can be made a day ahead of your party and *refrigerated.* They cannot be frozen.

They can be used for hors-d'oeuvre garnishes or to decorate many kinds of salad. They give a lift to cottage cheese. Use a pretty bowl, or one with an interesting shape. Line its border with crisp, washed and dried romaine, endive or Boston lettuce, stem ends upward. Fill the bowl with cottage cheese. With the bottom of a small juice glass, make an indentation in center of the cottage cheese and fill with parsley. Place a tomato rose on the parsley and sprinkle the cheese with paprika.

TURNIP FLOWERS

These are somewhat more difficult to make but worth the effort. Peel rather large turnips and slice horizontally, very very thin. Spread "petals" on cookie sheet and let stand for 30 minutes, until they feel limp.

Starting with the smallest slice, roll tightly to form the inside petals of the flower. Continue adding slices, turning the flower with each addition to layer it like the petals of a rose. Use toothpicks whenever needed to hold petals together. Partially fill quart jars with cold water. Add a few drops of different food colorings in each, and place turnip flowers in the jars. Add more water if necessary to immerse flowers completely. These cannot be frozen but they can be kept in the refrigerator, in the jars of cold water, for a day or two; they're better when made only the day before the party.

CARVED TURNIP ROSES

THESE can be frozen. The turnip flowers can't be. These are not merely flowers, but roses! Not only cut but carved. Practice and patience are the two prerequisites for making carved turnip roses. But the rewards for your perseverance will be worth it!

Pare the turnip and trim off evenly so that the surface is very smooth. Cut off stem to form a flat base. Using the tip of a very sharp paring knife, lightly outline the shapes of about five rounded petals. Keeping each slice thin, cut each petal completely away from turnip down to one-quarter inch from base. Continue around turnip until all five petals are formed. Pare inside of turnip just within petals again to make a smooth surface. Lightly outline the next row of petal shapes, spacing each one between two outside petals. Cut thinly, smoothing surface as you go along.

Cut as many layers as the size of turnip will allow, working toward center as far as possible. Remove a small piece of center and smooth it down, rounding it off a bit, if possible.

Tint water with vegetable coloring and place roses in colored water. Place in covered jars in refrigerator, or FREEZE. Under refrigeration only, the roses can be kept much longer than Turnip Flowers; but frozen, they can be used many times, refrigerating between uses.

GRAPEFRUIT- AND ORANGE-PEEL FLOWERS

Follow directions for tomato rose. Use sharp paring knife, make a slit in the peel, and cut in a circular manner so that peel forms a spiral whirligig flower. That's all there is to it. Put in jars of water with tinted vegetable coloring. These grapefruit- and orange-peel flowers can be used many times over if stored in jars or coffee cans in the freezer, allowing 2 inches at the top for expansion of water during process of freezing. Remove cans from freezer to defrost the day before a party. Save colored water in the cans. Flowers can be replaced in them and refrozen.

SUGAR AND CREAM

Only 1 out of 5 people uses sugar and cream. This makes a difference if you're renting equipment for your party, especially teaspoons. At 10 to 12 cents per spoon rental, this adds up to a hefty sum you can live without, especially if your guests don't use cream or sugar.

FOOD COLORING AND TINTS

Throughout these party menus, you will notice I use a great many food colorings and tints for decorative purposes, usually specifying the color to use. The one color you should avoid is *blue*. For some reason nature doesn't produce foods in blue, except blueberries which really are more deep-violet (like Elizabeth Taylor's eyes) than true-blue. We have red apples and strawberries, yellow bananas and lemons, green limes and avocados, purple plums, pink grapefruit, oranges, et cetera, but no blues in food. Perhaps because nature has a way of dictating these things, a blue food coloring, tint, or candied decorative dainties would look incongruously out of place on *food*.

A SUMPTUOUS COCKTAIL PARTY

(For 30)

MENU

Herring Tidbits in Wine
Marinated Artichoke Hearts
Smoked Oysters
Tiny Shrimps
Imported Boneless Sardines
Liver Pâté with Truffles
Pickled Melon Rinds
Sweet Midget Gherkins
Large Stuffed Olives, Mammoth Ripe Olives
Raw Cauliflowerets, Carrot Sticks
Quartered Hard-Cooked Eggs
Cubed Imported Swiss Cheese
Cubed Sharp Cheddar Cheese
Sliced Baked Ham
Sliced Italian Salami
Tuna-Stuffed Cherry Tomatoes
Assorted Crackers
Wedges of Imported Cheeses
Thin Rye Bread
Genuine Pumpernickel Bread, thin sliced
Crab Crêpes
Tenderloin of Beef Sandwiches
Orange Suzettes
Mocha Brownies
Coffee, Tea

This is my favorite kind of cocktail party because it's the easiest to do. All you need is a strong arm to open cans and jars. And for a change, you can count on spending more time in the market than in the kitchen.

There are no casserole dishes, no quick bake-and-serves, nothing to pop into the oven at the last minute. It's the easiest menu for even an amateur hostess to handle. Not even a gelatin mold to unmold!

All you have to do is set it all out on the table, let your guests help themselves when they please (no announced eating time), and keep the platters replenished.

With most of the foods already prepared, the crab crêpes and desserts made ahead and frozen, there will be nothing for the hostess to prepare before the party except the tenderloin of beef sandwiches.

The menu contains quite a few items; that's what makes it a Sumptuous Cocktail Party. What a warm feeling of hospitality you can create for your guests with a table laden with attractive dishes, bursting with variety and color! You can let your imagination run wild in choosing a few way-out items as well as some basic ones and imported treats. You'll enjoy arranging your own smorgasbord table and you can be sure your guests will enjoy it too.

EQUIPMENT WORK SHEET FOR A SUMPTUOUS COCKTAIL PARTY

containers of various sizes and shapes (dishes, platters, bowls, trays)
serving forks and spoons
12 cocktail forks for various items except finger foods
3 or 4 butter spreaders for pâté and cheeses
serving fork for crêpes
electric warmer
large round tray
cake stand
large oblong tray
60-cup coffee maker
silver coffee service
cocktail glasses
cocktail napkins
canapé trays or bread and butter plates
36 salad plates
36 coffee cups and saucers
12 teaspoons
36 spreaders
36 forks
ice cubes for cocktails
bartending supplies
ashtrays
silent butler

MARKETING WORK SHEET FOR A SUMPTUOUS COCKTAIL PARTY

1 quart milk
5 cups coffee cream
1½ pounds butter
½ pound Switzerland Swiss cheese
½ pound sharp Cheddar cheese
wedges of genuine French Roquefort, Camembert, Brie
3 dozen eggs
2 beef tenderloins, butt portion, 6 to 8 pounds each

1 pound sliced baked ham
1 pound thin-sliced Italian salami
1 head of cauliflower
1 pound carrots
2 pints cherry tomatoes
1 whole celery stalk
1 onion
6 large oranges (for rind and juice)
1 jar (1½ lbs.) herring in wine sauce
4 cans (4½ oz. each) small shrimps
2 cans (3⅔ oz. each) smoked oysters
2 cans (4 oz. each) boneless sardines
2 cans (7 oz. each) white meat tuna
2 cans (7½ oz. each) crab meat
1 can (3¼ oz.) liver pâté with truffles
1 can (15 oz.) marinated artichoke hearts
1 jar (10 oz.) pickled watermelon rind
1 jar (10 oz.) pickled cantaloupe rind
1 jar (22 oz.) sweet midget gherkins
1 jar (11 oz.) large stuffed olives
2 cans (7¾ oz. each) mammoth ripe olives
1 can (8 oz.) chopped ripe olives
1 can (3 oz.) sliced pimientos
1 pint mayonnaise
5 dozen Parker House rolls
1 loaf of thin-sliced cocktail rye bread
2 packages (8 oz. each) thin-sliced pumpernickel bread
2 boxes (12 oz. each) crackers, not highly seasoned
6 ounces vanilla wafers
½ pound shelled walnuts
½ pound sugar cubes
½ cup honey
2 cakes of compressed fresh yeast
rum
vermouth
liquor
mixes

STAPLES LIST FOR A SUMPTUOUS COCKTAIL PARTY

salt
white pepper
paprika
prepared horseradish
prepared mustard
garlic
granulated sugar
light brown sugar
powdered (confectioners') sugar
instant coffee powder
cocoa powder
all-purpose flour
baking powder
packages of active dry yeast if you are not using fresh yeast
vanilla extract
coffee
tea or tea bags
bar supplies

ARRANGEMENT: Place an extremely large round tray, or a plywood board cut to resemble a tray and covered with aluminum foil, in the center of table. Place a centerpiece of fresh flowers or one made of flowers carved from turnips or grapefruit peel (pp. 181–184) or any creation of your own imagination in the center of tray. Open cans and jars of various items, placing their contents into dishes and containers of various shapes and sizes. Place them in spokelike fashion around and radiating from the centerpiece.

Slice ham and salami very thin. Roll each slice into shape of a cornucopia. Lay close together, petal fashion, on dishes. Place crackers and rye bread on the tray in spaces between the dishes and containers.

Wash cauliflower, break apart into flowerets; peel carrots, cut into sticks; place half of each vegetable in 2 dishes. Place them on trays on opposite sides, preferably close to the black olives for color contrast.

Recipe Continues . . .

'Make a border in the front of tray with the stuffed tomatoes.* Place wedges and cubes of cheeses on a small cheese board or tray. Place small-size serving forks (such as cocktail forks) and long-handled spoons (such as ice-tea spoons) in most of the dishes; however, keep in mind that it is easier to pick up certain foods such as olives and raw vegetables with the fingers.

TENDERLOIN OF BEEF SANDWICHES

60 Sandwiches

2 beef tenderloins, butt portion, 6 to 8 pounds each
1 garlic clove, peeled
1 tablespoon paprika
¼ pound butter or margarine

½ cup mayonnaise
1 teaspoon prepared horseradish
1 teaspoon prepared mustard
5 dozen Parker House rolls

Preheat oven to 375°F. Cut garlic into thin spears and insert into beef in various places. Rub beef all over with paprika. Bake for about 1 hour, or if using a meat thermometer bake to 140°F., unless rare beef is desired. Allow meat to completely cool before slicing. A slicing machine is desirable, but if you do not have one, at least a very sharp knife is a necessity in order to slice the beef thin enough to allow 2 slices per sandwich, the slices weighing 1½ ounces combined.

Combine butter or margarine and mayonnaise; beat in the horseradish and mustard. Split the rolls and spread rather generously with this mixture. Fill rolls with slices of beef, allowing 2 slices per sandwich. Arrange on a tray and cover with wax paper and a damp towel until serving time.

(*For tomato filling, use recipe for tuna pinwheels, Chapter V, Tea Party, p. 134.)

ORANGE SUZETTES

8 Dozen tiny rolls

1 cup milk	4 egg yolks, beaten
1 cup warm water (105° to	2 tablespoons grated orange rind
115°F. for dry yeast, 80° to	8 cups all-purpose flour
90°F. for fresh yeast)	2 teaspoons salt
2 packages active dry yeast or 2	20 sugar cubes, crushed
cakes of compressed yeast	1 tablespoon rum
½ cup orange juice	¼ pound butter, melted
½ cup honey	Butter for muffin tins
¼ cup melted margarine	Orange Icing (recipe follows)

Scald milk and cool to lukewarm. Measure warm water into a large bowl and sprinkle or crumble in yeast, stirring until dissolved. Add lukewarm milk, orange juice, honey, melted margarine, beaten egg yolks and 1 tablespoon grated rind, reserving remainder of rind for filling. Combine half of the flour and the salt, and sift into yeast mixture; stir until well blended. Add remainder of flour gradually to make a stiff dough.

Turn out onto a floured board and knead several times with the palms of the hand. Grease a bowl, place dough in it, then quickly flip over so that what was the under side is now the top. Grease well again. Let stand at room temperature for about 2 hours, or until doubled in bulk.

Punch dough down. At this point the dough can be refrigerated and used within a few days or used immediately. If refrigerated, allow 3 to 4 hours for the dough to stand at room temperature before using.

While dough is rising, prepare the Suzette filling: Crush the 20 sugar cubes with a rolling pin. Spread out onto a sheet of wax paper. Scatter on the reserved 1 tablespoon grated orange rind and sprinkle the rum all over.

Divide dough into 8 portions, keeping unused portions covered with a damp cloth. Roll 1 portion at a time to a sheet 12 x 5 inches. Spread with melted butter and scatter some of the Suzette

Recipe Continues . . .

filling over the surface. Roll tightly jelly-roll fashion into a long roll; cut into 12 one-inch portions. Place cut side down in well-buttered 1½-inch muffin tins. Cover and let rise until doubled. Continue this same method with the remaining 7 portions of dough.

Preheat oven to 350°F. Bake rolls for 15 minutes. Remove from pans while still warm. Brush rolls with Orange Icing.

Place rolls in very small paper muffin cups; arrange on serving trays.

Orange Icing

1¼ cups sifted powdered sugar   ¼ cup orange juice, heated

Combine sugar and juice and stir until glossy and smooth.

MOCHA BROWNIES   36 Brownies

⅓ cup sifted flour
⅓ cup vanilla wafer crumbs
1 teaspoon instant coffee
  powder
⅓ cup packed light brown sugar
¾ cup chopped walnuts
⅓ cup butter
¾ cup sifted flour
⅓ cup cocoa powder
1 tablespoon instant coffee
  powder

1 teaspoon baking powder
½ teaspoon salt
2 eggs, well beaten
¼ pound butter or margarine,
  softened
¾ cup packed light brown sugar
2 teaspoons vanilla extract
Powdered sugar

Preheat oven to 425°F. Combine the first 5 ingredients. Blend in ⅓ cup butter. Press into a well-greased 8-inch square pan. Bake for 5 minutes. Remove from oven. Lower temperature to 350°F.

Sift together next 5 ingredients. Blend the eggs, softened butter or margarine, ¾ cup brown sugar and the vanilla. Combine with flour mixture. Mix well. Spread over baked layer. Bake for

40 to 45 minutes. Cool for a few minutes. Cut into 36 squares. Remove the pieces to a serving tray and sprinkle generously with powdered sugar.

FLO CHART FOR A SUMPTUOUS COCKTAIL PARTY

Again, you can figure out this easy Flo chart for yourself. A happy note: Everything except the tenderloin of beef sandwiches can be set up the DAY BEFORE the party, if covered well with plastic or foil wrap and refrigerated.

The crab crêpes can be made a week or two in advance and frozen. See recipe for this in Chapter IX.

Your only major chore on the DAY OF THE PARTY will be to prepare the tenderloin of beef sandwiches. Put meat in the oven about noon and plan to slice it about 4 P.M., or 2 hours before the party. Don't forget to remove sandwich spread from refrigerator and let soften before spreading on Parker House rolls. Sandwiches can be made and arranged on tray, covered with wax paper and a damp towel until serving time.

After most of the guests have arrived, add to the table the Crab Crêpes, placed on an electric warmer, and shortly after the tenderloin of beef sandwiches. Later, on a sideboard or table set up for the purpose, bring out your coffee, Orange Suzettes and Mocha Brownies.

If you've paid attention to other Flo charts, you will, of course, have prepared all your fresh vegetables (cauliflowerets, carrot sticks, stuffed tomatoes) the DAY BEFORE THE PARTY and had a dress rehearsal of your table setting arrangement. It should be a snap for you to get it all together on the DAY OF THE PARTY and create a table setting that is both sumptuous and beautiful. A truly delightful cocktail spread for your guests with a minimum of fuss and flurry.

CHAPTER VII

· · · · · · · · · · · · · · ·

A Bountiful Buffet

· · · · · · · · · · · · · · ·

This is a *sui generis,* one-of-a-kind party menu for a *very* special occasion. I've served it often for New Year's Eve parties. But it definitely should not be limited to calendar holidays. You can choose any day of the week, any time of the year, for this Bountiful Buffet. The menu itself transforms the party into a Special Occasion.

My crystal ball tells me this will become one of the most used party plans in the book. And why not? It has those good old American favorites, meat and potatoes, corn and tomatoes, that hearty appetites love, plus a Salad Smorgasbord and Glorious Fruit Platter for the diet-conscious, topped off with my mother's own heavenly Apple Strudel that *nobody* can resist. In fact, Kirk Douglas is so hung up on it that he claims *he* invented it. But I'll get to that later.

A BOUNTIFUL BUFFET

(for 30)

MENU

Salad Smorgasbord
Roast Beef Supreme
  Horseradish Sauce
Baked Tomatoes and Corn
Stuffed Potatoes
Glorious Fruit Platter
Assorted Rolls
Butter Balls
Coffee, Tea
Dessert:
  Kirk Douglas's Apple Strudel
  Sweet Tooth Pastries (optional)

EQUIPMENT WORK SHEET FOR A BOUNTIFUL BUFFET

12 to 16 feet of table length for dinner buffet
8 feet of table length for dessert buffet
tables and chairs to seat all guests
tablecloths
dinner napkins
large salad bowl
9 bowls of various sizes and shapes for vegetables
3 bowls and small ladles for salad dressings
3 bread or roll trays or baskets
large round platter for Crab Mousse Ring
meat thermometer
carving board
sharp carving knife
gravy boat or bowl for Horseradish Sauce
shallow bowl for butter balls
warming element and tray

round platter for stuffed potatoes
round 10- to 12-inch tray for baked tomatoes
large platter for fruit
large compote dishes ⎫
2 or 3 tiered trays ⎪ for assorted dessert
medium-size trays and platters ⎬ (optional)
cake and pie servers ⎭
coffee maker and coffee servers
serving spoons and forks
salad plates
dinner plates
dessert plates
cups and saucers
silverware: forks, knives, teaspoons, butter spreaders, dessert or salad
   forks
salt and pepper shakers for each table
sugar and creamer for each table
ashtrays for each table

MARKETING WORK SHEET FOR A BOUNTIFUL BUFFET

½ cup light cream
5 cups coffee cream
6 cups whipping cream
2 quarts dairy sour cream
3 pounds butter
1 pound margarine
3 eggs
2 eye of the rib beef roasts, 14 to 16 pounds each
6 pounds cabbage
5 pounds carrots
1 whole celery stalk
1 onion
30 medium-size tomatoes
6 large tomatoes for salad bar
1 pint tiny cherry tomatoes
30 medium-size baking potatoes

3 heads of lettuce
3 heads of romaine lettuce
2 heads of curly endive or escarole, or a combination of other available
greens
3 bunches of parsley
1 bunch of fresh chives, or 1 container of frozen chives
4 pounds eating apples, preferably McIntosh
5 pounds cooking apples for strudel
4 large pineapples
6 grapefruits
6 oranges
12 lemons
8 bananas
grapes for decoration
3 cans (12 oz. each) garbanzo beans (chick-peas)
3 cans (12 oz. each) cut green beans
3 cans (10 oz. each) sliced carrots
2 cans (14 oz. each) shoestring beets
5 cans (12 oz. each) whole-kernel corn
5 jars (4 oz. each) marinated artichoke hearts
5 cans (15 oz. each) whole peeled nectarines
4 cans (16 oz. each) pear halves
3 jars (8 oz. each) maraschino cherry halves
4 jars (1 lb. each) herring fillets in sour cream
3 cans (7½ oz. each) crab meat
1 can (26 oz.) tomato juice
1 can (10 oz.) red madrilène soup
1 quart mayonnaise
6 bottles (12 to 16 oz. each) of 3 varieties of salad dressing (2 bottles of
each kind)
2 jars (5 oz. each) cream-style horseradish
2 packages (3½ oz. each) dehydrated onion-soup mix
1 pound marshmallows
1 pint strawberry preserves
1½ pounds shelled walnuts
12 ounces Angel Flake coconut
6 ounces vanilla cookies
1 loaf of thin-sliced cocktail rye bread

1 pound thin-sliced pumpernickel bread
2 boxes (12 oz. each) crackers
gold spray paint

STAPLES LIST FOR A BOUNTIFUL BUFFET

salt
white pepper
paprika
ground cinnamon
grated nutmeg
garlic
dried dillweed
granulated sugar
powdered (confectioners') sugar
Worcestershire sauce
flour
vanilla extract
unflavored dry bread crumbs (be sure you have at least 2 cups)
envelopes of unflavored gelatin (be sure you have at least 4 envelopes)
vegetable oil
coffee
tea or tea bags

SALAD SMORGASBORD

Coleslaw
Apple-Marlow Salad
Mixed Greens
   Bowls of canned:
    *Garbanzo Beans
    *Cut Green Beans
    *Sliced Carrots
    *Shoestring Beets
    *Your choice of three
     dressings
     Quartered tomatoes

*Herring Fillets in Sour Cream
Crab Mousse Ring
Celery and Carrot Sticks (p.
157)
*Marinated Artichoke Hearts
*Assorted crackers, thin-sliced
rye bread, pumpernickel
bread, butter squares

Everything for this elaborate salad table can be made ready the day before, covered and refrigerated. *The asterisk-marked items require no preparation, merely chilling, placing in bowls, and setting out on the salad table. See marketing list (p. 196ff.) for suggested quantities.

The mixed greens (varies in different parts of the country) can be washed the day before and refrigerated in plastic bags. Allow approximately 1 cup greens per person.

COLESLAW

**30 Servings,
½ cup each**

6 pounds solid cabbage
1 pound carrots
1 medium-size onion
1 tablespoon salt

1 teaspoon freshly ground pepper
½ teaspoon dried dillweed
3 cups mayonnaise

Shred cabbage finely into a large mixing bowl. Peel carrots and onion and grate onto the cabbage. Add seasoning and mayonnaise.

Mix all together; refrigerate. This is best when made 1 day before serving in order that the flavors become married.

APPLE-MARLOW SALAD

30 Generous servings

4 pounds eating apples, preferably McIntosh
1 pound marshmallows
1 quart sour cream
1 cup shelled walnuts, chopped

2 jars (8 oz. each) maraschino cherry halves
¾ cup powdered sugar
2 teaspoons vanilla extract

Pare and seed half of the apples; cut into small cubes. Seed and cut up the other half, but do not pare, as the red peel will add color to the salad. Tear marshmallows into small pieces; add to apples with the sour cream. Stir all together. Add remaining ingredients and toss all together. Refrigerate. Serve cold.

This salad is best when prepared at least 24 hours before serving in order that the marshmallows and sour cream blend together. I prefer using the torn pieces of marshmallow rather than marshmallow bits, as they meld into the sour cream more readily.

CRAB MOUSSE RING

One 3-quart mold

First Layer:

2 envelopes unflavored gelatin
½ cup coffee cream
½ cup hot water

3 cans (7½ oz. each) crab meat
½ cup chopped chives
1 quart whipping cream

Second Layer:

2 envelopes unflavored gelatin
1 cup tomato juice, cold
2 cups tomato juice, hot
1 cup canned red madrilène
1 tablespoon lemon juice

1 cup finely chopped celery
Curly endive
8 lemons, quartered
Parsley sprigs
1 pint tiny cherry tomatoes

Lightly brush a 3-quart mold with vegetable oil (not olive oil). Tap upside down on paper towel to remove excess oil. Set aside.

Put the first 2 envelopes of gelatin in a mixing bowl, stir in coffee cream, and let stand for 5 minutes. Pour in the ½ cup of hot water and stir well until gelatin is completely dissolved. Drain crab meat, remove cartilage, and crumble into the gelatin. Add chopped chives. Whip cream until stiff. Fold into the crab-gelatin mixture. Mix until all ingredients are well blended. Pour into the oiled mold and chill.

Prepare the second layer. Soften the second 2 envelopes of gelatin in 1 cup of cold tomato juice; let stand for 5 minutes. Heat 2 cups of tomato juice, pour over softened gelatin, and stir well until gelatin is completely dissolved. Stir in the madrilène, lemon juice and celery. Chill until slightly set. Spoon onto firmly set first layer. Refrigerate.

To serve, unmold on large round platter. Fill center with a clump of curly endive or other curly lettuce and place 30 to 32 lemon quarters on the greens. Surround outer edge of platter with clumps of parsley. Scatter on the parsley 1 pint of tiny cherry tomatoes. Slice the mousse in wedges about 1½ inches wide.

ROAST BEEF SUPREME   30 Servings

2 whole eye of the rib roasts, 14   2 garlic cloves, slivered
  to 16 pounds each   2 tablespoons imported paprika

Do not confuse this cut of beef with one called eye of the round, for the eye of the rib is the most choice of all cuts of beef. It is marbleized, tender and juicy, especially when cooked only to the rare stage.

A most essential kitchen tool for properly cooking this, or any cut of meat, is a meat thermometer. Keep in mind that even after the roast is removed from the oven, it will cook to 5 to 8 degrees more from within. Also, meat can be carved more easily if it stands for 10 to 12 minutes after removing from heat.

Insert slivers of garlic in the fatty surface of the meat, taking care not to pierce the meat and thereby lose valuable juices. Rub entire surface with paprika.

Recipe Continues . . .

Insert meat thermometer in thickest portion of the meat, making certain that the tip does not strike the metal of the pan.

Place in a preheated 375°F. oven and roast for 1 hour and 45 minutes; or for 1 hour and 30 minutes for *very rare;* or for 1 hour and 40 minutes for *rare;* or for 1 hour and 50 or 60 minutes for *well done.*

To serve, place on a carving board which has been heated in a warm oven for 10 minutes before you need it. Carve the meat only as the guests wish to be served.

Serve with Horseradish Sauce prepared especially for this gorgeous eye-of-the-rib roast.

Horseradish Sauce Supreme · 5 Cups sauce

2 cups whipping cream
2 jars (5 oz. each) cream-style
  horseradish
1 tablespoon Worcestershire
  sauce
½ teaspoon salt

Whip cream until stiff, then fold in remaining ingredients. This can be prepared a day or two in advance and refrigerated. However, before serving, allow the sauce to stand at room temperature so it will not be chilled enough to cool the meat.

BAKED TOMATOES AND CORN · 30 Stuffed tomatoes

30 medium-size firm
  tomatoes
2 packages (3½ oz. each)
  dehydrated onion soup mix
5 cans (12 oz. each) whole
  kernel corn
6 ounces butter
½ cup bread crumbs

Cut a ¼-inch slice from stem end of each tomato. Scoop out pulp and seeds. Discard seeds and combine pulp with corn; set aside. Sprinkle insides of tomatoes with onion soup mix. Divide butter into 60 pieces. Put 1 piece in each tomato shell. Fill each shell with the corn and tomato-pulp mixture. Sprinkle tops with bread crumbs. Dot tops with remaining 30 pieces of butter. This preparation can be done several hours before serving. Bake in a preheated 375°F. oven for 20 minutes.

To serve, transfer tomatoes to a serving tray set upon a warming element to keep the vegetables warm. If one is not available, it is advisable to serve half of the servings at a time, as they cool rather quickly. Keep the second half warm in the oven with the heat turned off.

STUFFED POTATOES

30 Stuffed potatoes

30 medium-size baking potatoes
15 carrots
½ pound butter, melted
½ pound margarine, melted
1 tablespoon plus 2 teaspoons
  salt

1½ teaspoons white pepper
1½ cups flour
1½ cups dry bread crumbs

Peel potatoes. Using an apple corer or other round instrument, remove a round center from each. Peel carrots and cut off 2 inches from the bottom (save for other use). Cut remaining portion into halves slantwise. Place in pot with water to cover, with 2 teaspoons salt added. Cook for 8 minutes. Cool. Stuff potatoes with partially cooked carrots. Combine melted butter and margarine in a deep bowl. Mix together remaining salt, the pepper, flour and bread crumbs in another bowl. Dip potatoes into melted shortening, then roll in crumb mixture; place in well-buttered baking pans. Drizzle remaining melted butter and margarine over the tops of the potatoes. Bake in a preheated 375°F. oven for 50 minutes.

To avoid last minute preparation, the potatoes may be baked several hours in advance. In that event, allow 20 minutes to reheat them. Drizzle more melted butter and margarine over the tops to restore their shiny, crusty appearance.

To serve, arrange potatoes in a circle on a round platter centered with parsley.

GLORIOUS FRUIT PLATTER   30 Servings

Each time I have served a large and colorful fruit platter, I am complimented on the beauty of it. I always reply, "It is not my doing, but nature's, in her glorious and colorful splendor." There is no need to try to improve on nature. The arrangement of a variety of fruits, as the season allows, is a beautiful addition to every buffet.

No dressing is necessary. Serving the fruits *au naturel* particularly pleases the diet-conscious guests who prefer to return for "seconds" at dessert time, and who consider this their grand finale to a wonderful dinner.

The following is planned with some fresh fruits. By all means, do add whatever fresh fruits are available in your region during the season you are giving your party.

4 large fresh pineapples	3 cups sour cream
6 grapefruits	1 tablespoon powdered sugar
6 oranges	2 cups Angel Flake coconut
5 cans (15 oz. each) peeled whole nectarines	15 maraschino cherry halves
4 cans (1 lb. each) pear halves	Gold spray
4 drops of red food coloring	Parsley sprigs
8 bananas	Grapes

Leave 1 pineapple whole for decorating the platter. Cut off tops of the 3 remaining pineapples and remove enough peel to remove all brown spots. Cut lengthwise into 4 quarters. Cut away center core and slice each quarter into 4 slices.

Peel grapefruits and oranges in a spiral fashion so as to make flowers (p. 184) of the peels to use later in decorating the platter. Remove all white membranes. Slice each grapefruit and orange horizontally into 5 slices. Drain nectarines. Place pears with juice into a deep bowl; add red food coloring. Let stand until pears take on a light red color; then drain. Divide bananas into fourths; stir together the sour cream and lemon juice; pour into a shallow pan and stir in the powdered sugar. Spear each piece of banana with a fork, dip into sour cream, then roll in coconut. Chop cherries fine, set aside to scatter over bananas after they have been placed on platter.

All fruits except the bananas should be refrigerated and can be made ready the day before they are served. With the component parts set out and readied, it will take a short while to fix the bananas 2 to 3 hours before serving. Adding the lemon juice to the sour cream will help keep the bananas from turning a dark color.

ARRANGEMENT: Spray the whole pineapple with gold paint, covering the top with foil so it retains its green color. When dry, place in a mound of parsley in center of a large platter; surround it with colored flowers made of the grapefruit and orange peels. Divide the platter into 5 sections, using parsley laid in rows radiating from the gold pineapple to separate each section. Lay each variety of fruit in one section; alternating slices of grapefruit and oranges in one section and scattering the chopped cherries over the bananas. Embed more fruit flowers in the parsley at the edge of the platter.

APPLE STRUDEL

The recipe for this is in Chapter X, *FAVORITES OF THE FAMOUS* (p. 267).

I have also suggested Sweet Tooth Pastries as dessert optionals for this menu. Recipes for these are in Chapter V.

Never flop ice cream on apple strudel. This puts it in the same category with apple pie; while no patriotic American is going to knock apple pie, true strudel buffs (and there are many!) would be aghast to see apple strudel assaulted with ice cream. Pie à la mode is fine for pies, but please, gentle readers, omit the à la mode from my strudels!

FLO CHART FOR A BOUNTIFUL BUFFET

This is a party plan for which you should allow enough time, a minimum of 1½ to 2 hours, for your guests to enjoy the salad smorgasbord with their drinks before dinner, since there are no hors-d'oeuvre. If you invite guests at 7 o'clock, plan on dinner at 9, and schedule your timetable so the meat will be ready by then.

Here are some pointers for your Flo chart:

THREE WEEKS BEFORE Decide on invitations, decorations, music, bar arrangements, hired help. Check Equipment Work Sheet. Do you have enough tables and chairs to seat 30? Rental equipment should be ordered now. Check Marketing and Staples lists, bar supplies, purchase or order *all* basics or staples; do anything and everything that can be done this far ahead instead of leaving it till the week before the party.

Important: Decide now what kinds of breads and optional Sweet Tooth desserts you want for the menu. Make SUPPLE-MENTAL Marketing Lists for these specific recipes, do your marketing, and start your baking.

Suggestion: For your assorted rolls on this menu, I recommend the Sesame Loops (Chapter III, *My Favorite Brunch*), Tiny Brioches (Chapter III, *A Simple Brunch*), Potato Parker House Rolls (Chapter IV, *A Buffet Luncheon*), French or Sourdough Roll Slices (Chapter VI, *A Cocktail Supper*). (See Index for pages.)

If you're ambitious, and have enough freezer space, you may want to try all of these, to give your guests a variety. If you must make a choice, though, between breads and optional desserts, I recommend for this Bountiful Buffet that you treat your guests to some of the *Sweet Tooth* treats from Chapter V (pp. 142 and ff).

TWO WEEKS BEFORE Complete all baking and freezing items, except Apple Strudel. You may want to set aside 2 or 3 days this week only for baking, or you may prefer to do it all in one day and get it over with. Also this week, leave some time to make and freeze your turnip roses, grapefruit- and orange-peel flowers. (See Fancies and Furbelows, Chapter VI, p. 181 ff.)

ONE WEEK BEFORE With so much behind you, there is now plenty of time left to concentrate on the major menu preparations without any hassle. To play safe, order your eye of rib roast now. Double-check on hired help, music, rental equipment, Marketing List.

TWO DAYS BEFORE Purchase fresh fruit and vegetables. Make butter balls.

ONE DAY BEFORE Pick up (or have delivered) eye of rib roast. Prepare Coleslaw, wash all salad greens, spray pineapple, cut fruits. Prepare Apple-Marlow Salad, Crab Mousse Ring, Horseradish Sauce; refrigerate. Set out all equipment for your Smorgasbord Salad. Mark all trays, bowls and platters with scotch tape reminders as to what they are to be used for. This is one occasion where it's very important to have a DRESS REHEARSAL with your buffet table, accessories, arrangements, decorations, etc.

DAY OF THE PARTY Early in the day, prepare tomatoes and potatoes for baking; leave at room temperature. Remove strudel from freezer and let set all day at room temperature. Don't forget breads, desserts, other items in freezer; set out or refrigerate according to instructions. Get everything ready for your fruit platter.

Plan on 1½ to 2 hours in late afternoon, starting around 5:30, to finish necessary last-minute preparations and set out your salad smorgasbord. Prepare meat and let stand at room temperature. Plug in coffee maker at 6, keep warm. Smorgasbord should be completed a few minutes before 7 and meat should be placed in oven at 7, just in time for you to greet guests, and to act like one of them. There's nothing to do now until 8 o'clock, when the stuffed potatoes go in the oven; and at 8:40 the stuffed tomatoes.

At this time your helpers should start removing the salad smorgasbord dishes and set up the buffet for the main course. Your Glorious Fruit Platter with the gold-sprayed pineapple in the middle can serve as your centerpiece; you don't need a floral centerpiece.

At 8:50 remove meat from oven and set on buffet table.

At 9 o'clock transfer potato and tomato dishes from oven to

buffet; turn off oven and set strudel in so it will be nice and warm by the time guests are ready for dessert.

Then, at a propitious time you can commission someone to wheel in your surprise flower garden cart of mind-blowing Sweet Tooth treats. It makes a nice denouement for the perfect party.

SETTING A BUFFET TABLE

Two questions should guide you in setting up a buffet table: *Does it look pretty? Is it functional?* A buffet table always looks better if more bountiful than bare, but it should never look overcrowded. Decorative pieces such as ice carvings, candelabra, floral arrangements should be used only if you have a sufficiently large table to accommodate them along with the main menu dishes. It is usually best to set out a first course of appetizers or, as in the case of this Bountiful Buffet, a salad smorgasbord, and then remove these dishes and set up the buffet table with the main-course dishes. Also it's often more practical to use a fruit bowl or platter arrangement as your centerpiece rather than flowers. It's not only a space saver but saves money, too, and can have as much eye appeal as a floral centerpiece. Besides which, you can eat it! From a functional standpoint the most important factor is to arrange everything on the buffet table so it will be easily accessible to your guests without a jam-up in the food line, and easy for them to handle either with or without a helper, though in most cases I recommend a helper or two to assist in serving at a buffet table. With this menu, for instance, you would definitely need someone to assist in carving and serving the roast beef.

CHAPTER VIII

·················

Dinners: Formal and Not-So-Formal

·················

There comes a time when you may want to give a formal sit-down dinner party for 12, if for nothing more than to haul out and show off your fine Spode or Rosenthal chinaware, your tinkling crystal glasses, your 12 place settings of sterling silver (if you haven't lost any!) and all that sort of thing.

Not many people do this anymore. The trend is increasingly toward more informal and casual entertaining. But if the occasion calls for it or you're in the mood for a more formal type of dinner party, you will need a menu and perhaps instructions on how to serve it properly.

Formal dinner parties needn't be stiff and strained; they should be festive occasions, emphasizing the difference between eating and dining. Many people *eat* simply because it happens to be that time of day to do so. *Dining*, however, is a most pleasurable experience when the food is prepared tastefully and served properly.

Wines accompanying each course are part of the ritual of more formal dining. When properly chosen, they enhance the flavors of

209

even the best seasoned foods. (A dry white wine is most compatible with chicken, fish, creamed dishes; dry red wine with beef; a rosé with ham or veal.) Champagne served throughout dinner adds an elegant touch as do wines accompanying desserts, such as Port and Cream Sherry.

To do justice to your dinner, whether formal or not-quite-so-formal, serve only enough tidbits with cocktails to satisfy that "hungry edge," but not too many to dull the appetite. Choose one or two recipes from Chapter VI (*Cocktail Parties and Suppers*).

Any formal or semiformal sit-down dinner party, in my opinion, requires extra help, even more so than large buffets. The host and/or hostess must sit down with the guests. They can't be jumping up and down, running into the kitchen, passing or serving a vegetable dish, meat platter, gravy boat or casserole. Such a *modus operandi* is *verboten* at proper sit-down dinner parties. It makes guests uncomfortable and hosts conspicuous with the busy business of being a host or hostess instead of a guest at their own party, particularly if it's a sit-down dinner party for 12. (You can disappear more easily to turn the oven on or off or tell your kitchen helper to bring out the butter balls if you're in a crowd of 30 or 60. Don't try it with only 12.)

My advice up front is *not* to plan a formal sit-down dinner until or unless you have *extra help* you can count on.

With that in mind, you should have no problems with the following two menus, both of which are flexible and adjustable to either a formal dinner party or one not so formal.

Please note that some of the recipes make 15 servings; that gives extra portions for your hired help.

A FORMAL DINNER

(For 12)

MENU

Consommé-Filled Papayas
  Cheese Biscuits
  Butter Balls
Breast of Chicken Mystique
  Grape Mandarin Sauce
  Mushroom Croquettes
  Artichoke Casserole
  Burgundy Pears
    Croissants
Celery Victor Salad
Grape Juice Charlotte Russe
Demitasse Coffee

EQUIPMENT WORK SHEET FOR A FORMAL DINNER

tables and chairs
tablecloths
dinner napkins
floral centerpieces
candlesticks
silverware: forks, knives, 2 teaspoons, butter spreaders, salad forks, dessert forks
water glasses
Champagne glasses and other wineglasses
service plates
salt and pepper shakers
sugar and creamer
roll or biscuit tray
tray for Chicken Mystique
gravy boat and ladle for Grape Mandarin Sauce
double boiler for heating sauce

tray for Mushroom Croquettes
small double boiler for heating sauce
3-quart casserole
platter with raised sides or flat bowl for Burgundy Pears
glass or silver platter for Charlotte Russe
serving pieces
salad plates for Consommé-Filled Papayas
bread and butter plates
dinner plates
salad or glass plates for Celery Victor
coffee maker
demitasse cups and saucers
demitasse spoons
paper doilies
ashtrays (optional)

MARKETING WORK SHEET FOR A FORMAL DINNER

1 quart milk
2 quarts whipping cream
1 cup dairy sour cream
2 pounds butter
1 pound margarine
¾ pound Cheddar cheese
¼ pound Parmesan cheese
1 dozen eggs
15 boned (but not skinless) chicken breast halves, 6 to 7 ounces each
1½ to 2 pounds cooked pickled tongue
2 pounds onions
2 heads of romaine lettuce
13 whole celery stalks
1 green pepper
¾ pound fresh mushrooms
1 bunch of parsley
1 bunch of watercress
1 bunch of fresh chives
6 papayas

8 lemons
4 packages (9 oz. each) frozen artichoke hearts
2 cans (16 oz. each) pitted ripe olives
3 cans (16 oz. each) pear halves
1 can (14 oz.) seedless grapes
1 can (7 oz.) mandarin orange sections
2 cans (1½ oz. each) rolled anchovy fillets with capers
1 jar (3 oz.) caviar
1 can (3 oz.) pimientos
3 cans (10½ oz. each) cream of mushroom soup
2 cans (10½ oz. each) beef consommé
1 can (6 oz.) frozen orange juice concentrate
1 pint grape juioe
4 ounces orange-flavored honey
1 bottle (12 oz.) corn syrup
1 package (15 oz.) seedless raisins
1 loaf of white bread
1 package (8 oz.) refrigerated crescent dinner rolls
2 dozen ladyfingers
12 candied violets (available at specialty shops)
1 bottle Marsala wine
1 bottle red Burgundy wine
1 bottle white wine
table wines

STAPLES LIST FOR A FORMAL DINNER

salt
black pepper
white pepper
black peppercorns
celery seeds
dried thyme
grated nutmeg
garlic
granulated sugar
vinegar

salad oil
vegetable oil for frying
capers
green olives
sweet gherkins
envelopes of unflavored gelatin (make sure you have at least 3 envelopes)
vegetable shortening
flour
cornstarch or arrowroot
baking powder
cornflake crumbs
dry bread crumbs (make sure you have at least 2 cups)
dark-roast coffee for demitasse

CONSOMMÉ-FILLED PAPAYAS

12 Servings

6 firm ripe papayas
1 envelope unflavored gelatin
1½ cans (10½ oz. each) beef
  consommé
1 cup dairy sour cream

1 jar (3 oz.) caviar
3 lemons, quartered
1 bunch of watercress
12 paper doilies, 6 inches across

Cut papayas lengthwise into halves. Trim off a very thin portion of the outer skin of the bottoms to prevent them rolling as they are served. Remove seeds. Chill.

Jellied Consommé

Sprinkle gelatin over 1 cup consommé. Heat slowly in small saucepan until gelatin is dissolved. Pour remaining consommé in a shallow dish. Add hot consommé. Mix well. Refrigerate at least overnight; can be done 2 days in advance.

To serve, place papayas on doilies on salad plates. Cut consommé into small cubes. Spoon into cavities of papayas. Top each with 1 tablespoon sour cream, and drop a bit of caviar from the end of a teaspoon onto the cream. Lay a wedge of lemon alongside, together with a sprig of watercress.

CHEESE BISCUITS   36 Biscuits

4 cups sifted flour
½ teaspoon salt
4 teaspoons baking powder
¼ pound margarine or vegetable
  shortening

2 cups grated Cheddar cheese
1⅞ cups milk

Preheat oven to 450°F. Sift dry ingredients together into a large bowl. Cut in margarine or shortening with 2 knives or pastry blender until mixture resembles cornmeal. Blend in the cheese. Add milk gradually until a soft dough is formed. Drop by teaspoons on ungreased cookie sheets. Bake for 12 to 15 minutes.

If baked several weeks or days in advance, wrap securely in airtight containers, and freeze for future use.

To serve, allow to defrost at room temperature; heat just before serving.

BUTTER BALLS   13 Butter balls

¼ pound butter

Using a firm but not too hard stick of butter, cut it into 13 squares with a butter cutter. Separate squares on a sheet of wax paper. Have handy a bowl with water and ice cubes; also a tall glass with water and ice cubes; and another tall glass with hot water. Your essential tool is a pair of ribbed butter paddles, available in all housewares departments. Pick up each butter square in your hands and shape into a round ball. Immerse the paddles in the glass of cold water; then place a butter ball in the center of one paddle, tap with the other paddle and roll until a nice round scored ball is formed. Drop butter ball into bowl of ice water. Immerse paddles

Recipe Continues . . .

in the glass of hot water, then in the cold water, and repeat with another butter ball.

Once you get the hang of this, you can do it in no time at all. Plan to make ½ pound or even a whole pound of butter balls at one time. Remove balls from ice water. Refrigerate in shallow pans. Cover with plastic wrap or foil. They will keep in refrigerator for several days. (Should not be frozen.)

BREAST OF CHICKEN MYSTIQUE
15 Servings

15 boned (but not skinless) chicken breast halves, 6 to 7 ounces each
1½ teaspoons salt
Paprika
½ pound butter, each quarter cut into pencil sticks

½ cup chopped parsley
3 eggs
¼ cup water
2 cups finely crushed cornflakes
Oil for deep-frying

Mystique Filling

2 medium-size onions, chopped
2 ounces butter or margarine
2 cups finely chopped cooked pickled tongue
1 cup raisins

1½ cups chopped ripe olives
1 teaspoon salt
⅓ cup sugar
½ cup Marsala wine

Okay, so now maybe the pickled tongue stops you. If so, flip over to Part III, Chapter X, *Favorites of the Famous,* and see what Eleanor Roosevelt said about it.

First make the Mystique Filling: Sauté onions in butter or margarine. Add all remaining ingredients except the wine. Cook slowly for 8 to 10 minutes. Add wine. Cook for 5 minutes longer. Cool.

Lay the boned chicken breasts, skin side down, on a board and flatten them and spread open as wide as possible. Sprinkle with 1 teaspoon salt and a little paprika. Roll butter sticks in chopped parsley. Lay 1 stick down the center of each breast. Place 1 tablespoon filling on top of butter. Tuck in all uneven edges. Then roll lightly, completely enclosing the filling. Pull a portion of the skin tightly to the underside and over to one side. Press to make sure it stays in place, or secure with a toothpick. Chill for at least 2 hours before frying.

When ready to fry, beat lightly the eggs, ¼ cup water and ½ teaspoon salt. Carefully dip the stuffed breasts into the egg-water mixture. Roll in 2 cups finely crushed cornflakes. Deep-fry in oil heated to 380°F. on a frying thermometer for 10 to 12 minutes. Drain on absorbent paper towels.

All of this can be done 2 or 3 days in advance. Chicken breasts can be wrapped and refrigerated. They also can be prepared weeks or months in advance, and frozen, using care to wrap them very well. Defrost by allowing them to stand at room temperature for 4 to 5 hours. Place in well-buttered 3-inch-deep pans. Heat in a 350°F. oven until plump, moist and golden brown, for 35 to 40 minutes.

This Breast of Chicken Mystique is not only a delicious and easy to-do entrée for a formal dinner but is good to keep in your freezer bank for unexpected guests and drop-ins.

Grape Mandarin Sauce
About 4 cups sauce

1 can (14 oz.) seedless grapes
1 can (7 oz.) mandarin oranges
1 can (6 oz.) frozen orange
   juice concentrate, defrosted
¼ cup lemon juice

1 tablespoon cornstarch or arrowroot
¼ cup white wine

Drain the juice of the grapes and oranges into the top part of a double boiler. Set aside the fruit. Add the undiluted orange juice and the lemon juice; heat over direct low heat. Put the cornstarch or arrowroot in a small bowl; stir in the wine to make a smooth

Recipe Continues . . .

paste. Add to the heated juice. Cook, stirring constantly until sauce begins to thicken. Add drained fruit.

This can be prepared 3 to 4 days in advance; store in refrigerator.

To heat, set over the bottom pan of the double boiler filled with hot water. Heat until warm, stirring occasionally.

To serve, place warmed sauce in chafing dish or casserole that can be kept warm by canned heat; set alongside Chicken Mystique breasts, which have been placed on a serving tray ornamented with turnip roses, grapefruit- and orange-peel flowers, and clumps of parsley. This eye-appealing dish is delicious and easy for guests to handle; each boneless breast can be cut easily. The piquant sauce adds elegance and mystique.

MUSHROOM CROQUETTES   15 Croquettes

30 slices of white bread	1 onion, chopped
¼ pound butter or margarine	½ teaspoon salt
¾ pound mushrooms, washed	¼ teaspoon grated nutmeg
thoroughly	1½ tablespoons flour

Coating

3 eggs	½ teaspoon salt
¼ cup water	1½ cups bread crumbs

Sauce

1 can (10½ oz.) cream of	½ cup milk
mushroom soup	

Using a round cookie cutter or top of jar which measures 4 inches across, cut a round circle from each slice of bread. Set aside.

Melt butter or margarine in a large pan; slice mushrooms together with their stems into the pan. Toss until they are slightly coated. Add chopped onion, salt and nutmeg. Cook over low heat until the onions are soft and glossy. Remove from heat. Sprinkle on the flour and stir until well blended. Lay out 15 of the bread circles. Place 1 heaping tablespoon of the mushroom mixture in the center of each circle. Lay the remaining 15 bread circles on top. Seal together by pressing edges firmly with the tines of a fork.

Lightly beat together the eggs, water and salt. Spread out the bread crumbs on wax paper. Dip each filled bread circle into the egg mixture, then roll in crumbs to coat all over. French-fry a few at a time until golden brown. Turn onto paper towels.

Important: Croquettes can be frozen in a well-wrapped container and kept in freezer for several months, or in refrigerator for 5 or 6 days before using.

To serve, preheat oven to 350°F. If croquettes are frozen, remove from freezer the day before. If refrigerated, remove to room temperature about 1 hour before heating. Place on top shelf of oven and heat for 30 minutes.

Combine soup and milk; stir until well blended while heating. When smooth and heated, turn heat very low to keep sauce warm. At serving time, place a gravy boat or bowl in the center of serving tray. Surround with heated croquettes. Dribble some of the sauce over tops of croquettes. Place remainder in container in center of the tray.

I'll wager most of your guests will say, "These are absolutely delicious—what are they?"

Just tell them it's your magic mushroom wand!

ARTICHOKE CASSEROLE

One 3-quart casserole

I think I've received more requests for this recipe than for anything else I have ever served. It's Dinah Shore's favorite, as well as an oft-repeated request from other clients. This recipe is quite ample for a dinner party of 12, allowing for second helpings. It can be easily doubled or tripled for larger buffet parties; can be made a day or two before the party but cannot be frozen.

Recipe Continues . . .

4 packages (9 oz. each) frozen
artichoke hearts
1 teaspoon salt
2 onions
½ celery rib
1 green pepper
¼ pound buttter

1 teaspoon salt
½ teaspoon freshly ground pepper (scant)
1½ cans (10½-oz. cans) cream of mushroom soup
½ cup bread crumbs
½ cup grated Parmesan cheese

Cook artichokes in salted water according to package directions. Drain and set aside. Chop, rather fine, the onions, celery and green pepper. Sauté in butter, reserving about 2 tablespoons of the butter to use later on the tops of the casserole. Add salt and pepper and cook until vegetables are tender and slightly browned. Distribute a portion of the drained artichoke hearts in the bottom of a 3-quart casserole, just enough to cover the surface. Spoon half of the sautéed vegetables in a layer over the artichokes, then spoon on some of the undiluted soup. Repeat the layers, ending with artichokes on top, covered with a thin layer of soup.

Sprinkle on the bread crumbs and top with the grated Parmesan cheese. Dot with reserved butter. Heat in a 350°F. oven for 40 minutes.

BURGUNDY PEARS   15 Servings

3 cans (16 oz. each) pear halves
¼ pound butter or margarine

1 cup red Burgundy wine
½ cup corn syrup

Drain pears, set aside. Combine butter, wine and syrup in a heavy saucepan. Stir until smooth and well blended. Bring to a boil. Remove from heat. Carefully immerse pear halves in wine sauce, turning occasionally. Cool and transfer to a large bowl. Store in refrigerator to chill.

To serve, place pear halves, core side down, in a shallow bowl or serving tray with raised sides. Spoon enough wine sauce over the pears to add color to this dish but not so much that your guests dribble as they are served.

CROISSANTS

16 Small croissants

1 package (8 oz.) refrigerated
   Crescent Dinner Rolls
2 ounces butter, softened

2 egg yolks
2 teaspoons water

Preheat oven to 375°F. Unroll 1 package at a time. Separate dough into the 8 scored triangles. Cut each into halves, making 16 triangles. Spread lightly with softened butter. Starting at wide end, roll. Place point side down on ungreased cookie sheets; curve to shape crescents. Beat egg yolks and water just to combine. Brush tops of rolls lightly with the egg mixture. Bake for 10 to 12 minutes. Can be made in advance; wrap well and freeze.

    To serve, defrost at room temperature for 2 to 3 hours. Keep wrapped. Heat shortly before serving. Serve warm.

CELERY VICTOR SALAD

12 Servings

Serving a salad course *after* the main entrée is a European custom adopted by some Americans for formal dinner parties. I have served different kinds of salad as an after-entrée course, such as hearts of palm, spinach salad, tossed butter lettuce salad. However, the Celery Victor Salad seems to be the most favored.

12 celery hearts
1 tablespoon celery seeds
1 teaspoon black peppercorns
1 sprig of dried thyme
2 teaspoons salt
4 cups Vinaigrette Dressing
   (p. 50)

2 heads of romaine lettuce
12 rolled anchovies with capers
1 can (3 oz.) pimientos
Freshly ground pepper

Wash celery hearts, trim off about ¾ inch from the bottom and a bit off the top. Cut lengthwise into halves. Select a deep, narrow pot (such as an asparagus cooker). Stand the celery hearts upright in it and fill pot with water to within 2 inches of the tops.

Recipe Continues . . .

Cut a square of cheesecloth, 3 to 4 inches, and lay on it the celery seeds, peppercorns and thyme. Gather the 4 corners of the cheesecloth to form a bag. Hold securely with a rubber band or string. Immerse in the water and add the salt to the water. Cook over medium-high heat until celery is barely tender, approximately 20 minutes.

Carefully remove the celery hearts and lay them in a deep, narrow pan. Cool. Pour over the celery enough of the Vinaigrette Dressing to cover. Chill for several hours, preferably overnight.

To serve, line 12 salad or glass plates with washed and dried leaves of romaine. Lay 2 halves of celery hearts, well drained, across the center of each plate. Cut pimientos into strips. Lay one on each side of the anchovy in a slantwise position. Sprinkle all lightly with freshly ground pepper. Serve well chilled.

GRAPE JUICE CHARLOTTE RUSSE
16 Portions

1½ envelopes unflavored gelatin
1 cup cold water
1 cup boiling water
1½ cups grape juice

Juice of 2 lemons
2 quarts whipping cream
2 dozen ladyfingers
12 candied violets

Soak the gelatin in cold water. Pour in the boiling water and stir well until gelatin is completely dissolved. Add grape juice and lemon juice. Set the container of gelatin in a bowl of cold water or crushed ice to thicken slightly, stirring occasionally. Whip 1 quart of the cream until thick. Fold into gelatin mixture. Lightly butter two 10-inch springform pans with removable sides. Line bottoms and sides with ladyfingers. Turn in the creamy grape-juice filling. Refrigerate several hours, preferably overnight, or even for 2 days in advance of party.

To serve, unmold on serving trays. Whip remaining cream stiff. Spoon into a decorating bag fitted with a star tip. Pipe down sides between ladyfingers. Decorate top with large stars, covering it completely. Place candied violets on top. Voila! It looks like a piece of Dresden china!

DEMITASSE   15 Servings

A demitasse cup of coffee is a small cup of black, double-strong coffee served following dinner. Use ½ pound coffee and 16 cups water. Prepare in usual manner. Serve piping hot from service set out in the living room.

FLO CHART FOR A FORMAL DINNER

THREE WEEKS BEFORE A formal dinner, even for only 12 persons, requires a written invitation. Be sure to specify if black tie. Check hired help.

TWO WEEKS BEFORE Order chicken breasts, pickled tongue. Check Equipment and Marketing Lists. Purchase all canned goods, frozen items and wines.

ONE WEEK BEFORE Bake and freeze cheese biscuits, croissants, mushroom croquettes.

THREE DAYS BEFORE Prepare artichoke casserole, cover well, refrigerate. Cook tongue (unless purchased precooked). Prepare consommé for papayas; Burgundy pears, Grape Juice Charlotte Russe (except the decorating whipped cream and candied violets); the breasts of chicken and the grape sauce. Refrigerate. Make butter balls. Purchase papayas; if not ripe, do not refrigerate but leave out at room temperature.

ONE DAY BEFORE Double-check everything, especially hired help. Prepare celery and the vinaigrette dressing. Chill.

DAY OF THE PARTY Early afternoon, set tables complete with service plates, place-settings, place cards, etc.

Three hours before remove chicken, artichoke casserole, grape sauce from refrigerator. Cut papayas, place in refrigerator. Assemble Celery Victor salads on plates; refrigerate. Prepare sauce for mushroom croquettes; put in double boiler.

Two hours before place chicken breasts in buttered pans. Set grape sauce over hot water in double boiler. Heat on very low heat. Also heat sauce for mushroom croquettes. Put cheese biscuits and croissants on cookie sheets.

One-and-a-half hours before preheat oven to 350°F.

45 minutes before place chicken breasts in oven. Make coffee for demitasse. Put artichoke casserole in oven.

30 minutes before put mushroom croquettes in oven. Set papayas on plates; fill with chilled consommé. Remove butter balls from refrigerator, place on each bread and butter plate with a clump of parsley. Remove Burgundy pears from refrigerator, transfer quickly to serving bowl or tray.

8 minutes before put cheese biscuits in oven.

DINNER TIME As soon as guests are seated, place a filled papaya (from left side) on everyone's service plate. Immediately follow with the heated cheese biscuits. Turn oven off. When the papaya course is finished, the service and salad plates are removed and dinner plates set. Remove chicken, artichoke casserole, mushroom croquettes from oven; place on appropriate trays. Transfer sauces to serving bowls. Put croissants in oven to warm.

After this main course, clear the table. Serve the Celery Victor Salad. At dessert time, remove Charlotte Russe from the refrigerator, pipe with whipped cream, decorate with candied violets. Adjourn to the living room and serve the demitasse.

FORMAL TABLE SETTINGS

The usual number for formal and semiformal dinners is 12, because place settings of crystal, china and silverware come in 12, an even dozen. You may be lucky enough to have 3 or 4 dozen of any fine pattern. The average hostess is lucky to have an even dozen of all the formal place settings that belong on a formal dining table. (Some are inevitably lost or broken.) For that matter, the average hostess is lucky to have a table large enough to seat 12, even with extension inserts. Long formal dining tables are almost obsolete in today's smaller houses and more informal style of living. For that reason, and for a more relaxed ambience at formal dinners, I recommend using round tables seating 6 each, with the host at one table, the hostess at the other, and guest (or guests) of honor to the right as dictated by protocol.

There is no reason a formal dinner can't combine proper protocol in accoutrements and serving with a certain warmth and conviviality generally associated with more informal parties.

But by no means should the formal or semiformal dinner party be confused with the casual cocktail or buffet party.

NOT-SO-FORMAL DINNER

(For 12)

MENU

First Course
   Seafood-Stuffed Avocado
   Cucumber Canapés
Buffet
   Wine-Glazed Cornish Hens
   Eggplant Stuffed with Ham
   Wheat Pilaf
   Glazed Carrots
   Honey Beets
   Fruit Kabobs
   Potato Parker House Rolls
   Butter Curls
Dessert
   Lemon Angel Freeze
   Coffee, Tea

At an informal dinner, the first course is served to guests seated at the table, or tables. When the first course is finished, guests are then asked to get up and proceed to the buffet table to be served their main course. There definitely should be someone to serve them; the semiformal dinner should not have a self-help buffet. When the main course is finished, plates are removed and guests are served the dessert while remaining at their tables.

Incorporating the buffet into a semiformal dinner has certain advantages over the more proper formal sit-down (all the time) dinner. For one thing, of course, buffet tables, with their colorful and artistic arrangements of food platters and trays, certainly are more pleasing to look at than those individual platters (often too large) that must be passed around at formal sit-down dinners, and sometimes squeezed uncomfortably between you and the person next to you.

Moreover, it seems easier to get people up to the buffet table if the first course is sit-down. When it's finished, the host or hostess (or helper) merely gives the signal that guests must now step up to the buffet, and they do.

Protocol requires place cards at a formal dinner; I prefer them at a semiformal dinner as well, both for small and large groups.

Protocol also requires 3 glasses, for wine, water, and Champagne; and all place settings and china should match, or be of one pattern, at both the formal and semiformal dinner tables.

The two menus in this chapter are interchangeable, can be used for either the formal sit-down-only dinner, or the not-so-formal dinner by incorporating the buffet.

Both menus also lend themselves to larger groups by simply doubling or tripling the recipes; but in this case your party might come in the category of casual rather than formal unless you're loaded with all the proper formal accoutrements.

For that matter, you could plan formal and semiformal dinner parties with other menus in this book. The difference between formal and informal entertaining is not so much in the menu as in the style and manner of serving.

This not-so-formal dinner menu, with buffet main course, is still formal enough to justify bringing out your best china and silverware. With practically everything prepared in advance, except for last-minute heating, again you can plan to relax and be a guest at your own dinner party!

EQUIPMENT WORK SHEET FOR NOT-SO-FORMAL DINNER

tables and chairs (For both formal and semiformal dinners, I recommend
    2 round tables seating 6 each.)
tablecloths
dinner napkins
floral centerpiece for each table
silverware: forks, knives, teaspoons, butter spreaders, salad forks, dessert
    forks
water glasses
Champagne glasses and other wineglasses
salt and pepper shakers for each table
sugar and creamer for each table
cloth for buffet table
candles or candelabra for buffet table
serving tray for canapés
2 platters or trays for Cornish hens
3-quart casserole for pilaf
large round tray for vegetables, or separate vegetable dishes
large bowl or punch bowl for fruits
1 roll tray
glass bowl
serving pieces: large spoons, large forks
24-cup coffee maker
teapot
salad plates
dinner plates
bread and butter plates
dessert plates
cups and saucers
ashtrays (optional)

MARKETING WORK SHEET FOR NOT-SO-FORMAL DINNER

2 cups coffee cream
1 quart whipping cream
1½ pounds butter
¼ pound margarine
6 ounces Parmesan cheese
½ cup chicken fat or shortening
1 pound cooked crab meat
1 pound shrimps, 22 to 24 to the pound
12 Rock Cornish game hens
1 pound cooked ham
6 avocados
12 oranges
12 lemons
2 grapefruits
1 pineapple
½ pound seedless grapes, or 1 can (7 oz.) grapes
½ pound pitted dates
½ pound pitted prunes
1 pint fresh strawberries, or 1 jar (4 oz.) red maraschino cherries
24 medium-size carrots
5 onions
2 large eggplants
¾ pound fresh mushrooms
2 cucumbers
2 ounces shallots
1 head of lettuce
1 whole celery stalk
1 bunch of parsley
1 bunch of mint leaves
1 pound cracked wheat or bulgur
2 cans (29 oz. each) whole baby beets
2 cans (14 oz. each) chicken broth

1 can (10½ oz.) cream of chicken soup
1 jar (8 oz.) preserved kumquats
1 jar (4 oz.) green maraschino cherries
1 jar (4 oz.) red maraschino cherries
1 small jar of sweet pickles
1 pint mayonnaise
8 ounces orange-flavored honey
1 box (15 oz.) light raisins
3 packages (3¾ oz. each) lemon pudding and pie filling
4 ounces slivered blanched almonds
1 loaf of unsliced white sandwich bread
2 quarts bread cubes
1 baked angel-food cake, 14 ounces
1 bottle red Burgundy wine
1 bottle white wine
table wines

STAPLES LIST FOR NOT-SO-FORMAL DINNER

salt
pepper
dried thyme
dried sage
dillweed
ground ginger
garlic
sugar
light brown sugar (be sure you have at least ½ pound)
flour
packages of active dry yeast
chili sauce
canned tomato sauce
coffee
tea or tea bags

SEAFOOD-STUFFED AVOCADOS

12 Servings

See my notes on buying and using avocados in Chapter IV.

6 avocados
4 lemons, quartered
1 pound cooked crab meat
1 cup finely chopped celery
4 tablespoons mayonnaise
4 tablespoons chili sauce
2 teaspoons chopped sweet
 pickle

¼ teaspoon salt
1 pound shrimps, 22 to 24 to
 the pound, cooked and
 cleaned
1 head of lettuce

Split avocados into halves, carefully removing the large pit. Quarter 2 lemons and squeeze juice over cut surfaces of avocados to prevent them turning black.

Combine the crab meat with the next 5 ingredients. Pile into the cavities of the avocados. Divide the shrimps among the 12 filled avocados, overlapping the shrimps on the edges. Refrigerate until serving time. This preparation can be done about 2 hours in advance of serving.

To serve, core lettuce; place a large leaf on each salad plate. Set a stuffed avocado on center of lettuce. Cut remaining 2 lemons into 6 portions each. Place one alongside the stuffed avocado. Pass cucumber canapés for a refreshing accompaniment.

CUCUMBER CANAPÉS

24 Canapés

1 unsliced loaf of white sandwich bread
3 tablespoons mayonnaise
1 teaspoon grated onion

⅛ teaspoon dried dillweed
1 or 2 cucumbers, yielding 24
 slices

Cut bread lengthwise into 6 half-inch-thick slices. With a 2-inch round cutter cut 4 circles from each slice of bread. Place circles on a buttered cookie sheet and toast lightly in 400°F. oven for 8 to 10 minutes. Cool. (Note: Use some of bread for stuffing for Cornish Hens.)

Combine mayonnaise, onion and dillweed; spread on surfaces of toast rounds. Peel cucumbers, slice, and cut into rounds with the same cutter as used to make the toast rounds. Place a slice on each toast round. (Any cucumber larger than the bread round should be cut to fit.)

If made a few hours before serving, place on serving trays, cover with plastic wrap, and refrigerate.

WINE-GLAZED CORNISH HENS
12 Servings

½ cup chopped onion
4 tablespoons slivered blanched
   almonds
2 ounces butter
8 cups dry bread cubes
4 medium-size oranges, peeled
   and diced

½ cup light raisins
1 teaspoon salt
12 Rock Cornish Game hens, 1
   pound each
Salt, pepper, paprika
½ cup melted butter
Wine Glaze (recipe follows)

Cook onion and almonds in 2 ounces butter, stirring, for about 5 minutes. Toss with bread cubes, oranges, raisins and 1 teaspoon salt. Rinse hens; pat dry. Season with sprinkling of salt, pepper and paprika. Lightly stuff birds with the bread mixture; do not pack. Skewer shut; tie legs together; tie legs to tail. Place hens, breast side up, on a rack in shallow roasting pan. Brush with a little melted butter. Cover loosely. Roast in a preheated 375°F. oven for 30 minutes.

Uncover. Baste with wine glaze. Bake for 45 to 55 minutes longer, basting frequently. To make sure they are done, test whether drumstick can be twisted easily. (Preparations can be done in advance.)

Recipe Continues . . .

Wine Glaze   1¾ Cups

¼ pound butter or margarine   1 cup red Burgundy wine
¼ cup orange juice

Melt the butter in a small saucepan and pour in orange juice. Heat, then pour in wine. Keep the glaze warm but do not let it boil. Use to baste Cornish hens or other poultry.

EGGPLANT STUFFED WITH HAM   12 Servings

2 eggplants, cut lengthwise into halves
2 large onions, chopped
¾ pound fresh mushrooms, chopped
1½ ounces margarine
2 garlic cloves
½ teaspoon salt
½ teaspoon freshly ground pepper

¾ cup white wine
1½ cups diced cooked ham
3 tablespoons tomato sauce
¾ teaspoon sugar
¾ cup bread crumbs
1½ ounces butter
6 ounces Parmesan cheese, grated

Scoop out pulp of eggplants to within ½ inch of outer skin, leaving a boatlike shell. Set shells aside. Cut pulp into ½-inch cubes, immerse in cold water, and soak while preparing other ingredients of the filling.

Lightly sauté the onions and mushrooms in the margarine. With garlic press, add the garlic, and sauté for a few more minutes while adding the salt and pepper. Add the wine; simmer slowly for 5 minutes. Add the diced ham, tomato sauce and sugar, and stir to blend all the ingredients.

Drain and squeeze all water out of the eggplant pulp. Add to ham mixture; cook covered for 8 minutes. Season with more salt if necessary. Set eggplant shells in a baking pan. Stuff them with ham and eggplant mixture, rounding off the tops. Sprinkle with bread crumbs, dot with butter, and sprinkle with about half of the Parmesan cheese, reserving remainder to serve at the buffet. This preparation can be done the day before it is served. Bake in a preheated preheated 350°F. oven for 45 minutes.

To serve, set out on serving tray, preferably on a warming element, with a bowl of the remaining Parmesan cheese close by.

WHEAT PILAF

12 Generous servings

1 pound cracked whole-wheat kernels or bulgur
½ cup chicken fat (preferred) or other shortening
1 large onion, chopped
2 ounces shallots, chopped
2 cans (14 oz. each) chicken broth, heated

1 teaspoon salt
¼ teaspoon dried thyme
¼ teaspoon dried sage
1 can (10½ oz.) cream of chicken soup

Sauté the wheat in ¼ cup chicken fat or other shortening in a heavy-bottom pan with a cover. Stir constantly to prevent burning. When lightly browned, remove from heat. Set aside.

Sauté onion in remaining ¼ cup fat until opaque. Add chopped shallots, stirring constantly, until both vegetables are lightly browned. Combine with the cracked wheat or bulgur in a 3-quart casserole. Place over low heat. Add seasonings to heated broth, and slowly pour broth over wheat until all the liquid is absorbed. Cover, and cook over low heat for 20 minutes. Transfer to a 3-quart casserole. This can be made a few days ahead and refrigerated.

To serve, cover top of casserole with undiluted cream of chicken soup. Heat uncovered in a 350°F. oven for 30 to 35 minutes.

GLAZED CARROTS   12 Servings

24 medium-size carrots   ½ pound light brown sugar
2½ teaspoons salt   ⅛ teaspoon ground ginger
2 tablespoons butter   2 teaspoons lemon juice
1 tablespoon margarine   2 teaspoons grated lemon rind

Peel carrots. Cover with boiling water with 2 teaspoons salt in a covered saucepan and cook until just tender, 10 to 15 minutes. Drain. Melt butter and margarine in a large skillet; add brown sugar, ginger, lemon juice and rind and ½ teaspoon salt. Stir well, add carrots, and turn until well glazed. Transfer to an ovenproof serving dish with a cover.

This can be prepared 2 or 3 days in advance and refrigerated. Remove from refrigerator a few hours before serving. Let stand at room temperature. Reheat in a preheated 350°F. oven for 35 to 40 minutes.

To serve, use a large round tray; arrange carrots in a circular fashion, allow the center to remain free to fill with Honey Beets (following recipe). If serving carrots as a separate vegetable dish, fill center of tray with parsley and Grapefruit Flowers (p. 184).

HONEY BEETS   12 to 14 Servings

1½ ounces butter or margarine   2 oranges
¼ cup orange-flavored honey   2 cans (29 oz. each) whole baby
⅓ cup sugar   beets

Melt butter or margarine or a combination of both in a large saucepan. Add honey and sugar, stir to blend well, and cook over very low heat for 5 minutes. Wash and thinly slice oranges; remove seeds. Add to butter and honey mixture; remove from heat. Add drained beets. This preparation can be done several hours in advance.

To serve, place over low heat for 15 minutes, stirring occasionally. Spoon onto center of glazed carrot arrangement (preceding recipe). Drizzle every drop of honey glaze over the top for a delicious and shiny effect.

FRUIT KABOBS   16 Kabobs

1 fresh pineapple	2 grapefruits
½ pound pitted dates	1 pint fresh strawberries, or 1
2 oranges, sectioned into	jar (4 oz.) stemmed red
eighths	marashino cherries
½ pound seedless grapes, or 1	16 extra long bamboo skewers*
can (7 oz.) grapes	Crushed ice
1 jar (8 oz.) preserved kumquats	1 bunch of mint leaves
½ pound pitted prunes	
1 jar (4 oz.) stemmed green	
marashino cherries	

Peel and core pineapple and cut into chunks. Peel oranges and grapefruits and section into eighths. Cut prunes into halves; drain canned or jarred fruits; wash strawberries, leaving stems on.

Thread fruits on bamboo skewers in order listed above, ending with strawberries (stems left on) on top end. Gently push the fruit to top of skewer, leaving bottom section of skewer bare. Carefully lay the kabobs on cookie sheets and refrigerate until serving time. These can be made the day before and covered tightly with plastic wrap.

ARRANGEMENT: At serving time, fill a large bowl, such as a punch bowl, with finely crushed ice. Insert skewers into the crushed ice in a rather helter-skelter fashion. Lay sprigs of mint leaves on the ice at the base of the Fruit Kabobs.

*Available at most markets and party goods stores.

Recipe Continues .

To serve, use the tines of a fork to aid in lifting the skewers from the ice, keeping the fruit intact.

For the last items on this menu (bread, butter, and dessert), refer to other sections as follows:

Potato Parker House Rolls, Chapter IV, *Buffet Luncheon* (p. 121)

Butter Curls, Chapter III, *A Simple Brunch* (p. 55)

Lemon Angel Freeze, Chapter V, *Sweet Tooth Party,* (p. 148, 285)

FLO CHART FOR NOT-SO-FORMAL DINNER

THREE WEEKS BEFORE Mail or telephone invitations. Organize Equipment and Marketing Lists. Hire help. Check bar supplies, including wine for recipes as well as wines for serving with dinner.

TWO WEEKS BEFORE Buy staples. Order Cornish game hens. Bake and freeze Parker House rolls; prepare Lemon Angel Freeze.

ONE WEEK BEFORE Check hired help. Order floral centerpieces.

FOUR DAYS BEFORE Purchase avocados; if ripe, they should be refrigerated. If hard, allow 4 days to ripen. Prepare toast rounds for canapés; store in tightly covered cannisters.

THREE DAYS BEFORE Prepare Wheat Pilaf, butter curls.

TWO DAYS BEFORE Finish marketing.

ONE DAY BEFORE Prepare Eggplant Stuffed with Ham, Glazed Carrots, Honey Beets. Set up buffet and tables.

DAY OF THE PARTY In the morning, prepare Cornish hens; bake for 30 minutes. Let stand at room temperature. Remove all prepared items from refrigerator, Parker House rolls from freezer.

Two hours before arrange fruit on skewers. Fix Cucumber Canapés and crab-meat filling for avocados. Refrigerate. Halve avocados; squeeze lemons over them and refrigerate. Plug in coffeepot, keep warm.

45 minutes before put Cornish hens and stuffed eggplants in oven.

30 minutes before put pilaf in oven. Remove Lemon Angel Freeze from freezer; place on cutting board (it should be out at least an hour before serving).

15 minutes before warm carrots and Honey Beets on low heat. Set out butter curls and Parker House rolls on buffet table. Stuff avocados with crab meat; arrange each salad with the shrimps.

5 minutes before place avocados at each place, announce dinner. When guests are seated, pass Cucumber Canapés. Helper turns oven off, sets out platter of Fruit Kabobs on buffet, followed by main course. When guests have finished first course, they proceed to buffet table while helper removes the salad plates. Guests carry filled dinner plates to tables. Helper serves rolls and butter on bread-and-butter plates. Later helper serves Lemon Angel Freeze with coffee.

Note: Incidentally, this Cornish Hen menu is an excellent one to halve if you want a small intimate but elegant dinner party for 6. You may wish to try this before going more formal.

STRAWBERRIES

When cleaning strawberries, I prefer to leave the stem on. The little green touch is decorative. Wash them only an hour or two before using.

PART III

....

THE PARTY
CONNECTION

....

Chapter IX

....

Quiches and Crêpes

....

Up to now, I have planned all the menus for your parties. Now it's your turn.

I'm turning you loose with a number of recipes that can flow (no pun intended) in and out of any party plan. You should be able now to plan a menu, make out your own Equipment and Marketing Work Sheets, as well as those all-important timetables.

This section will deal only with *recipes* for separate dishes, not entire menus. The recipes range from main entrées through salads and desserts, from quiches and crêpes to tarts, tortes and trifles, with a lot of Favorites of the Famous included as a bonus for you to use as special party treats when you can fit them in.

In previous chapters you have learned how certain foods and flavors go together to complement each other, but there are no hard and fast rules. A great deal of the personal pleasure in cooking and planning a party comes from your own individual creating, improvising, and perhaps even *improving* on the original recipe or menu. So go right ahead. I don't mind at all if you throw out my suggestions (well—not *all* of them!) and substitute some of your own.

QUICHES

The quiche (pronounced keesh) is a French egg-custard pie that has zoomed to popularity in America in recent years as an hors-d'oeuvre and/or entrée delicacy. I think I was serving it a long time before it really became stylish, mainly because two of my clients wanted it, Frank Sinatra and Eva Gabor.

I started with my Mushroom Quiche for Sinatra because he was daffy for mushrooms. I had catered three parties for him in rapid succession and was running out of fresh ideas of things to do with fresh mushrooms, so I decided to put them into a quiche.

I first served my Mushroom Quiche as an hors-d'oeuvre. Now it has become a favorite main dish on party supper and dinner menus. I think the reaon is that more young people now are gung-ho vegetarians; they're into health foods, alfalfa sprouts, no meat. A quiche can be a very satisfying meal with the right salad, and no meat. In fact, I have discontinued making any kind of meat quiche; there's no demand for it. However, I have many special-order requests for a seafood quiche.

The real beauty of a quiche, quite apart from the fact that it happens to be mouth-watering delicious, is that it can be made ahead of time and put in your freezer. So, you can make one or two or five or ten, as the mood strikes you, and have them ready for your bridge party or for when your husband unexpectedly brings the boss home for dinner.

Important: The quiche must rest for 10 minutes after it is removed from the oven, which gives the cheese a chance to solidify and makes it easier to serve.

It tastes even better if made 2 to 4 days ahead of time and kept in the refrigerator, then reheated for 20 minutes before serving. The marriage of flavors will be much more pronounced.

It's best to cut the quiche while it's cold, before reheating.

This makes it easier to serve especially when used as finger food. My recipe makes a quiche so firm that it can be picked up with the fingers and put on a cocktail napkin. But there should be no problem in serving it from the dish as a main entrée, using a small spatula or cake knife, if you let it set out of the oven for 10 minutes.

Although a quiche *can* be frozen, I generally do not recommend it unless absolutely necessary, as it tends to lose some of its solidity in defrosting. However, if you choose to freeze it, then it is best to let it stand at room temperature, not in the refrigerator, until it is completely defrosted before heating. If an emergency requires you to take a quiche from the freezer and bake without defrosting, allow 1 to 1½ hours at 350°F. for it to be heated properly. I suggest also that you lay a sheet of foil loosely over the top of a frozen quiche during the first half hour of heating. In general, if you plan ahead properly, there should be no reason for you to freeze quiche, as it keeps quite well in the refrigerator for several days to a week.

PIECRUST (Pastry Shell)

Enough for one 9-inch deep single crust

If baking a piecrust overwhelms you, use the frozen ones from the market if you can find one deep enough. Most are too shallow. I prefer baking my own, and you'll find it's not all that difficult.

1 cup all-purpose flour	¼ cup ice water
½ cup shortening	pinch of salt

Combine flour and shortening with a pastry blender or 2 knives until tiny particles are formed. Add the ice water and salt. Stir until mixture forms a ball. Chill for at least 1 hour.

Roll out on a pastry cloth or floured board. Fit into quiche dish or round straight-sided cake pan. Trim ½ to 1 inch beyond edge. Fold excess under and flute the pastry edge. Prick bottom and sides with tines of a fork. Cover with a sheet of wax paper. Scatter

Recipe Continues . . .

on raw rice or beans to cover surface. This keeps the crust from puffing up. Bake in a preheated 350°F. oven for 7 minutes. Remove wax paper. Return to oven. Bake for 3 minutes longer. Cool.

MUSHROOM QUICHE
(A la Sinatra)

6 to 8 Servings

1 prebaked 9-inch pastry shell	1 ounce butter
2 cups grated Swiss or Jack cheese	½ teaspoon salt
½ pound mushrooms, chopped	⅛ teaspoon white pepper
3 shallots, chopped	4 eggs
1 tablespoon chopped green pepper	1¼ cups cream

Scatter half of the grated cheese on the bottom of the prebaked pastry shell. Combine the chopped mushrooms, shallots and green pepper. Sauté in the butter. Add seasonings. Cook gently for 8 to 10 minutes.

Combine eggs and cream. Beat together for about 2 minutes. Distribute the cooked mushroom mixture over the layer of grated cheese. Pour on the egg-cream mixture. Scatter the remaining half of grated cheese on top. Bake in a preheated 350°F. oven for 50 minutes. Remove from oven; let set for 10 minutes before serving.

After you've done it once, you'll see how simple it is to make 3 or 4 or more quiches for your larger parties.

Tips: If shallots are not available, substitute 1 garlic clove, *not* green onions, as they would change the flavor; and of course you know enough not to use canned or dried mushrooms, only fresh.

MUSHROOM DUXELLES

Duxelles is one of the terms of classic French cooking; it is the name of a mushroom mixture. It usually means finely chopped or minced mushrooms sautéed in butter with shallots. The shallot is a small onion shaped like garlic and with just a hint of garlic flavor, very delicate. This is why it is important *not* to substitute green onions if shallots are not available in your market. This mushroom quiche recipe requires a delicate garlic flavor, but not too strong. Substitute only 1 garlic clove for the 3 shallots if latter are not available.

When preparing mushrooms, remember they have a lot of water in them already, so after washing them, lay them out on a paper towel and lightly squeeze or pat so all the water comes out.

QUICHE AUX ESCARGOTS
(A la Eva)   6 to 8 Servings

Snails are not everyone's cup of tea so you should be sure of your guests' tastes before trying this one on them. But it was Eva Gabor's absolute favorite. The first time she asked me to cater a party for her, she told me, "I don't care what else you do, but just make sure you have the *escargots.*" It is rich and perhaps a little flamboyant for some parties, but surprisingly I have a lot of calls for it. I make it only on special order, and you may want it only for a special occasion.

1 prebaked 9-inch pastry shell	4 eggs
1½ cups grated Gruyère cheese	¾ cup cream
1½ ounces butter	¼ cup vermouth
2 shallots, minced	¼ teaspoon salt
2 garlic cloves, minced	⅛ teaspoon white pepper
4 ounces cooked snails (if canned, drain well)	¼ teaspoon seasoned salt

Scatter ¾ cup grated cheese on bottom of prebaked pastry shell. Melt the butter, add the shallots and garlic, and sauté for 5 minutes. Add the snails. Cook gently for 3 to 4 minutes. Scatter snail mixture over grated cheese layer. Beat eggs, cream and vermouth for 1 minute. Add seasonings. Beat for 1 minute. Pour over

Recipe Continues . . .

snails. Scatter on remaining ¾ cup grated cheese. Bake in a preheated 350°F. oven for 50 minutes. Remove from oven. Let set for
10 minutes before serving.

CLAM AND ANCHOVY QUICHE
6 to 8 Servings

This is another quiche you have to be careful about. Some people
just turn up their noses at clams and anchovies. Your guests will
either like it a lot or not eat it at all. But I've been told by many
that my clam and anchovy quiche is the tastiest of all. I think this
is because of what I call my "secret ingredient" that makes it
smell like corn-on-the-cob. Smell is very important in cooking and
entertaining. And many people just don't like the smell of fish,
especially seafoods such as clams. I use as my "secret ingredient"
a can of plain old store-bought creamed corn to disguise or eliminate the smell, or to transform it to that delicious aroma of corn-on-
the-cob. It really does make a difference in the taste, too.

1 prebaked 9-inch pie shell
1½ cups grated Swiss cheese
1 can or frozen package (6½
   oz.) clams, well drained
¼ cup cream-style corn
1 can (1½ oz.) flat anchovy fillets

4 eggs
1 cup cream
¼ teaspoon salt
⅛ teaspoon pepper

Scatter half of the grated cheese on the prebaked pastry shell.
Combine the drained clams, corn and anchovy fillets. Stir to combine. Spread over layer of cheese. Beat the eggs slightly. Add the
cream and seasonings. Beat for 1 minute. Pour over clam and
anchovy mixture. Scatter on top remaining ¾ cup of grated
cheese. Bake in a preheated 350°F. oven for 50 minutes. Remove
from oven. Let set for 10 minutes before cutting and serving.

FIESTA CHILI/CHEESE QUICHE

6 to 8 Servings

This is a very big favorite as an hors-d'oeuvre or main entrée at parties.

1 prebaked 9-inch pastry shell
1½ cups grated Swiss cheese
1 cup dry cottage cheese
2 ounce chopped green mild chilies
1 tablespoon chopped ripe olives

1 tablespoon flour
¼ teaspoon baking powder
¼ teaspoon salt
4 eggs
1 cup cream

Scatter ½ cup of grated Swiss cheese on the bottom of the prebaked pastry shell. Combine cottage cheese, chilies, olives, flour, baking powder and salt. Beat eggs and cream for 2 to 3 minutes. Stir into the chili-cheese mixture until well combined. Spread evenly over grated cheese layer. Scatter the remaining ½ cup of grated Swiss cheese on top. Bake in a preheated 350°F. oven for 1 hour. Remove from oven. Let stand for 10 minutes before serving.

SPINACH QUICHE

6 to 8 Servings

This is a standby favorite of confirmed vegetarians as well as those who simply want something deliciously meatless for a change.

1 prebaked 9-inch pie shell
2 cups grated Jack cheese
1½ ounces butter or margarine
1 medium-size onion, chopped
1 package (10 oz.) frozen spinach
½ teaspoon salt

¼ teaspoon pepper
½ teaspoon freshly grated nutmeg
½ teaspoon Pernod liqueur, or ¼ teaspoon anise extract
4 eggs
1 cup cream

Scatter 1 cup grated cheese in prebaked pastry shell. Melt butter or margarine in medium-size frying pan. Add the onion and cook for

Recipe Continues . .

10 to 15 minutes, or until onion is tender but not brown. Set aside. Cook spinach in a saucepan until tender; do not overcook. Drain and squeeze until all visible water is removed. Stir into the sautéed onion. Add the seasonings, liqueur or extract. Spread mixture over layer of grated cheese. Beat the eggs slightly. Add the cream and beat for 2 minutes. Pour over the spinach mixture. Scatter on remaining 1 cup of grated cheese. Bake in a preheated 350°F. oven for 55 to 60 minutes. As with the other quiches, allow to stand for 10 minutes before cutting and serving.

WHAT TO SERVE WITH QUICHE

Quiche is a deliciously satisfying meal of mostly proteins—eggs, cheese, milk—and it needs only a beautiful and tasty salad to complement it, though I often also suggest croissants. You can buy these at your favorite French bakery, or if you're feeling energetic, follow my recipe for croissants on page 221. Perhaps you're wondering why I would recommend any kind of bread-roll when the quiche itself has a pastry shell. But its crust should be tissue-thin, like paper; and croissants should be feathery light. Quiche and croissants just seem to go together.

As for a salad, you can serve either a beautiful fruit platter, and go as wild as you like on this with anything that is in season: grapefruits, oranges, fresh pineapple, melons, strawberries, or serve a salad of mixed greens, tossed with finely chopped red onion and a small can of mandarin oranges, chilled and drained. If you want dessert, keep it light—a parfait, sherbet, or a half papaya squirted with juice of a fresh lime.

CRÊPES

Nothing is more party fun than crêpes when you learn how to do them. Nothing is more versatile. From hors-d'oeuvre to desserts, for breakfast, brunch, luncheon, teatime, cocktail hour through the most formal dinners, these crazy little pancakes (for that's really what they are) all gussied up in party finery, could give some stiff competition to quiches, casseroles, and other convertibles for entertaining.

They're marvelous as main entrées (brunches, luncheons), they make fabulous desserts, and they're perfect for informal do-it-yourself entertaining.

THE PROPER PAN FOR CRÊPES
Crêpes have become so popular that there are now on the market many different types of pans in which to prepare them. So okay, maybe I'm just old-fashioned but I'm still using the one I bought in a Palm Springs hardware store twenty years ago; and with all due respect to the new-fangled pans of the crêpes craze, I still think mine is the best.

It's a black, heavy iron skillet that has never been washed since its initial "seasoning," and I've never had a crêpe that didn't just slide right out of it. Whoosh!

So buy yourself a crêpe pan, and carefully follow the instructions on "seasoning."

SEASONING AN IRON CRÊPE PAN
Scrub the new iron pan with steel wool and scouring powder. Rinse thoroughly and dry completely. Fill the pan almost to the rim with vegetable oil. Set the pan over medium heat and heat it until the oil begins to smoke. Remove pan from heat and let it stand overnight with the oil in it. Next day discard the oil and wipe out the pan with paper towels. If the paper towels are not clean, pour in 3 tablespoons oil and 2 tablespoons salt and scrub the pan again. Discard oil and salt, then once again fill with oil, heat to smoking, cool overnight, and once again wipe clean with paper towels. From this time, do not wash the pan with water or any kind of soap, simply wipe clean with a paper towel after each use. Reserve this pan only for crêpes. Do not use it for frying bacon, scrambling eggs, or any other use. Also, very important, do not

touch the pan with a fork. The grooves made by a fork scratching the surface of the pan can ruin your crêpes. Batter sinks into the grooves and makes it difficult to turn out the finished crêpe. If your recipe requires crêpes browned on both sides, use a wooden spatula to flip the crêpe over, or turn by hand so quickly that your fingers are not burned. If you have a well-seasoned crêpe pan, you will have no problem turning out the finished crêpe; it will slide out as soon as browned.

CRÊPE BATTER   65 Crêpes

6 eggs	2 cups milk
1½ cups flour	1 tablespoon melted butter
½ teaspoon salt	

Count on 2 crêpes per person, with a few extra.

Optional: Grated orange rind: For most crêpes I like to add just that little extra touch of grated orange rind in the batter, especially for fruit fillings such as apple, pineapple, cherry or strawberry. It's also a nice extra touch for your cheese blintzes, as well as for crab crêpes.

To make batter, break eggs into blender or medium-size bowl if you're using a rotary beater. Combine flour and salt. Add dry ingredients, alternating with the milk, mixing continuously. Add butter and orange rind.

Refrigerate batter. *Important:* The most important step in the success of the batter itself is to *refrigerate it.* I suggest letting the batter rest in the refrigerator for 2 to 4 hours, or longer. Better yet, if possible, make the batter a day ahead of time. It's so much better, and it will stick far less if you refrigerate it overnight. It will thicken a little, but that's fine. Just add a little more milk to the batter to thin it to the consistency of a heavy cream, no more than that.

When you're ready to use the batter, stir vigorously again. Then start cooking in your well-seasoned, nonstick, preheated skillet. Be sure skillet is hot enough; test it with dancing water drops. Be sure to tilt skillet as you pour the batter from a lipped pourer. Be sure to cook for only 15 to 20 seconds until the edges are slightly brown. Be sure to loosen the crêpe, slide it out easily, stack finished crêpes gingerly. Now they're ready to serve if your fillings are ready, or to prepare for freezing.

HOW TO REFRIGERATE, FREEZE AND DEFROST CRÊPES

Put small pieces of wax paper between each crêpe so they don't stick together. Stack in bundles of 10 or 12. Wrap well with foil so there's no chance of a freezer burn, or drying out at the edges. Because they're so thin, the edges will have a tendency to dry even at room temperature unless they are very well covered. If crêpes are properly separated with wax paper, stacked and well wrapped with foil, there should be no problem in storing these neat little bundles in your freezer.

There should be no problem either when you're ready to un-freeze them. Simply put the foil-wrapped packages in a 225°F. oven for 15 to 20 minutes; remove, let them stand for 10 minutes, and you'll be able to separate them easily.

Alternative: It isn't necessary to freeze crêpes for future use. You can follow this same prefreezing procedure—separate with wax paper, wrap with foil—and simply stick in the refrigerator where they'll keep for several days. I have often kept mine in the refrigerator for as long as 10 days without freezing them.

ANOTHER ALTERNATIVE: BAKED CRÊPES:

Real honest-to-gosh crispy crêpes, of course, are *always* fried on top of the stove and on hot burners. The word "fried" is now anathema to health cults. For those who want no truck with frying pans or my old-fashioned skillet, I can recommend, albeit reluc-tantly, oven-baked pancakes, or do-it-the-easy-way crêpes. There's nothing to it after you've made the batter. Just pour the circlets on a well-buttered cookie sheet, stick in a 350°F. oven and bake for 5 minutes.

FILLINGS FOR CRÊPES

The marvelous thing about crêpes is the way they can be changed by the kinds of fillings you use and the accompaniments, for so many varied occasions.

For a do-it-yourself crêpe party with wine and cheese, for example, you could have several bowls of different fillings—seafoods, fruits, and nut-flavored concoctions such as almond cream filling for your guests to choose from. Your stacks of already-made frozen or refrigerated and reheated crêpes should be placed on a platter surrounded by the bowls of fillings, so guests can help themselves and roll up their own crêpes. They'll have a ball!

If you're using the crêpes as a main entrée for an informal party, it could be complemented with an appropriate salad, such as The Day Before Salad. (The recipe is at the end of this chapter.)

CRAB FILLING

Enough for 30 crêpes

1½ ounces butter	1¼ teaspoons white pepper
½ cup flour	½ cup dry vermouth
2½ cups hot milk	2 cans (7½ oz. each) crab meat,
½ teaspoon salt	drained

Melt butter in heavy-bottomed pan. Gradually stir in flour. Cook the thick paste for 2 minutes, stirring constantly. Add the hot milk slowly, using a wire whisk to beat to a smooth consistency. Add seasonings. Remove from heat and slowly beat in the vermouth. Remove cartilage from crab meat. Crumble crab into sauce and stir together. Fill crêpes, bake, and place on the serving tray that is to be set on electric warmer.

I have never served these without hearing the same raves, "Divine! Divine!" That makes it worth all the trouble.

Important Note: Unfrozen crêpes should first be placed on

well-buttered cookie sheets and warmed in a 400°F. oven for 15 minutes before being filled and served. Also put 1 tablespoon filling on the front edge of crêpe and roll rather tightly, not turning in the sides so they will be long and narrow.

You can substitute other seafoods for the crab meat, such as shrimp, lobster or even tuna.

APPLE FILLING

Enough for 20 to 22 crêpes

8 medium-size apples (Pippin or McIntosh), pared and cubed
¼ pound butter or margarine
6 tablespoons brown sugar
1 teaspoon ground cinnamon
3 tablespoons granulated sugar
1 teaspoon vanilla extract

1 tablespoon sherry or brandy (If you do not wish to use an alcoholic seasoning, substitute apple juice or apple cider.)
Juice and grated rind of 1 medium-size orange

Sauté apples in butter or margarine only to the point where they're translucent. Add brown sugar and cinnamon. When this is melted in with the apples, add granulated sugar, stir, and cook for only a minute or two longer. Remove from heat. Add vanilla, sherry, orange juice and rind. Let cool. Put 1 tablespoon of filling on a crêpe about ½ inch from the front edge and roll it one full turn. Turn the sides in and continue rolling. Press crêpe down slightly and place seam side down on a buttered cookie sheet.

When you're ready to serve, heat crêpes in 350°F. oven for, about 20 minutes, until they're warm inside. Both crêpes and apple filling should be warm when served. They're marvelous to keep on hand in your freezer but allow plenty of time for the apples to thaw out. Serve with vanilla sauce (from a package of vanilla pudding) with a little rum flavoring. Yummy!

PINEAPPLE AND APRICOT FILLING

1 small to medium-size pineapple, peeled
3 ounces butter
½ cup rum or sherry, or pineapple juice

¼ teaspoon rum or vanilla extract
½ cup apricot preserves

Cut pineapple into small chunks. Sauté pineapple in butter; add flavoring, then add apricot preserves. The pineapple and apricot combination is delightful. Mix and cook together until pineapple is tender. Cool. Roll into crêpes. This too can be made and frozen for future use.

CHERRY FILLING

1 cup cherry preserves
¼ cup Cherry Heering liqueur or cherry wine

Juice and grated rind of 1 lemon

Nothing much to this. Just heat together the cherry preserves, cherry liqueur or wine, lemon juice and rind, and voila! A quick filling for a different kind of crêpe. Also good for your freezer bank.

Important: When freezing crêpes with fillings, be sure to use the wax-paper separations and wrap well with aluminum foil. Even with the fillings crêpes are still small enough to store and freeze in quantities of 10 to 20 to a package, so when people pop in unexpectedly you'll be ready for them with a real party-time treat.

THE DAY BEFORE SALAD

10 to 12 Ample servings

This is one of those hard-to-classify but so easy-to-do salads that can be made the day before and remain fresh, crisp and delicious for your party. Try it with your crab crêpes or a quiche, or incorporate it into a buffet luncheon or dinner party. It might almost make a main dish for salad aficionados.

1 pound fresh spinach (usually sold in a bunch)
1 head of red-leaf or butter lettuce
1 head of iceberg lettuce
2 packages (2 oz. each) herb-flavored salad dressing mix
2 cups mayonnaise

2 cups sour cream
1 package (10 oz.) frozen peas, thawed
1 bunch of green onions, chopped
4 hard-cooked eggs, grated
½ pound bacon, cooked crisp and crumbled
1 cup grated Cheddar cheese

Wash all the greens and dry thoroughly. Tear into small pieces; toss together. Place half of the greens in the bottom of an oblong dish, 11 x 9 x 2½ inches, or 13 x 7 x 2½ inches. Combine herb dressing. Mix mayonnaise and sour cream. Spread half of the mixture on the mixed greens. Scatter on the peas, green onions, grated eggs and crumbled bacon. Cover with remaining mixed greens. Spread remaining mayonnaise mixture on top. Distribute the grated cheese evenly over the top. Cover with plastic wrap. Refrigerate overnight. Serve cold, cut into squares.
Note: The thawed, uncooked peas help keep it more crisp than the average salad.

CHAPTER X

. . . .

Favorites Of The Famous

. . . .

So many people have asked me what it's like to cater parties for some of these Very Important People, public figures such as His Royal Highness Prince Philip and that other HRH of the entertainment world, Sinatra. Aren't they extremely difficult to please?

On the contrary. I have found that the more important they are, the nicer they are. And while this is a party book and I have no wish to become embroiled in personality controversies, I would like to go on record here as stating unequivocally that, in spite of his public image, Frank Sinatra is one of the most considerate and generous persons I have ever had the pleasure of working for—and I have catered many of his parties.

As for Prince Philip, he was an absolute doll!

PRINCE PHILIP'S ROYAL REPAST

My menus for Prince Philip were planned with his Colonel, who approved and accepted every one of my suggestions, including

256

serving California wine instead of French wine. I purposely wanted him to have American rather than European food and menus. He was charming and enthusiastic about some of the dishes; he told me he had never tasted French Fried Cauliflower before; he was most interested in my Wheat Pilaf and Date Ramaki.

I had to plan all the breakfast, luncheon, and dinner menus for three days, plus a banquet for 250, the big event of their stay. The banquet for 250 was held at 1 o'clock in the afternoon—a lunchtime hour, but I was asked to serve a dinner menu.

The setting was in the lush gardens and terrace, the rather formal patio and pool area of the private home where the Prince and his entourage were staying. I had arranged to have umbrella tables for the guests, with yellow-and-white-striped umbrellas, white tablecloths fringed in yellow, and floral decorations of yellow and white. The florist did a beautiful job, turning the entire area into a sunburst display.

In a shaded area on the upper level of the patio I had one table set up banquet style for ten people. This was intended for the Prince and other dignitaries such as the Mayor, and some celebrities, including Danny Kaye, who, as it turned out, was apparently quite chummy with the Prince. I had gone to a great deal of trouble to try to make my Royal Banquet Table a little nicer than the others. I had brought my own sterling silver from home, my best china, and had personally supervised an especially beautiful arrangement of flowers. All of the tables looked very pretty, of course, but this one was extraspecial. Can you blame me?

At the appropriate time, when we had everything on the buffet tables and the hosts gave the green light, we asked the Colonel to invite the Prince, who made his royal entrance to the buffet table with Danny Kaye in tow, or vice versa. They were the first two in line. The Prince seemed royally impressed with many of the arrangements, particularly a long tray laden with freshly cut California fruits—melons, strawberries, citrus, etc. He had a great curiosity, asked many questions as he went down the buffet line looking everything over.

Meanwhile, busy with other things, I turned my back for a moment, and looked up to see—to my horror—His Royal Highness and Danny Kaye heading for a little table for two stuck in the farthest corner of the patio. It didn't even have an umbrella over it! The Prince and Danny seemed so absorbed in their own tête-à-tête that no one else had the nerve to interrupt or join them.

Of course I was disappointed. But even more so, I'm sure, were those who had looked forward to sitting ringside at Prince Philip's banquet table. They probably could have cheerfully wrung Danny Kaye's neck.

The next day the Prince was treated to a tour of a Hollywood movie studio where Danny Kaye was making a picture. A luncheon was held for him on the studio lot. I wasn't there but I got a first-hand report from some who were. During lunch, the Prince leaned over to Danny and said, "Listen, if you have any interest in this studio, you'd better get that little lady from Palm Springs to come in and teach them a few things about cooking."

It made my day!

You won't need all the menus I planned for Prince Philip. Here are a few of his favorites to work into your own.

A ROYAL BREAKFAST

Grapefruit Bar-le-Duc
Salmon Steaks in Fluffy Sauce
Cheesy Crispy Potatoes
Baked Tomatoes
Assorted thin toast
Butter Curls
Yorkshire Fruit Loaves
Coffee and hot milk

GRAPEFRUIT BAR-LE-DUC

If you're lucky enough to live in Palm Springs, in the Coachella Valley known for its citrus orchards, you take grapefruit for granted. But most good markets everywhere nearly always have grapefruit available, from Texas, California, or Florida, even sometimes those delicious Texas pinks.

Cut chilled grapefruits into halves. Remove seeds and cut around each section of pulp close to the membraneous walls or partitions. With a serrated grapefruit knife, carefully free the membrane from the sides and bottom of the skin; lift it out, leaving the pulp in place. Put a spoonful of Bar-le-Duc currant preserves in the center. Serve well chilled.

SALMON STEAKS IN FLUFFY SAUCE 10 Servings

3 pounds fresh salmon steaks, ¾ inch thick	½ cup grated Cheddar cheese
1 cup mayonnaise	3 egg yolks
2 tablespoons drained sweet pickle relish	1½ teaspoons salt
	3 egg whites
	Lemon wedges

Preheat oven to 350°F. Butter well 1 large or 2 medium-size baking pans. Lay fish in a single layer in the pans. Bake uncovered for 10 minutes. Cool. (This can be done a few hours ahead.)

Combine mayonnaise with remaining ingredients except the egg whites and lemon wedges. Beat the whites until stiff enough to hold in peaks. Carefully fold into the mayonnaise mixture. Completely cover fish with sauce. Bake until cheese topping is firm and golden brown in color. This should take about 45 minutes. Set the baking pan on a serving tray as it is difficult to transfer the fish and keep the beautiful soufflé-fluffy topping intact.

Surround with lemon wedges. Serve immediately. I sincerely hope your guests will enjoy this dish as much as the Prince did.

Recipe Continues . . .

Although he had it for breakfast, it's an excellent dish for brunch, luncheon, a buffet supper or dinner party.

CHEESY CRISPY POTATOES   10 Servings

3½ cups grated raw potatoes
6 ounces butter, melted
3 eggs
2 teaspoons chopped chives or tops of scallions
1 teaspoon salt

½ teaspoon pepper
½ teaspoon paprika
¾ cup milk
¾ cup grated sharp Cheddar cheese

Drain and squeeze potatoes to remove any water. Mix potatoes with the melted butter. Beat eggs, add chives and seasonings, and mix well with the potato-butter mixture. Place in a well-buttered casserole and pour the milk over all. Preheat oven to 350°F. Bake for 40 minutes. Remove from oven and sprinkle with grated cheese. Return to oven and bake until the cheese melts and turns a golden brown. Serve immediately.

Important note: With this recipe it's always advisable to have all your ingredients right there and handy so your raw potatoes won't turn black. The casserole can be made several hours ahead (potatoes won't turn black after they're cooked) or even the day before. It won't have the fluffiness of the freshly made dish but will have all the flavor. This is another one of those convertibles that can be served for breakfast, luncheon, or dinner.

BAKED TOMATOES   10 Servings

5 large beefsteak tomatoes
2 ounces butter or margarine, melted
1½ teaspoons fine herb seasoning

½ teaspoon salt
1 teaspoon garlic powder
2 teaspoons ground coriander
1 teaspoon ground cuminseed
1 cup bread crumbs

Preheat oven to 350°F. Wash and stem the tomatoes and cut cross-wise into halves. Lay cut side up in a shallow baking dish. Combine all other ingredients. Spread surfaces of tomatoes with this mixture. This can be done a few hours ahead. Bake uncovered for 20 minutes, or until lightly browned. Tomatoes should remain firm enough to handle in serving, yet tender enough to eat with a fork. Transfer to a shallow serving bowl. Serve while hot and puffy.

YORKSHIRE FRUIT LOAVES   2 Loaves

1 cup milk	1 teaspoon salt
¼ pound butter	1 teaspoon ground ginger
2 ounces margarine	½ teaspoon ground mace
1 teaspoon and 1 cup sugar	1 cup sultana raisins
1 cake of compressed fresh yeast	½ cup seedless raisins
or 1 package active dry yeast	1 cup dried currants
3 eggs	½ cup candied citron peel
6 cups flour	1 cup English walnuts

Scald the milk and pour half of it into a mixing bowl. Add butter and margarine and stir until melted. Pour remaining milk into a small bowl and allow to cool to lukewarm (80° to 90°F.) if using fresh yeast, and moderately warm (105° to 115°F.) for dry yeast. Add the 1 teaspoon sugar and the yeast. Set aside until foamy. Beat the eggs well, gradually add the 1 cup sugar, and blend well. Add this mixture to the milk and melted butter in mixing bowl. Add dissolved yeast and beat all together well. Combine dry ingredients and sift into yeast mixture. Beat well. Cover dough with a damp towel and let rise at room temperature until doubled, about 2 hours.

While dough is rising, place all the fruits except citron in a colander over hot water and steam for 10 minutes. Turn out onto paper towels and pat dry. Chop together with the citron and walnuts. When dough has risen, punch down and beat into it the

Recipe Continues . . .

chopped fruits and nuts. Divide dough into 2 well-greased loaf pans, cover, and let rise for 1 hour.

Bake in a preheated 325°F. oven for 1½ hours, until loaves are golden and shrink slightly from the sides of pans. Remove to cooling rack. Let stand for 10 minutes before removing from pans. Cool well before slicing. As a matter of fact, these loaves should be made a day ahead before serving. They can be sliced more easily and the fruits will "ripen," enhancing the already delightful flavor of the loaves.

DATE RAMAKI

This is something I invented many years ago when I had to do a party for a date growers' convention and was trying to think of everything possible I could make out of dates. Simply fill a pitted date with a small piece of pineapple, fresh or canned; wrap bacon around it, and broil. The saltiness of the bacon cuts the sweetness of the date, a surprise sweet-salt blend that people love. Prince Philip flipped for it!

SINATRA'S MUSHROOM KICK

I have already given you my recipe for Mushroom Quiche (p. 244), which I often made especially for Sinatra. There are two other mushroom dishes I created for him, good for anyone else who may love mushrooms as much as he does. One is Mushroom-Stuffed Mushrooms, which I made for 500 guests—and that's a lot of mushrooms!—at a wedding reception for golf pro Ken Venturi and his bride, which Sinatra hosted.

Frank's generosity on this occasion was quite evident. He gave me *carte blanche* to cater the reception, with only one instruction: He wanted the best. And he got it! I was quite pleased with the whole setting. It was both romantic and spectacular. Frank arrived a few minutes ahead of the guests, surveyed the scene, gave me a great big smack on the cheek, and said, "Thanks! It's great! You're great!"

You'd be surprised at how many people forget to say thanks. Not Sinatra. He later pulled me aside and asked what I had inside the mushrooms. "Your favorite, mushrooms," I told him. He grinned and said, "Terrific!"

A couple of months later, for his birthday in December, songwriter Jimmy Van Heusen and his wife gave a party in his honor at their home and asked me to come in and cater it. What could I do for an encore, after giving him mushrooms stuffed with mushrooms? I was, as they say, in a twit. So I wracked my noodle and came up with strudel, if you'll pardon the poetic license. I took some license, too, with my mother's old-fashioned recipe for apple strudel. I substituted mushrooms for apples. Why not?

I was in the kitchen gathering the ingredients for after-dinner Café Brûlot when Mrs. Van Heusen rushed in and said, "Please, quick! You must come out to the dining room. Mr. Sinatra wants to see you."

My first reaction was, Oh, no! I'd been there for hours, I must look like a mess, I should freshen my lipstick, fix my hair. But Mrs. Van Heusen wouldn't let me waste a second. She literally propelled me into the dining room, and there was Frank already standing with a glass of Champagne in his hand. When he saw me, he said to everyone, "Stand up. Let's drink a toast to Florence for this fabulous dinner, and here's an extra toast to her Mushroom Strudel!"

It's the only time in my life I ever received a standing ovation.

Later I was invited to join the guests and listen to Jimmy Van Heusen play his latest composition, which he had written especially for Sinatra, as he has many other songs that Sinatra has made famous, including "Chicago," "All the Way," "Nancy," and many others. As I watched Jimmy Van Heusen play the song and then hand his sheet music to Frank, I couldn't help thinking, this is how a song is born. For the life of me I can't even remember the song, except that it was something about a lonely man in a bar. I wasn't concentrating on the words or the music. I still had tingles all over from that standing ovation.

MUSHROOM STRUDEL À LA SINATRA

15 Pieces, 3 inches wide

Strudel dough and directions for stretching this dough are the same as given for the Apple Strudel (p. 267).

Mushroom Filling

3 medium-size onions, chopped	1 tablespoon salt
1½ pounds butter	2 cups bread crumbs
2½ pounds fresh mushrooms, chopped	

Sauté the onions in ½ pound of butter in a large frying pan. Cook until shiny, 8 to 10 minutes. Add the chopped washed mushrooms, including the stems. Add salt. Stir and cook for 5 minutes so that the mushrooms are only partially cooked. Remove from heat.

Melt remaining 1 pound of butter. Use ½ cup of melted butter to coat generously a baking pan or cookie sheet approximately 15 x 18 inches and ½ inch deep.

After dough has been fully stretched (directions, pp. 267–268), pour remaining butter over the entire surface. Scatter the bread crumbs over the buttered surface. Then scatter the mushrooms on in the same manner as the apples for the apple strudel. Roll, shape, and bake as for apple strudel.

Serve warm.

This strudel freezes very well. When ready to use, remove from freezer a day ahead and allow to defrost, then refrigerate until time to heat. Heat in a preheated 350°F. oven for 20 minutes.

If made a day or two in advance, strudel will keep well in the refrigerator. Heat as above.

The perfect strudel if you're off your noodle for mushrooms!

MUSHROOM-STUFFED MUSHROOMS À LA SINATRA

6 to 8 Servings

16 large fresh mushrooms
2 ounces butter or margarine
2 tablespoons chopped onion
1 garlic clove, minced
1 large celery rib, finely
    chopped

¼ teaspoon salt
⅛ teaspoon pepper
⅛ teaspoon grated nutmeg
½ cup dry bread crumbs
½ cup grated Parmesan cheese

Wash mushrooms. Remove stems by merely twisting them off. Chop stems and set aside. Melt butter or margarine in a medium to large frying pan. Add the chopped stems, onion, garlic, celery and seasonings. Cook for 10 minutes, or until the juices are almost ready to evaporate. Place mushroom caps, web side up, in a shallow baking dish. Fill cavities with chopped mushroom stems and vegetable mixture. Combine bread crumbs and cheese; sprinkle over filling. Set aside until ready to use.

When made a day ahead, cover with plastic wrap and refrigerate. Broil 4 to 5 inches from the source of heat for 6 to 7 minutes, or until tops become brown and bubbly.

KIRK DOUGLAS'S APPLE STRUDEL

Two of the nicest clients I ever had were Anne and Kirk Douglas. She's a very good cook in her own right but she always made me feel that whatever I prepared was so special. I don't suppose Kirk spends any more time in the kitchen than it takes to walk through it to the garage. But he and I had a little thing going. He always told his guests that *he* made the apple strudel. I never let on that he was spoofing. They're a very warm, affectionate family, and as far as I'm concerned Kirk can take credit for my mother's apple strudel any time he wants to.

And so can a few fine chefs in and around Vienna!

Several years ago I spent the summer in Europe with the sole purpose of learning things that would add a bit of a European touch to my menus. I was staying in a hotel about halfway between Salzburg and Vienna and spending a lot of time observing the chefs in the kitchen. They were very friendly, welcomed me in at any time, and so it happened that one very busy morning as I stood by quietly observing, the manager of the hotel ran in frantically waving his arms and sputtering.

The president, the chairman of the board, and all the directors of the corporation that owned that hotel, along with a whole string of the finest hotels in Austria, were on their way, arriving in the early afternoon, within about two hours. He beseeched the poor chefs to hurry up and make something special. With the sole purpose of wanting to be helpful, and totally unaware of the incongruity of my proposal, I volunteered to make apple strudel. The manager looked at me aghast. In the first place, I was a woman, which was obviously *verboten* in their kitchen. In the second place, I was an American offering to make the Austrian native dish!

After his initial shock, he was polite about it. And so I proceeded to make my mother's apple strudel.

It turned out fine, dinner was served, with my strudel for dessert. I was chatting away in my broken German with the chefs when the manager came running in, grabbed my arm, pulled me into the dining room and introduced me to all those very distinguished hotel men. They were quite extravagant in their praise of my apple strudel and surprised me with an invitation to come and spend a week or so at one of their hotels in Vienna, one of the finest in Europe, as their guest!

The invitation had only two strings attached: (1) I was to demonstrate to their chefs how I prepared the strudel; and (2) Please, would I not tell *anybody* when I returned home that I, an American, had shown the Austrians how to make their favorite dessert.

Well, I've kept their secret all these years, which is long enough for any woman to keep a secret.

APPLE STRUDEL

**2 Strudels,
32 servings**

Strudel Dough

4 cups sifted flour
2 teaspoons salt
3 eggs, at room temperature

1 cup water
6 tablespoons vegetable oil

Apple Filling

¾ pound butter, melted
6 ounces vanilla cookies or ani-
mal crackers, finely crushed
1½ cups sugar
2 teaspoons ground cinnamon
½ teaspoon grated nutmeg

Grated rind of 2 lemons
5 pounds cooking apples,
peeled and cut into small
cubes
1 pint strawberry preserves
Powdered sugar

Sift flour and salt onto a bread board or other wooden surface. With the fist, make a well in the center, building up the sides. Lightly beat the eggs; gradually add the water and the oil to the eggs. Slowly pour this mixture into the center of the flour mound, incorporating some of the flour as it is added. When all the liquid has been used, there should be a sticky mass of dough. With floured hands, lift the dough and holding it high above the head, throw it hard onto the board. Repeat flouring the hands each time until dough can be handled without sticking to them. Throw the dough about 20 times, or until smooth and elastic. Place dough on center of a lightly floured tablecloth covering a table approximately 6 x 3 feet. Cover with an inverted bowl which has been warmed by rinsing with hot water and then well dried. Let dough rest for 1½ hours. During this time, prepare filling.

Remove bowl, taking care not to bump against the dough. Gently roll dough with lightly floured rolling pin from center outward in all directions until the dough is slightly thinned. Gently lift the dough to make certain it is not adhering to the tablecloth. With the back of the hands, stretch the dough, a little at a time, working

Recipe Continues . . .

from the center all around the table so that the dough is stretched in 4 directions. Anchor the dough on one of the corners of the table and continue stretching until the entire table top is covered with the now very thin dough. Trim off all overhanging dough. Carefully brush on half of the melted butter. Scatter cookie crumbs over entire surface. Mix the sugar, cinnamon and nutmeg, and scatter over the dough with the lemon rind. Cut down center to divide dough into 2 strudels.

Using three quarters of the cubed apples, make a thick row at edge along the length of the table; scatter remaining quarter of apples over remaining surface. Spoon the strawberry preserves, in small dabs, onto the apples. Turn in the 4 sides of the tissue-thin dough. Grasp tablecloth with both hands held up high and allow the strudel to roll into shape as you lift the tablecloth and draw it away from you. Using half of remaining butter, generously butter 2 cookie sheets. Carefully lift strudels into pans. Fashion into a horse-shoe shape. Lightly brush tops with remaining melted butter. Bake in a preheated 375°F. oven for 40 minutes.

These strudels can be frozen or baked a few days in advance and refrigerated. In either case, it is most important that the strudels be heated slightly so they can be served warm and thereby bring out their marvelous aroma and buttery flavor.

To serve, sprinkle generously with powdered sugar. Cut into 1½-inch slices.

Should you have a commercial oven which will accommodate a pan 26 x 17 inches, do not cut the stretched dough in half; make 1 large strudel.

MY HAWAIIAN CHICKEN

This is the *Hawaiian Chicken* I had to send out an SOS for on the night I ran out of Jolie Gabor's Hungarian Goulash. It's one of my all-time favorite party entrées, and I've often served it for some of my all-time favorite hosts and hostesses.

My *Hawaiian Chicken* can serve as the main entrée for informal buffet dinners as well as for more casual entertaining. It is especially appropriate for a "theme" party, especially if the theme is an Hawaiian luau, where guests can come in bright shirts and muu-muus. Also it's an excellent recipe to have on hand if you just want to have another couple, or two or three, over for dinner and you're fresh out of chicken ideas.

HAWAIIAN CHICKEN   10 Servings

2 broiler-fryer chickens, 2½ to   8 cloves
   3 pounds each, quartered   4 bay leaves
2 teaspoons salt   1 celery rib
2 onions

Place cut-up chicken in a large pot. Sprinkle with salt. Add water to cover. Stick 4 cloves in each onion; add to the pot along with the bay leaves and celery. Bring to a boil, cover, and simmer for 45 minutes, or until tender. Remove chicken and cool. Strain broth; set aside. Discard the vegetables and bay leaves.

Remove bones and skin from chicken and cut meat into bite-size pieces. Cover and set aside.

Prepare sauce, following directions for the sauce used for the Sweet 'n Sour Meatballs (Chapter VI, *Strictly for Cocktails*, p. 158). Add to the sauce 1 green pepper, cut into strips; omit the mustard and substitute half of the pineapple juice with the chicken broth.

Place chicken in two 1½- to 2½-quart casseroles, or 1 large casserole, 4 to 5 quarts. Sprinkle lightly with salt. When sauce thickens, add pineapple chunks and pour over chicken. Cover.

This can be prepared 2 to 3 days in advance and refrigerated.

To serve, preheat oven to 350°F. Bake, covered, for 40 minutes. Serve over chow mein noodles.

The recipe can easily be doubled or tripled.

GOVERNOR REAGAN'S OVEN-FRIED CHICKEN

I have catered many parties at which former Governor Reagan and his wife Nancy were guests, and at least one that I remember where they were the host and hostess. This was a dinner for a group of Republican governors who were staying in Palm Springs.

The only request the Governor made was for some crisp, golden-brown chicken, moist but not greasy. Of course I was delighted when he told me it was done just the way he liked it. I hope you will like it as well.

It's a simple way to fix chicken for a large party but the recipe can be easily cut to half or a third.

GOVERNOR REAGAN'S OVEN-FRIED CHICKEN

15 to 17 Servings, 36 portions

9 frying chickens, 2 to 3 pounds each, quartered
½ cup salt
2 teaspoons garlic salt
2 pounds butter

5 pounds cornflake crumbs
4 ounces dried parsley flakes
1½ pounds finely grated American cheese
Parsley sprigs

Remove the skins from each piece of washed and drained chicken, except the hard-to-remove portions, such as the wings. Sprinkle a pinch of salt and garlic salt, combined, over all chicken portions. Melt butter in a deep skillet. Combine the cornflake crumbs, parsley flakes, another pinch of salt and cheese in a deep bowl. Using some of the melted butter, generously grease cookie sheets or shallow pans. Bathe the chicken portions in the melted butter, a few pieces at a time, then drop into bowl of crumb mixture. Place coated pieces with meaty side down on cookie sheets. Bake in a preheated 375°F. oven for 50 minutes.

Remove pans from oven. Turn chicken portions over, lifting with them whatever crusty portions adhere to pans.

This preparation can be done the day before serving, by covering well and refrigerating.

To serve, allow chicken to stand at room temperature for about 1 hour before heating if it has been prepared and refrigerated. Heat in a 350°F. oven for 30 minutes.

ARRANGEMENT: Lay the similar sections of chickens in rows for easy identification and a more orderly looking platter. Divide the rows with clumps of parsley. Decorate the 4 corners with turnip flowers (p. 183). Set serving tray on an element using dry heat rather than over hot water, so the chicken will not lose its crispiness.

LUCY'S CHICKEN SALAD

Lucille Ball is one of my favorite party people, maybe because she flipped for my favorite chicken salad recipe. She's also a great backgammon player, and a very clever and funny lady even without a script.

LUCY'S CHICKEN SALAD   10 Ample servings

3 frying chickens, 2½ to 3 pounds each
3 teaspoons salt
1 celery stalk
2 carrots
3 bay leaves
7 hard-cooked eggs, grated
1½ cups mayonnaise
2 teaspoons chicken base seasoning

1 cup drained canned grapes, or fresh if available
1 can (8 oz.) drained pineapple chunks
¼ cup toasted sliced almonds (not slivers)
1½ tablespoons chopped pimiento
1½ teaspoons dry mustard

Cut chicken into quarters, and place in a large kettle with enough water to cover. Add 1½ teaspoons salt; the top of the celery ribs, which will be used later in the salad; 2 carrots; 3 bay leaves. Cover pot and cook slowly for 1½ hours. Strain the chicken broth and

Recipe Continues . . .

save for another occasion (i.e., chicken soup). Also save liver and giblets for another recipe.

When chicken has cooled somewhat, but *not* chilled, remove all meat from bones onto a chopping board. Cut—do *not* chop— into approximately ½- to 1-inch cubes, good bite-size pieces. Place in a large mixing bowl. Lightly salt with about 1½ teaspoons of salt. Add the 7 hard-cooked eggs, grated; the 1½ cups of mayonnaise (*not* salad dressing); 2 heaping teaspoons chicken base seasoning (*not* bouillon). (You'll find chicken base in small jars in the condiment section at your market.) Then add the drained canned grapes, or fresh if available; the drained pineapple chunks; the sliced almonds; chopped pimiento; dry mustard; and the reserved, celery ribs, chopped fine.

You will note that the directions for this are very similar to my recipe for the breast of turkey salad in the Buffet Luncheon, Chapter IV (p. 115). Again I suggest that you mix your dry seasonings, particularly chicken base and dry mustard, into the mayonnaise. Then spoon mayonnaise into the other ingredients and mix well.

This chicken salad should be prepared the day before the party. It may absorb most of the mayonnaise overnight; if so, add more to give it a nice consistency. Serve with light dainty rolls. It's a delicious salad for luncheon parties, buffet suppers and would also be appropriate for a wedding reception.

WALTER ANNENBERG'S POACHED SALMON

I suppose everyone has heard about Sunnylands, the baronial estate of former Ambassador Annenberg, which is said to be bigger than the principality of Monaco and lies just a helicopter hop over the oleanders from Sinatra's Tamarisk compound. Sunnylands has its own 18-hole golf course, pink gazebo, and security gates that admit only the high and mighty.

My first experience at Sunnylands was a memorable one. I was overwhelmed by the gold door knobs; but I was more impressed and really touched by a small human gesture at the end of a rather strenuous evening. I had finished my catering chores. My husband and I were driving out the back gate when a security guard stopped us and said, "Wait here." Presently a golf cart drove up behind us and out jumped Ambassador Annenberg and his wife just to thank us and say goodnight. They had been busy with other departing guests, as we could see, but not too busy to remember the amenities some people forget. It must have been around midnight; still they expended the extra time and effort to drive all the way out in their golf cart to catch us and say "Thank you." It was a lovely experience, and even more so because they made a special point of praising my poached salmon! I have served it at many parties since then. It can be used in many ways—for first course, luncheon, buffet, or formal dinner party.

POACHED SALMON À LA ANNENBERG
30 to 34 Servings

1 salmon, 14 to 18 pounds	2 teaspoons peppercorns
1 celery stalk	Garnishes
4 large carrots	Parsley sprigs
2 large onions	Lemon twists
4 bay leaves	

Wrap salmon in triple-strength cheesecloth, bring ends to top, and tie ends in a heavy knot. Place in a very large pot, unless you are so fortunate as to have a poacher, and fill with water to cover the salmon. Add the vegetables, bay leaves and peppercorns. Cover and poach over low heat. Do not allow the water to boil; cook just above the point of simmering, allowing 15 minutes to the pound. Carefully lift out the salmon and transfer to a pan to cool. Unwrap the cheesecloth and refrigerate the fish. This preparation can be done a day or two before serving. Keep under refrigeration.

Recipe Continues . . .

Arrangement: Place chilled salmon on a large oval platter. With kitchen scissors cut top skin 2 inches from the edge in a scallop design. When skin has been cut all around the fish, lift off and discard the large cut-out portion, thus exposing the flesh. Scrape off the layer of dark meat to expose the more colorful surface, the true salmon color. Decorate with cream cheese, tinted a pleasant light orange; using a pastry bag with a star tip, outline the scalloped edge. With light-green tinted cream cheese in a pastry bag fitted with a leaf tip, decorate the scalloped border further with leaves placed in several places.

Place very thin strips of green pepper, or the tops of scallions, down the center indentation of the salmon. Cut a hard-cooked egg into halves; place one half cut side down on center of fish. Dot with small stars using the same colored cream cheese as used on the scalloped edge. Simulate 2 leaves on each side by cutting leaf shapes from a green pepper. Surround entire fish with parsley onto which lay twists of lemon.

To serve, cut top half of salmon into individual servings as each guest desires, rather than in advance, so as to keep the beautiful fish intact as long as possible. When top half has been served, the entire center bone can easily be removed and then the bottom half cut and served as was the top half. Serve with Cucumber Cream Sauce (recipe follows).

Cucumber Cream Sauce   6 Cups

4 cucumbers
3 green onions (scallions)
1 quart dairy sour cream

2 teaspoons dry mustard
2 teaspoons dillweed

Peel and dice the cucumbers. Chop the green tops off the scallions; add the sour cream. Add the dillweed. Serve well chilled.

Note: Chopped chives can be used in place of green onions, which are not always available.

IKE'S FAVORITES

Mamie Eisenhower once came up to me and asked to take home some of my cookies for the General. She said they were his absolute favorite. Here's the recipe:

IKE'S FAVORITES   40 Squares

½ pound butter	½ teaspoon salt
1 cup sugar	1 teaspoon vanilla extract
1 egg, separated	1 cup finely ground filberts (ha-
2 cups sifted flour	zelnuts)
¼ teaspoon ground cardamom	

Cream butter and sugar well. Add egg yolk; beat well. Sift the flour together with other dry ingredients. Beat into the butter-sugar mixture. Beat in the vanilla. Stir in ground filberts. Blend until well mixed. Press into a buttered pan, 15 x 10 inches. Beat egg white slightly. Brush over top of batter. Bake in a preheated 275°F. oven for 1 hour. While warm, score in squares 2 by 1¾ inches. When completely cold, store in tightly covered container.

These cookies should not be frozen.

Note: I always served Ike's Favorites at the Ahmonson parties where the Eisenhowers were always guests.

GERRY FORD'S HOLE-IN-THE-HEAD CAKE

I met President Ford in one of Life's Most Embarrassing Moments. He was then Vice President, and I was asked to cater a small dinner party in his honor at the Fred Wilsons' Thunderbird home. It was to be quite intimate, only 28 people, but the Wilsons wanted it to be elegant and asked me to dream up something special as a surprise for Mr. Ford's birthday.

So I dreamed up a cake with a silk-screen portrait of Mr. Ford in the middle of it. This, I must tell you, was not the easiest thing in the world to do. I have a friend who does silk screening. After many consultations, designs, drawings and experiments, and working from a photograph of Vice President Ford, we were able to figure out how to apply the silk screening process to a cake with a portrait of Gerry Ford in color, and with the exact color of his eyes, hair and skin tones.

I had a large cake made and decorated the outer edge with red, white and blue. The portrait would be right in the middle of the cake.

We held our breath until the silk screening was completed. It turned out magnificently; it looked like a hand-painted portrait. I delivered the cake personally to the Wilsons' house early in the afternoon. I wouldn't trust it to my helpers. I left it on a table in the breakfast room area off the kitchen, with a word of caution to guard it carefully. I had other details to attend to for the dinner.

When I returned and walked into the kitchen, it seemed unusually quiet. The other household help were there, and the Wilsons' pretty young daughter, but they all had a strange look on their faces as I started getting things organized with my helpers: This goes in the refrigerator. That goes in the bar. Why were they all just standing there?

Finally the host's daughter blurted out, "Mrs. Lowell, I have something horrible to tell you. Please don't faint. I'm *so* sorry . . ."

She burst into tears as she gestured toward the breakfast area and the cake. I almost broke into tears too. There was my beautiful cake with a big hole in Gerry Ford's head, slashed from the temples just above the eye and right to the bottom of the cake.

For a moment I couldn't believe it. It had to be a dream. But it wasn't. The host's daughter explained: her three-year-old son apparently had wandered into the kitchen when nobody was watching and, probably intrigued with the picture on the cake, stuck his thumb in it and slashed a big gaping hole in it.

When I recovered from the initial shock, everyone started asking, "What are you going to do?"

"Just leave me alone," I said. "I'll figure out something." I told myself, Calm down, don't panic, take it easy. You'll never think of anything if you let yourself get worked up. (Remember, it's called *coping!*)I studied the picture on the cake and thought: his hair is light cocoa color. And it suddenly struck me—cocoa. I looked in a cupboard and found a can of instant cocoa. The cake had a very wide border of frosting at the bottom, fluted. I found a spatula and stole some of the frosting from the back to fill the hole. I couldn't fill it completely, just enough so it was level with the cake. I smoothed it over, then put some cocoa in the palm of my hand, spread my fingers apart and blew the cocoa through my fingers onto the side of the Vice President's head where the hole had been. The cocoa was almost the same color as Mr. Ford's hair, and by blowing it through my fingers it looked like streaks of hair on the side of his head, the way it was supposed to look, almost a perfect repair job.

It was all finished by the time the photographers came.

I was asked to pose with Mr. Ford in some of the pictures. During the photo session, he was very warm, cordial, and complimentary about the cake. Should I tell him about the hole in the head? I hesitated. Then I told him about the cake. He roared with laughter.

When the photographers finished their pictures, he took me aside and whispered, "Is there anything else you might serve for dessert? I'd like to take this cake back to Washington. I know a lot of people there who would like to cut me up. I'll give this to them. And they'll love knowing about the hole in my head."

The next day, escorted by his security officers, I personally deposited the Vice President's hole-in-the-head birthday cake aboard *Air Force I* bound for Washington. I later received a nice thank-you letter from him, which I treasure.

GERRY FORD'S HOLE-IN-THE-HEAD CAKE

1 Cake
15 servings

(Omitting the hole)

¼ pound butter
¼ pound margarine
2 cups sugar
5 eggs, separated
2 cups flour
2 teaspoons baking powder
½ teaspoon salt

1 cup buttermilk
1 teaspoon baking soda
1 teaspoon vanilla extract
1 cup chopped walnuts
1 cup flaked coconut
Creamy Frosting (recipe follows)

Cream together the butter and margarine with the sugar until light and creamy. Add egg yolks one at a time; beat well after each addition. Sift together flour, baking powder and salt. Pour the buttermilk into a 2-cup measuring cup and add the baking soda. Stir well and let it rise. Add to the egg mixture alternately with the dry ingredients, beginning and ending with the dry ingredients.

Beat the egg whites stiff but not dry. Fold into batter. Fold in the vanilla, walnuts and coconut. Pour into 3 greased and floured layer-cake pans.

Bake in a preheated 325°F. oven for 25 minutes.

When layers are cool, remove from pans. Fill and frost.

Creamy Frosting

½ pound cream cheese, softened
¼ pound butter, softened

1 pound powdered sugar
1 teaspoon vanilla extract

Combine all ingredients and beat until smooth. Spread on cake.

Keep out of reach of overactive three-year-olds!

DINAH'S TENNIS TORTE

I once catered a buffet dinner party in honor of Dinah Shore's birthday. (I've certainly done a lot of birthday parties, haven't I?) Her favorite dishes on the menu were my Artichoke Casserole, which I have already included in recipes for a Formal Dinner (Chapter VIII, p. 219) and my Apple Torte that I made for her instead of a regular birthday cake.

I decorated the top of the torte with a little tennis court, rackets and tiny tennis balls made out of cream cheese. She got a big bang out of that. Everyone called it Dinah's Tennis Torte.

Dinah is certainly one of the warmest and most gracious ladies I've ever met. She's well known for many things, of course, but not the least of her talents is cooking. She is considered one of the best cooks among the Hollywood celebrities (I think *the* best) and loves to give parties, does her own cooking, and has written a cookbook herself. I was flattered when she asked very modestly if I would mind giving her my recipes for the Artichoke Casserole and the Apple (Tennis) Torte. Later she wrote a nice thank-you note saying how much she appreciated my giving her the recipes. She added, "And I certainly take my hat off to you for knowing how to have enough food for everyone when such a mob shows up."

I had been told to prepare for 40 or 50 guests. Nearly a hundred dropped in! After they sang "Happy Birthday," she led a hand-clapping chorus of "Someone's in the kitchen with Dinah . . ." as a thank-you to me.

DINAH'S APPLE-TENNIS TORTE

1 Torte,
16 servings

This is the one I decorated for Dinah. You don't have to carry it that far! This recipe should be done a step at a time.

Preheat oven to 350°F. Butter a 9-inch springform pan with removable sides.

Recipe Continues . . .

1 pkg. (6 oz.) zwieback, rolled
   into crumbs
¾ cup granulated sugar

¼ pound butter, melted
½ teaspoon ground cinnamon
¼ teaspoon ground nutmeg

Combine all ingredients. Press half onto bottom and sides of the buttered springform pan. Reserve other half of crumbs for top of torte.

Apple Filling

7 large or 9 medium-size cooking or baking apples
4 tablespoons lemon juice
⅔ cup sugar

1½ ounces butter
½ teaspoon ground cinnamon
¼ teaspoon grated nutmeg

Peel and core apples. Cut apples into chunks, sprinkling lemon juice over them as you proceed. Add the sugar, butter and spices and cook over moderate heat until apples are slightly cooked and glossy in appearance. Do not overcook. Remove from heat and cool.

When cool, add the following:

5 eggs, well beaten
2 cups sour cream

½ teaspoon vanilla extract

Cook over moderate heat until slightly thickened, about 20 minutes. Stir occasionally to prevent scorching. Remove from heat and cool slightly. Pour filling into crumb-lined pan. Sprinkle remaining crumbs on top. Place pan on a cookie sheet and bake for 1 hour. Cool on a rack; do not remove sides of pan until torte is completely cooled.

This apple torte should *not* be frozen. It will stay fresh in the refrigerator for at least 5 days to a week and can be served with or without a whipped cream topping.

ELEANOR ROOSEVELT'S BREAST OF CHICKEN MYSTIQUE

I've already given you the recipe for this on the same Formal Dinner menu (Chapter VIII, p. 216) as Dinah's Artichoke Casserole, but I'll let you in on the secret of the "mystique." The hostess for the party in Mrs. Roosevelt's honor was one of those grand-lady types who like to put up a gilt-edged front, but keep the costs down, please. So I stuffed boned chicken breasts with an inexpensive kind of meat, camouflaged it with seasonings, prettied up the chicken breasts with a grape mandarin sauce, and named it Breast of Chicken Mystique. I did this purposely, thinking if anyone should ask about the filling, I would just smile and say sweetly, "It's a secret."

The "mystique" part of it was pickled tongue. It's not terribly exotic. I'm sure the hostess would have had apoplexy if she had known, but I had no intention of telling her nor anyone else.

Alas, Eleanor Roosevelt herself came up to me raving rather audibly, "Young lady, that is the best chicken I ever put in my mouth."

I thanked her profusely, at the same time trying to back off and avoid what I knew was coming. No luck. The inimitable, indomitable First Lady was not the type of woman to let go easily.

"Would you mind telling me," she pursued, still in sonorous tones, "how you made that filling. Or is it a secret? I'd like to have the recipe."

How could I lie to Eleanor Roosevelt? After all, she was the guest of honor. Besides, I was too flustered at the moment to think of anything else to say. So, in an anguished effort to compose myself, nearly swallowing my own tongue in the process, I simply smiled bravely and told the truth.

I'm sure the hostess never forgave me. I could have given it a fancier name than pickled tongue. But Mrs. Roosevelt, bless her heart, got me off the hook by fervently proclaiming she absolutely adored pickled tongue but mine was the best she'd ever tasted! She still insisted on having the recipe, so I gave it to her.

CHAPTER XI

. . . .

Tarts, Tortes and Trifles

. . . .

The difference, in my book, is: Tortes are made more like cakes; tarts are individual pastry servings; trifles are a combination of cake, pudding and whipped cream and anything else you feel like tossing into it, all well saturated with sherry.

There are also other differences—in the way they are used, their manageability and freezability. Some should not be frozen, others are better frozen. Some are strictly "Sweet Tooth" desserts, others are not so sweet, can be served for breakfast.

For my Sweet Tooth Party menu (Chapter V, p. 142 ff.) I selected what I believe to be the best easy-do recipes, particularly for large parties. If you're ambitious, you may wish to add or substitute some of the following recipes. However, two of the most popular tortes in my *Queen of Tarts* shops are made with vegetables—carrots and spinach—and therefore can't be called strictly Sweet Tooth desserts.

HAWAIIAN CARROT TORTE

**1 Large torte,
18 to 20 servings**

This is by far the most popular item on my *Queen of Tarts* menu of *Tarts, Tortes and Trifles*. I don't know what they all do with it, except eat it, apparently at any hour of the day or night. I even know people who eat it for breakfast, heaped with ice cream yet! Note: I'm not recommending that you serve it this way.

3 eggs
1½ cups granulated sugar

¾ cup vegetable oil
1 teaspoon vanilla extract

1 cup graham-cracker crumbs
1 cup all-purpose flour
1½ teaspoons baking powder
1 teaspoon baking soda

1½ teaspoons salt
½ teaspoon ground nutmeg
1 teaspoon ground cinnamon

1½ cups grated carrots (7 to 9 carrots)
½ cup crushed pineapple
½ cup chopped fresh apple
½ cup Angel Flake coconut

½ cup chopped walnuts
¼ cup flour to coat walnuts
Orange-Lemon Sauce (recipe follows)

Beat eggs well; gradually add sugar. When lemon-colored, slowly beat in the oil and vanilla. Next, combine the dry ingredients. Then combine the carrots, pineapple, apple and coconut. Add both mixtures alternately to the eggs-sugar mixture, beginning and ending with the dry ingredients. Coat the walnuts with the ¼ cup flour; fold into the batter. Transfer batter to a well-buttered 9-inch tubular angel-food pan. Bake in a preheated 350°F. oven for 50 minutes.

Let cool in pan before turning out. Turn torte top side up. Poke many tiny holes in top of cake with the tines of a meat fork or ice pick. Pour the Orange-Lemon Sauce on top.

Orange-Lemon Sauce

Juice and grated rind of 1 lemon   2 cups granulated sugar
Juice and grated rind of 2
   oranges

Bring all ingredients to a full rolling boil. Cook for 4 minutes. Let stand for 30 minutes. Pour over cake slowly so that sauce will seep down into the cake and soak into it like a sponge. This is the purpose of the holes, and oh, what flavor! This cake *can* be frozen but it doesn't need to be, as it will stay moist and fresh for over a week in the refrigerator, if it lasts that long. I've never heard of any that ever did.

SPINACH CAKE
1 Loaf, 9 x 5 inches

This is one of my most recent original creations, inspired by the popularity of the carrot cake. Why not spinach too? Even if you can't stand spinach, you'll like this.

¼ pound butter or margarine   1 teaspoon salt
1 cup sugar   1 teaspoon ground nutmeg
2 eggs   1 cup dairy sour cream
1 teaspoon anise extract   1 cup chopped fresh spinach
1½ cups sifted flour   ½ cup chopped walnuts
2 teaspoons baking powder   Icing (recipe follows)

Cream the butter or margarine with the sugar. Add eggs and flavoring. Beat for 2 minutes. Sift dry ingredients into the creamed mixture; blend well, but do not overbeat. Combine sour cream, chopped spinach and walnuts. Fold into the flour mixture. Transfer to a buttered loaf pan 5 x 9 inches. Bake in a preheated 350°F. oven for 1 hour. Frost cake while warm.

Icing for Spinach Cake

2 cups sifted powdered sugar
2 tablespoons melted butter

2 tablespoons hot water
1 teaspoon anise extract

Combine all ingredients. Beat until smooth.

LEMON ANGEL FREEZE

This has been one of my all-time hits for many years and the recipe is included in my Sweet Tooth Party Menu (Chapter V, p. 148) and need not be repeated here, although it deserves recognition again in this chapter since it is such as unbelievable best seller among my *Queen of Tarts* tortes. And ironically it's a recipe I discovered by accident, or somebody else's accident.

One day I whipped up a batch of these for a party I was doing that night. I left it for a helper to spoon into pans and to put in the refrigerator. Then I went off to do some errands.

The helper had been instructed to remove the tortes from my Lowell Manor refrigerator and bring them to the party. But when I arrived at the host house and began to assemble all the party preparations, I noticed the tortes were missing. The first helper had forgotten them, but she was busy at something else now, so I sent a second helper back to my shop to fetch them. He returned empty handed. He said he had looked all through the refrigerator and they weren't there.

The first helper, the woman who had spooned them into the pans, looked up puzzled and said, "Oh, yes they are. They've got to be. They're in the freezer right where you told me to put them."

Well, I had said refrigerator, not freezer, but that wasn't important at the moment. What was important was to get them quickly out of the freezer and defrosted in time to slice and serve as dessert, and hope they would be edible.

They weren't completely defrosted on time but I sliced and

served them anyway, and they were delicious, actually much better than the original. Since then I always freeze my lemon-angel "mishmosh" whatever-it-is. I'm not sure it's a proper torte, but thanks to my absent-minded helper, it's delightfully *different*. It has an icy-cool light and refreshing touch to the tongue that a merely refrigerated mishmosh, with all its various refinements, did not have. In fact, many people think it's made of ice cream or sherbet. And the freezing gives it a consistency that makes it easier to handle in slicing and serving. It will keep for weeks or months in the freezer, but it should be removed about 40 minutes before serving or transferred to refrigerator 2 hours before.

BUTTER LEMON TARTS

Enough for 6 to 8 tarts

Lemon Filling

½ pound butter
1 cup sugar
Grated rind of 2 lemons
½ cup lemon juice

3 whole eggs
1 extra egg yolk (The extra yolk acts as a thickener.)

Melt butter in the top part of a double boiler over simmering water. Add the sugar, lemon rind and juice; stir well. Beat whole eggs and egg yolk for 2 minutes. Pour into the butter-lemon mixture. Use a rubber spatula to help remove all the beaten eggs from mixing bowl, but stir custard with a wooden spoon to prevent the mixture separating. Cook for 15 to 20 minutes, stirring occasionally, until slightly thickened. Remove to a cooling rack.

When custard is cool, fill tart shells, or store in refrigerator in covered container. This will keep well for several days.

A border of whipped cream on each tart, centered with a tiny wedge of sliced lemon, is a nice finishing touch.

Tart Shells   8 to 10 Tart shells

1 cup all-purpose flour   ⅓ cup cold water
3 tablespoons vegetable shorten-
    ing, very cold

Combine the flour and shortening. Work with a pastry blender
until tiny particles are formed. Slowly add the cold water until a
ball forms. Refrigerate.

When dough is cold, roll out on a pastry cloth. Cut into circles
to fit tart pans.

Extra shells can be frozen. Or shells can be filled with Butter
Lemon Tart Filling and then frozen.

Note: As an alternative, you can buy frozen tart shells at the
market which will serve adequately for Butter Lemon Tart fillings.
(These are *not* the same as patty shells.) But I prefer to make my
own pastry shells, and it's really not all that difficult.

LEMONS
When grating a lemon, remember, the marvelous zest of a lemon
is in the outer portion of the rind; the bitterness is in the white
pulpy portion. Never grate a lemon beyond the yellow surface.
Just the top of the surface is best.

TRIFLES

Trifles are not trivia. They're a traditional English dessert with no
trifling amount of calories. What you need first is a very pretty
crystal or glass bowl. The elegant dessert is made with cake, pudding, whipped cream, and whatever else your inclination leads you
to toss into it, all saturated, as I've said, with a good amount of
sherry.

Start out with a layer of sponge cake (Sara Lee's will do)
about ½ inch thick in the bottom of the bowl. Sprinkle sherry over

Recipe Continues . . .

cake to saturate it. Then spoon a layer of vanilla pudding (either a package or your own favorite recipe) over the cake. Then spoon over it either raspberry preserves (if you want a raspberry trifle) or thick chocolate pudding (if you prefer chocolate). Top this with whipped cream and toasted sliced almonds.

Repeat from the beginning. When you get to the top, add another layer of sponge cake, sprinkle with more sherry (if you haven't nipped too much). Spread more whipped cream over the top, or for a prettier effect, make swirls of whipped cream out of a decorating bag and scatter sliced almonds again over the whole pretty creation.

And whoopee! You can diet tomorrow!

The trifle can be frozen and kept in the freezer indefinitely. The day before using, take it out of the freezer and place in the refrigerator section. Or allow it to stand at room temperature for at least 4 hours before using.

If bowl measures 9 inches across the top, it will yield 10 servings.

PART IV

....

ENCORE

....

CHAPTER XII

· · · · · · · · · · · · · · ·

Caviar Mousse

· · · · · · · · · · · · · · ·

I don't often play favorites, but now I'm breaking my own rules. Any woman who aspires to be the perfect hostess can take a tip from Betsy Hammes.

I have "catered" many parties in Betsy's home and I use the word *catered* in quotes here because Betsy doesn't really need a caterer or cateress—it would be more accurate to say that I assisted her at these parties.

First of all, Betsy has that rare gift *par excellence* of always being or appearing to be the *happiest* guest at her own party and she instills this feeling in others. It's contagious, it catches on, like an epidemic.

I know some of you reading this are going to say, So, okay, sure, rich people can afford to give great parties. But this has nothing to do with the real key to a party's success, which must lie within *you,* the host and hostess.

The degree of affluence and social standing, I'm convinced, is no barometer of one's abilities to be both a perfect hostess and guest at one's own party.

The Hammes house in Palm Springs, lends itself well to indoor entertaining with many unusual areas for setting up tables for food. Guests can be served in the living room, dining room, lanai room and a huge game room at the far end of the house, which is equipped with a professional-size bar as well as pinball machines, backgammon and ping-pong tables, and every conceivable kind of game for the guests' amusement and enjoyment.

I know there are women who don't like to clutter up their whole house for a party, but think about it and try it sometime. Your guests will have more fun when the party isn't confined to one area.

The best party in the world is one where there is food at all times and in different places.

No one expects a large cocktail supper or buffet to be a strictly formal affair but you can give it class and style by having many tables, all properly set, where guests can eat *when they are ready to eat.* There can be hot dishes set out on various tables as well, so that not everyone dashes to a table at the same time. If there is no announced beginning and end of a party, it sort of takes care of itself and the guests have more fun. Some parties fall apart and break up early after the food is served, unless there's music and dancing. This is especially true if guests feel confined or regimented within certain areas at certain hours for their food service.

Of course I am not speaking here of formal sit-down dinners where certain rules of protocol and courtesy prevail.

Betsy's secret of success, which any woman can emulate, is this: She actually *enjoys* giving a party and she actually *enjoys* cooking.

It isn't only the design and layout of her house that make her parties great fun; I've catered many parties in homes with more lavish layouts perfectly suited for entertaining. No matter if your house is big or small, it's the exuberant hostess who makes the difference.

We're not all constituted the same way. Not everyone has a natural instinct or inclination toward cooking and parties. Not everyone *enjoys* them but certainly almost everyone at some time in life must run up against the necessity of cooking and even giving a party. You can turn a pain-in-the-neck to pleasure when you have the confidence and know-how. This is the secret of being a good hostess and guest at your own party. Learn how—and *enjoy!*

CAVIAR MOUSSE   2 Cups

Traditionally, a Hammes party features a Caviar Mousse. Here's how to make it:

1 envelope unflavored gelatin	⅛ teaspoon pepper
2 teaspoons lemon juice	1½ teaspoons Worcestershire
2 teaspoons water	sauce
4 hard-cooked eggs	4 ounces black caviar
1 cup mayonnaise	2 teaspoons grated onion
2 tablespoons dairy sour cream	1½ teaspoons anchovy paste
¼ teaspoon salt	

Combine gelatin, lemon juice and water in a small bowl; set over a pan of hot water; stir until gelatin is dissolved. Put hard-cooked eggs through a grater: mix into gelatin. Stir in mayonnaise and sour cream. Remove gelatin bowl from pan of hot water. Add seasonings, stir into caviar. Add grated onion and anchovy paste; stir well. Transfer to a well-oiled (not with olive oil) 2-cup mold. Chill for 4 to 5 hours, or preferably overnight.

To serve, unmold on a platter; surround with Melba toast, finely chopped onions, sour cream, hard-cooked eggs and lemon wedges.

A TOAST

May your hours of entertainment be a pleasure and your pleasure be hours of entertainment.

Index